COMPASS AMERICAN GUIDES
An imprint of Fodor's Travel

YOSEMITE

and Sequoia / Kings Canyon National Parks

BY **SARA BENSON** · PHOTOGRAPHY BY
CHRIS FALKENSTEIN AND **ROBERT HOLMES**

Tuolumne
Meadows

1

2

Tenaya
Lake

Yosemite
Falls

Tioga Road

Big Oak Flat
Road

1 Mt. Conness
2 Lambert Dome
3 Mammoth Peak
4 Cathedral Peak
5 Half Dome
6 Washington Column
7 Glacier Point
8 Sentinel Dome
9 El Capitan
10 Leaning Tower
11 Cathedral Spires
12 Dewey Point
13 Valley View
14 Tunnel View

PANORAMA VIEW OF YOSEMITE NATIONAL PARK, LOOKING EAST

CATHEDRAL RANGE

LITTLE YOSEMITE VALLEY

TENAYA CANYON

Nevada Falls

Vernal Falls

Curry Village

Yosemite Village

Glacier Point Road

YOSEMITE VALLEY

Bridalveil Falls

Wawona Road

El Portal Road

BERANN

Sunset over Tuolumne River.

A skier on Dewey Point takes in the vista of Yosemite Valley and the High Sierra.

COMPASS AMERICAN GUIDES: Yosemite and Sequoia/Kings Canyon National Parks

COMPASS SENIOR EDITOR: Jennifer Paull
EDITOR: Debbie Harmsen
EDITORIAL CONTRIBUTOR: Paul Eisenberg

DESIGNERS: Tigist Getachew, Nora Rosansky, Chie Ushio
CREATIVE DIRECTOR: Fabrizio La Rocca
PRODUCTION EDITORS: Linda Schmidt, Evangelos Vasilakis
PHOTO EDITOR: Melanie Marin
ILLUSTRATIONS: William Wu
MAP DESIGN: Mark Stroud, Moon Street Cartography
PRODUCTION MANAGERS: Matthew Colbourn, Steve Slawsky

COVER PHOTO: Sunset on Half Dome after fall winter storm, from Olmsted Point
by Chris Falkenstein

First Edition

ISBN 978-1-4000-1933-5
ISSN 1943-0086

Compass American Guides, 1745 Broadway, New York, NY 10019

PRINTED IN CHINA
10 9 8 7 6 5 4 3 2 1

Giant sequoias in Mariposa Grove, Yosemite National Park. ▶ ▶

DEDICATION:
To all of the NPS
employees, especially the
hard-working seasonal
staff, who protect the
Sierra Nevada region.

Contents

MAPS AND CHARTS

Introduction

High in the glacier-carved Sierra Nevada mountain range in California near the western edge of the North American continent, there is a place of incredible beauty and heart's solace called Yosemite Valley. There waterfalls leap from the edges of cliffs into grassy meadows nourished by bubbling streams. The valley is overhung by natural masterpieces of weather-worn granite, including world-famous Half Dome and El Capitan. Above the timeless valley, the craggy peaks of the Sierra Nevada high country rise, liberally scattered with pristine alpine lakes, wildflower-strewn meadows, and hardy hiking trails that make you feel as if you are walking on the rooftop of the world. Both the high altitudes and the imperial panoramas will steal your breath away and make your blood course like a waterfall rushing with spring snowmelt.

JOHN MUIR

Before there were any artificial boundaries, these Western lands were inhabited by Native American nations, including the Miwok, Paiute, and Mono tribespeople who staked out summer camps in the elevated valleys and beat trading routes on foot over high mountain passes. Beginning in 1848, the California gold rush brought miners, ranchers, and pioneers into the American West. Slowly the parks began to lose their rich natural resources, especially as grazing livestock denuded meadows and many of the largest living trees on earth—giant sequoias—were cut down by loggers. In 1890, Yosemite and Sequoia national parks were established to preserve these lands, from the snowy heights of Tuolumne Meadows to the cloaked depths of the Giant Forest. That same year, General Grant National Park (which was later expanded into Kings Canyon National Park) was created to protect the nation's official Christmas Tree, a legendary giant sequoia that still stands. Today, these national parks together stand guard over a large swath of epic landscape and natural ecosystems along the spine of the Sierra Nevada, including Mt. Whitney (elevation 14,505 feet), the tallest peak in the United States outside of Alaska.

Even if you have only one brief chance to experience the Sierra Nevada mountains, it's worthwhile to visit these parks. Wildlife watchers, outdoor enthusiasts, photographers, and countless tourists return to the parks many times over to explore them in all four seasons. The best time to visit is in early summer, when wildflowers bloom in the high country, peaceful streams feed the verdant valleys and mountain meadows, and sunlight dapples the groves of giant sequoia trees. You can watch black bears and their cubs foraging for berries and acorns during the day, then see the stars of the Milky Way shine with startling clarity at night. Or just laze away an entire afternoon swimming in an alpine lake until sunset casts an alpenglow on skyscraping Sierra Nevada peaks. The opportunities for adventure are endless here.

"Climb the mountains and get their good tidings. Nature's peace will flow into you as sunshine flows into trees. The winds will blow their own freshness into you, and the storms their energy, while cares will drop off like autumn leaves."

–John Muir,
Our National Parks, 1901.

HOW TO USE THIS BOOK

Our guidebook opens with "Best Experiences," a photo-rich intro-duction to the most outstanding sights, activities, and places to stay in the three national parks. Our contributors share their favorite experiences and hope to inspire your trip planning. Next is a short overview of the history of the region, starting with its early Native American inhabitants and leading up to the political and environmental issues that the parks face today.

Each of the main regional chapters is devoted to an individual national park. These three park chapters are each subdivided into "Sights" and "Other Activities." The "Sights" sections follow the key driving routes around the parks. The "Other Activities" sections cover the most popular outdoor pursuits, listing them alphabetically. Star icons in these park chapters highlight the must-see attractions, which are especially handy to keep in mind if your time is limited.

Following the regional chapters are our recommendations for where to stay and eat in and near the national parks. Here, too, we star our top choices. The "Geology, Flora, and Fauna" chapter showcases the natural history of the region and includes a handy reference to the most noteworthy local plants and animals. Finally, our "Practical Information" chapter rounds up essential tips and contacts, plus a short list of recommended further reading.

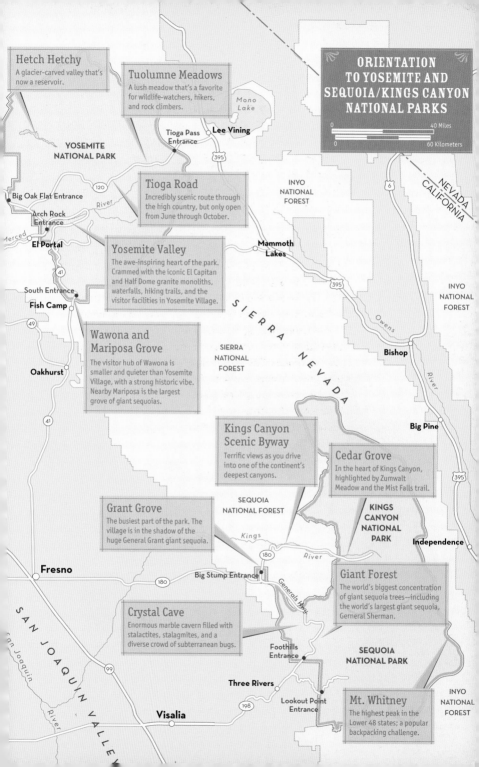

Hetch Hetchy
A glacier-carved valley that's now a reservoir.

Tuolumne Meadows
A lush meadow that's a favorite for wildlife-watchers, hikers, and rock climbers.

Mono Lake

Tioga Pass Entrance   Lee Vining

395

YOSEMITE NATIONAL PARK

Tioga Road
Incredibly scenic route through the high country, but only open from June through October.

120

Big Oak Flat Entrance

River

Arch Rock Entrance

Merced

El Portal

41

South Entrance

Fish Camp

49

INYO NATIONAL FOREST

Mammoth Lakes

395

NEVADA
CALIFORNIA

6

INYO NATIONAL FOREST

Yosemite Valley
The awe-inspiring heart of the park. Crammed with the iconic El Capitan and Half Dome granite monoliths, waterfalls, hiking trails, and the visitor facilities in Yosemite Village.

S I E R R A

Owens

Bishop

Wawona and Mariposa Grove
The visitor hub of Wawona is smaller and quieter than Yosemite Village, with a strong historic vibe. Nearby Mariposa is the largest grove of giant sequoias.

Oakhurst

41

SIERRA NATIONAL FOREST

N E V A D A

River

Big Pine

Kings Canyon Scenic Byway
Terrific views as you drive into one of the continent's deepest canyons.

Cedar Grove
In the heart of Kings Canyon, highlighted by Zumwalt Meadow and the Mist Falls trail.

395

KINGS CANYON NATIONAL PARK

Independence

Grant Grove
The busiest part of the park. The village is in the shadow of the huge General Grant giant sequoia.

SEQUOIA NATIONAL FOREST

Kings

180

River

ORIENTATION TO YOSEMITE AND SEQUOIA/KINGS CANYON NATIONAL PARKS

0   40 Miles
0   60 Kilometers

Fresno

180

Big Stump Entrance

Generals Hwy

Giant Forest
The world's biggest concentration of giant sequoia trees—including the world's largest giant sequoia, General Sherman.

Crystal Cave
Enormous marble cavern filled with stalactites, stalagmites, and a diverse crowd of subterranean bugs.

99

S A N   J O A Q U I N   V A L L E Y

San Joaquin

River

Foothills Entrance

SEQUOIA NATIONAL PARK

Three Rivers

198

Lookout Point Entrance

Visalia

Mt. Whitney
The highest peak in the Lower 48 states; a popular backpacking challenge.

INYO NATIONAL FOREST

Welcome to Yosemite, Sequoia, and Kings Canyon national parks, the wild heart of the Sierra Nevada mountain range. We want to share some of our favorite places in the parks with you, from thundering waterfalls and giant sequoias to hidden trails and backcountry vistas. Whether you're looking for a serene retreat or an adrenaline fix, here are experiences we think you'll love as much as we do. It's time to get ready for unforgettable adventures.

–Sara Benson, *author*
–Chris Falkenstein, *photographer*
–Robert Holmes, *photographer*

S T

EXPERIENCES

BEST
Scenic Drive

Tioga Road, Yosemite; *see p. 114*

"This route takes you up to Yosemite's high country, with **knockout** views at every turn. You'll wind through thick forests, pass Tenaya Lake (a perfect place to swim and picnic), and finally crest at Tioga Pass." —*Chris Falkenstein*

Splashy views from Tioga Road. ▶▶

INSIDER'S PICK

Kings Canyon Scenic Byway

"With sharp turns and drop-offs, this road dives into a canyon deeper than even the Grand Canyon. In spring, whitewater spray from the Kings River splashes my car!"

–Sara Benson, see page 238

BEST
Family
Adventures

Rafting and Tubing, Merced River; *see p. 151*
Skiing, Badger Pass; *see p. 153*

"While Yosemite can be a strikingly rugged place, Mother Nature's gentler side also emerges. The bubbling Merced River is one such place—take the kids on a dreamy summertime float. From the vantage point of an inner tube, you can crane your neck up at granite monoliths like Half Dome. In winter, join the generations of families who've learned to ski down the pint-sized slopes of Badger Pass, near Glacier Point."

—*Sara Benson*

Rafting on the Merced River in Yosemite National Park. ▶▶

BEST
Day Hikes

"If you're up for a challenging hike, **iconic** Half Dome is the ticket. It's a long day's effort but worth every step. Don't forget to take plenty of water, as there's none on the mountain." —Robert Holmes

Half Dome, as viewed from the south. ▶▶

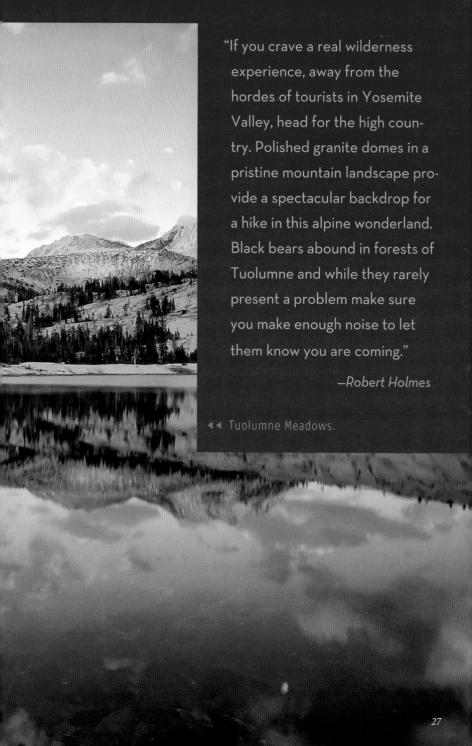

"If you crave a real wilderness experience, away from the hordes of tourists in Yosemite Valley, head for the high country. Polished granite domes in a pristine mountain landscape provide a spectacular backdrop for a hike in this alpine wonderland. Black bears abound in forests of Tuolumne and while they rarely present a problem make sure you make enough noise to let them know you are coming."

—*Robert Holmes*

◄◄ Tuolumne Meadows.

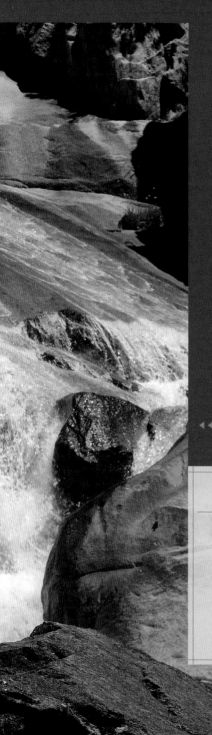

"Almost no other trail in the Sierra Nevada gives you so much in so short a distance: a deep canyon gorge, mossy pine forest, granite talus slopes, and finally, Mist Falls. For the full dramatic effect, hike in April or May, when you'll move through mist so thick it obscures the trail itself. You'll have to stand back to admire nature's handiwork—as if the scene were a painting hanging in a museum."

—Sara Benson

◄◄ Midway point on Mist Falls trail.

⊕ INSIDER'S PICK

Zumwalt Meadow,
Kings Canyon

"Misty spring mornings are best for spotting black bears foraging for berries and wildflowers alongside the river. Canyon views and great birding make it worth the trip." —Sara Benson, see p. 244

BEST
Waterfalls

Vernal and Nevada Falls, Yosemite
see p. 133

"The slick, knee-knocking miles of hiking—either up from the valley or down from Glacier Point— are worth the singular experience of getting **up close** and personal with these mighty waterfalls." —*Sara Benson*

Vernal Fall, Yosemite National Park. ▶▶

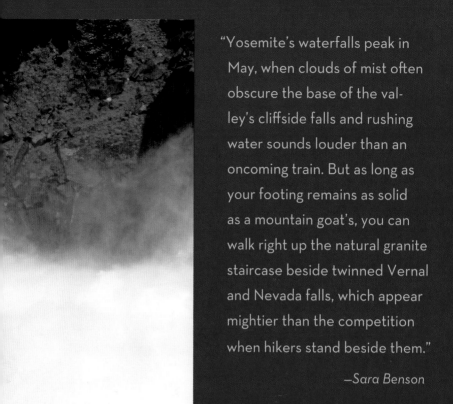

"Yosemite's waterfalls peak in May, when clouds of mist often obscure the base of the valley's cliffside falls and rushing water sounds louder than an oncoming train. But as long as your footing remains as solid as a mountain goat's, you can walk right up the natural granite staircase beside twinned Vernal and Nevada falls, which appear mightier than the competition when hikers stand beside them."

—*Sara Benson*

◄◄ Hiking between twinned Vernal and Nevada Falls.

INSIDER'S PICK

Wapama Falls, Yosemite

"In the hidden Hetch Hetchy Valley, a footpath thrillingly leads to the base of this triple cascade, which peaks in concert with the park's more famous falls in May." —*Sara Benson, see p. 128*

BEST
Extreme Thrill

Rock Climbing, Yosemite; *see p. 148*

"Climbers from all over the world seek the **challenging** routes in Yosemite Valley. There's a certain magic that develops as you climb here, Friendships are made and stories exchanged in our favorite home base, Camp 4."

—Chris Falkenstein

Legendary climber Ron Kauk works on a new route above Tuolumne Meadows. ▶ ▶

BEST
Campgrounds

High Sierra Camps, Yosemite; see p. 143
Hume Lake, Kings Canyon; see p. 240

"**You don't have to** carry a heavy backpack to explore the High Sierra Camps—what conservationist John Muir called his 'high pleasure-ground.' This alpine backcountry circuit of summer-only tent villages provides plenty of creature comforts, including canvas-sided tents, hot meals, and sometimes showers. The camps also free you from carrying anything but the most essential gear on day hikes. Just don't forget bug spray!"

—*Sara Benson*

(right) Camping by a lake near Tuolumne Meadows. (above) High Sierra Camp. ▶▶

Best Viewpoints

Glacier Point, Yosemite; *see p. 102*

"It feels like you can touch the sky here. Spread beneath you is the jaw-dropping beauty of Half Dome, Nevada and Vernal Falls, and the Yosemite Valley. I love to come here on full-moon nights, when it's easy to imagine the ghosts of John Muir and Teddy Roosevelt standing right beside me."   —Sara Benson

Olmsted Point, Yosemite; *see p. 119*

"This is one of my favorite places for watching sunsets. The view sweeps all the way from Half Dome to the domes of Tuolumne Meadows to the eastern high country. If you take the short nature trail south from the parking lot, you'll reach a small granite dome and even broader views of the surrounding mountains—a great photo op."
—Chris Falkenstein

Best Lodging

The Ahwahnee, Yosemite *(left)*; *see p. 95*

"Nowhere else is Yosemite's natural splendor better matched by human craftmanship. The hotel radiates a genteel, historic atmosphere—and let's not forget the spectacular views."
—Sara Benson

Curry Village, Yosemite; *see p. 88*

"For more than a century, families have been staying right here on the floor of Yosemite Valley. It's good old-fashioned summer-camp fun for everyone."   —Sara Benson

Best Backpacking

John Muir Trail, Yosemite (right); *see p. 142*

"Tracing the spine of the Sierra Nevada, this 211-mile route clambers through the high country that the namesake naturalist held so dear. If you go against the flow and hike north to south, it's easier to get a permit and you can finish triumphantly atop Mt. Whitney, the USA's highest peak outside of Alaska." —Sara Benson

High Sierra Trail, Sequoia National Park; *see p. 204*

"If you've ever wanted to brag that you've walked across the Sierra Nevada, this trail is unquestionably the way to do it. Though not the shortest trans-Sierra route, this 70-mile-plus route has glorious alpine scenery, wildflower meadows, and glassy lakes. It's also a handy back door to climbing 14,505-foot Mt. Whitney." —Sara Benson

Best Sequoia Trees

Giant Forest, Sequoia National Park; *see p. 181*

"A wonderful way to get a handle on man's insignificance is to walk beneath the sequoias of the Giant Forest. It's impossible to grasp how massive these trees really are until you're standing beneath one of the centuries-old behemoths. Even if you're somehow jaded, this is an awe-inspiring, don't-miss experience." —Robert Holmes

Mariposa Grove, Yosemite; *see p. 110*

"Walking among these giant sequoias, you'll feel like a hobbit—the trees are that immense and magical. My favorite area is the upper grove. It takes a little more effort to reach it, as you'll need to hike two miles from the parking lot, but you'll be rewarded with a much quieter and more solemn experience." —Chris Falkenstein

History of the Parks

The sun sets on Half Dome and El Capitan.

Today's battles over invasive tourism, wilderness management, indigenous land rights, water resources, and deforestation are, unfortunately, nothing new to the Sierra Nevada region and its big three parks. These are largely the same issues that have shaped the colorful, hardscrabble history of Yosemite, Sequoia, and Kings Canyon. One of the great aspects of visiting the region is the opportunity to trace the evidence of this past.

Bridalveil Fall flows year-round in Yosemite Valley, an area once home to the Ahwahneechees.

NATIVE
AMERICANS

SIERRA NEVADA
TRIBES & BANDS:
· Paiutes (tribe)
· Southern
  Miwouk (tribe)
· Monacheee
  (tribe)
· Waksachi
· Patwisha
· Wobonuch
· Yokut
· Ahwahneechee

⟲ NATIVE AMERICANS

While relatively little is known about many of the native peoples who lived in the Sierra Nevada, we do know that various tribes have lived in the area since prehistoric times. Signs of these early inhabitants include *morteros* (grinding holes in rocks, where acorn was turned into flour) and rock art—mostly pictographs, but petroglyphs, too. You can spot the *morteros* in all three national parks: keep your eyes trained along the walking trails in forests and valleys for rocks with the telltale scooped depressions. The best place to spy prehistoric rock art is in the southern reaches of Sequoia National Park.

Evidence suggests seasonal relocation as part of the prehistoric peoples' lifestyle. They moved around to stay ahead of the cold as well as to hunt game and gather edible plants at higher elevations in the summer. Later tribes in the Sierra Nevada foothills also followed this movement pattern. On the east side of the mountain range, especially around Mono Lake and the Owens Valley, lived the Paiutes; to the west were the Southern Miwok. Though the tribes sometimes intermarried and had occasional alliances, skirmishes between them were frequent. Historians likewise disagree about why the two warred, though it's typically assumed that common causes were hunting ground rights and a scarcity of resources, especially for the

Paiutes, who had to contend with the east side's demanding desert-like existence.

Farther south in what today is Sequoia National Park, the Monachee (or Western Mono) tribe was divided into different bands, with the Waksachi residing north of the Kaweah River and the Patwisha (Potwisha, or Balwisha) to the south. The Wobonuch band inhabited the foothills farther north at what is now Grant Grove in Kings Canyon National Park. In the lowest-elevation foothills and across California's central valley were the Yokut, whose role in the most significant event in the history of Yosemite, the engagement of the Mariposa Battalion, is described below.

In the Yosemite Valley, a distinct band of Native Americans who called themselves the Ahwahneechee ("dwellers of the gaping mouth," referring to the valley itself) eventually emerged. A fierce debate continues over whether these people were more closely connected to Miwok or Paiute tribespeople. This conflict helps prevent either tribe from achieving federal recognition as an indigenous tribe with rights related to the Yosemite Valley.

There can be no debate, however, that the Ahwahneechee ways of life showed significant cultural influences from both sides of the Sierra Nevada. This is demonstrated, for example, in their mixed artistic styles of basketry. The baskets reflect different traditional designs, interpretations, and materials. It's possible to see some of this basketry at the museum in Yosemite Valley, as well as other park interpretive centers. (It also can occasionally be bought at the gift shop in The Ahwahnee hotel in the Yosemite Valley.)

You can literally walk in the footsteps of some of these tribes. Still in existence are footpaths more or less as they were centuries ago, crossing formidable mountain passes. They're snowbound for most of the year but clear for a couple of months in summer.

EARLY EXPLORERS AND A RUSH FOR RICHES

On January 6, 1805, a Spanish expedition came across the great canyon of the Kings River, named by them in honor of the royals who stopped over in Bethlehem for the Feast of Epiphany. However, it is not known for certain who the first Europeans to set foot in the Yosemite Valley were. It may have been a bunch of frontiersman led by Joseph Reddeford Walker, who crossed the Sierra Nevada in 1833 and stumbled upon

Early inhabitants in the Sierra Nevada wove baskets. You can see demonstrations at the Yosemite Museum, near the Yosemite Valley Visitor Center.

In the 19th century, pioneers came to hunt in the area that would become Yosemite National Park.

what the group described as a vast valley with nearby groves of giant sequoia trees.

It wasn't until 1848 when James W. Marshall successfully panned for gold at Sutter's Mill that the pioneer boom really began. As word of the riches hidden in the Sierra Nevada spread eastward, gold seekers traveled by wagon train across the United States and many more arrived by ship in the San Francisco Bay. Perhaps in part because of the gold in them thar hills, California was quickly granted statehood in 1850.

Encounters between miners (for gold as well as mineral resources) and Native Americans were seldom friendly. The miners and other newcomers to the West, including the military, ranchers, and homesteading pioneers, introduced such foreign diseases as smallpox, influenza, and measles that decimated tribal populations, much as earlier Spanish Catholic missions had done elsewhere along the California coast. The U.S. federal government supposedly wanted to negotiate the peaceful relocation of local tribes, but Native Americans resisted being forcibly removed to reservations in California's central valley.

THE MARIPOSA BATTALION

In 1851 a militia called the Mariposa Battalion led by prospector James Savage entered Yosemite Valley, hell-bent on avenging an attack on trading posts by Miwok and Yokut tribespeople who had been working for immigrant miners. After successive campaigns, this militia captured Chief Tenaya, the leader of the Ahwahneechee people then living in Yosemite Valley.

The Ahwahneechee were taken to a reservation outside Fresno. Soon afterward, Chief Tenaya left the reservation to live with Paiutes near Mono Lake before returning in 1853 to Yosemite Valley, where he died violently during a confrontation with Southern Miwok tribesmen, allegedly over stolen horses. These events swung the pendulum from Native American dominance in the Yosemite region in favor of the expansion of the Western frontier. Today, the conflict's impact is signaled by the many landmarks bearing Native American names, such as Tenaya Lake in the Tuolumne Meadows highlands of Yosemite National Park.

HUNGRY FOR PROFIT

No rich veins of mineral ore were ever discovered in the Yosemite Valley or Kings Canyon, although mining operations were set up at Tioga Pass and Mineral King in the Sierra Nevada high country. After the mid–

19th century, once it was clear mining was not paying off, California immigrants became interested in exploiting the more abundant natural resources in the region, trying their hand at ranching—ranchers grazed herds of cattle and sheep in the mountain meadows and valleys—as well as logging.

The loggers found themselves in a no-win situation. They hacked down giant sequoias, but never profited from their labors because the wood of these trees becomes more brittle as the trees age, often causing them to break apart into useless pieces after being felled. Loggers didn't know that the trees would splinter until they started cutting them down, and even after the logged trees disintegrated, the loggers kept hoping they could profit by transforming the wood into differ-

Frustrated by shattering giant sequoias, some 19th-century loggers tried to turn the wood into toothpicks.

ent products (like toothpicks) or by trying different techniques. But ultimately, nothing proved profitable. Under the heading of history that you can unfortunately see, ugly fields of giant-sequoia stumps in Kings Canyon National Park and the Giant Sequoia National Monument of the Sierra National Forest testify to this brief, destructive period of local history.

⊙› PRESERVING THE PARKS

Not everyone who visited the Yosemite region during the late 19th century was just trying to make a buck. Painters and photographers soaked up the natural beauty of the uniquely shaped and unusually lush Yosemite Valley, while scientists and surveyors measured, observed, and cataloged the riches of flora and fauna. After concerns raised by early visitors and budding conservationists, President Abraham Lincoln signed the Yosemite Land Grant of 1864, which gave the Yosemite Valley and the Mariposa Grove of giant sequoias to the state of California to better protect them as a natural resource.

In 1866, Wawona-area pioneer Galen Clark was appointed as the guardian of the grant, a job that came with little authority; the job was ill-defined, so Clark had no official tasks. His duties consisted of wel-

Conservationist
John Muir called Kings Canyon
"a rival of the Yosemite."

coming visitors and providing them with some guidance. He in effect served as both an early park interpreter and an ad hoc law enforcement ranger, albeit one without power to enforce regulations. He was able to educate visitors in how to better preserve the wildlands in their natural state, even as ranchers, sheepherders, homesteaders, and tourism entrepreneurs continued to wreak havoc on the natural ecosystem of the area. Fragile meadows were eroded by grazing livestock and a burgeoning tourism infrastructure.

Fortunately today you cannot see the effects of this damage, as these areas have long since been restored within the national park boundaries. However, the past wasteful havoc is still felt by visitors confronting the fact that there are limited places to camp in Yosemite Valley.

JOHN MUIR, FATHER OF OUR NATIONAL PARKS

In 1868, Scottish-born naturalist and conservationist John Muir took his first life-changing trip into the Sierra Nevada mountains. He saw firsthand how grazing livestock (which he referred to as "hoofed locusts") and the logging of giant sequoias were ruining this mountainous region. Muir soon became an advocate of the need to further protect these public lands for future generations. His advocacy was popular with the U.S. populace, but not so much with the state and federal government or private entrepreneurs.

Theodore Roosevelt and John Muir stand at Glacier Point in Yosemite National Park.

Muir invited politicians and other well-known people of influence to accompany him on camping trips into the high country, including at Tuolumne Meadows and in Kings Canyon, which Muir called "a rival of the Yosemite." At the same time, partly in response to these grassroots efforts, Visalia newspaperman George Stewart had been campaigning for federal protection of the Giant Forest from timber logging interests. In 1890, the federal government established not only Yosemite National Park but also Sequoia National Park, encompassing the Giant Forest, and General Grant National Park, surrounding the General Grant Tree in Grant Grove, now part of Kings Canyon National Park. Two years later, Muir founded the Sierra Club.

Kitty Tatch, an 1890s waitress, and a friend celebrate on Yosemite's overhanging rock at Glacier Point. (top right) Ice skaters enjoy Mirror Lake. (bottom right) A stagecoach takes visitors through Yosemite Valley.

⊶ TOURISM TAKES ROOT

Visitors could pass through the Wawona Tunnel Tree between 1881, when the hole was carved out, until the winter of 1968-69, when it toppled due to the hole as well as the paving over of its roots. What's left of the felled tree lies in Mariposa Grove, Yosemite National Park.

Even before the national parks were established, pleasure-seeking visitors had started frequenting the Yosemite Valley, Giant Forest, Kings Canyon, and Mt. Whitney (named after Josiah Whitney, the leader of the ambitious California Geological Survey begun in 1860).

The first tourists arrived on foot or by horseback. Starting in 1886, a horse-drawn stage service reached Yosemite Valley from Wawona. The stage operated until 1907, when a railroad between Merced and El Portal allowed visitors access to the valley from the west. Tourist camps were built in both Yosemite Valley and in the Giant Forest of Sequoia National Park, while atop Glacier Point in Yosemite National Park a tourist hotel appeared that was accessible by hiking or on horseback via a 4-mile toll trail up from the valley below. The detrimental effects of this early tourism were slowly erased once the area came under the administration of the National Park Service.

By the turn of the 20th century, tourism in both parks, as well as in the nearby Kings Canyon, was well established. In 1906, the state of California gave back Yosemite Valley and Mariposa Grove to the

BUFFALO SOLDIERS: THE FIRST PARK RANGERS

Although Native Americans were the original protectors of the land, it was the U.S. military that was assigned to protect the new Sierra Nevada national parks that Congress created in 1890. African-American regiments of "buffalo soldiers" (so called out of respect by Native Americans in honor of their fierce fighting style, as well as the color of their skin and the feel of their hair) that had been established during the Civil War were assigned this peacetime duty.

Starting from San Francisco's Presidio, it took the soldiers about two weeks to journey overland into the mountains, where they set up camp during the summer in the Wawona area of Yosemite National Park and also in the giant sequoia groves farther south.

While most of the officers in charge of these black regiments were white, Captain Charles Young, the African-American son of freed slaves, was in charge of the soldiers assigned to Sequoia National Park as well as General Grant National Park (which would later be incorporated into Kings Canyon). In defense of the parks, these infantry and cavalry regiments chased off poachers, sheepherders, loggers, and miners until civilian rangers took over after 1914.

Unfortunately, few photos or other documents remain today to tell us more about this unique period in the parks' history.

Buffalo soldiers of the 25th Infantry.

federal government, thus expanding Yosemite National Park. The ever-increasing popularity of Yosemite, Sequoia, and General Grant national parks exerted pressures on the natural ecosystem as tourist development continued unchecked.

All that changed after the National Park Service (NPS) was founded in 1916. Under Director Stephen T. Mather and his successor Horace Albright, development of the parks was judiciously planned. Many private land in-holdings (privately owned parcels of land within the national park boundaries) were eliminated; park concessionaire businesses were consolidated; a network of trails and roads was built; and the tradition of ranger-led campfire programs and guided interpretive hikes began.

LESSONS OF HETCH HETCHY

The NPS was too late, however, to save the Hetch Hetchy Valley of Yosemite National Park from being environmentally affected by

Yosemite's Hetch Hetchy Valley held a special place in John Muir's heart, but try as he did, he was not able to stop it from being dammed. The water that floods the valley provides water and energy for San Francisco.

the building of a dam, which had been under construction for three years before the NPS was founded. When it was completed after 10 long years in 1923, the O'Shaughnessy Dam flooded the Hetch Hetchy Valley and began supplying water and generating power for the rapidly growing San Francisco Bay Area. John Muir had tirelessly campaigned against the dam, but lost out to political interests from the city of San Francisco.

Also in the 1920s, a similarly alarming plan by the city of Los Angeles proposed damming the nearby Kings River watershed.

However, conservationists had begun advocating not only for the enlargement of Sequoia National Park (to which the Kern River Canyon and Mt. Whitney were successfully added in 1926), but also for legal protection of the Kings Canyon from logging and ranching interests. Much political wrangling over all of these environmental concerns ensued.

The controversy over the creation of the third national park in the Sierra Nevada ended in 1940, when Congress established Kings Canyon National Park, which swallowed up smaller General Grant National Park. In 1965, the proposed dam sites of Cedar Grove and the Tehipite Valley were also safely added to the new national park, saving them from Hetch Hetchy's fate.

BUILDING UP THE PARKS

The advent of automobile travel sparked the greatest changes to the national parks. Auto-friendly paved roads quickly connected the parks

President Teddy Roosevelt stands with some companions at the base of the Grizzly Giant tree in Yosemite National Park's Mariposa Grove, 1903.

to towns and cities in California's central valley and provided greater access to the parks' interiors.

The first cars entered Yosemite Valley in 1913. Soon afterward director Stephen T. Mather purchased the privately owned Tioga Road, a historic wagon route, across Yosemite's high country. Then in 1926, Generals Highway opened between the Sierra Nevada foothills and the Giant Forest area of Sequoia National Park. In the 1930s, convict labor was used to build a stunning scenic byway into the Kings Canyon to connect Grant Grove with Cedar Grove along the

FREE FOR ALL

"There is nothing so American as our national parks. The scenery and wildlife are native. The fundamental idea behind the parks is native. It is, in brief, that the country belongs to the people, that it is in the process of making for the enrichment of the lives of all of us. The parks stand as the outward symbol of this great human principle."

"It took a bitter struggle to teach the country at large that our national resources are not inexhaustible and that, when public domain is stolen, a twofold injury is done, for it is a theft of the treasure of the present and at the same time bars the road of opportunity to the future."

—President Franklin D. Roosevelt in a radio address, 1934.

South Fork of the Kings River. Because of its hairpin turns and sheer cliff drop-offs, it was a hazardous byway to build as well as drive. The breathtaking, twisting road is still used today by drivers going from Grant Grove to Cedar Grove.

In the same decade, President Franklin D. Roosevelt created the Civilian Conservation Corps (CCC), which employed three million young men mostly on forestry and flood-control projects, some of which were in the national parks during the Great Depression. The CCC brought hundreds of thousands of workers into the American West to help pave over parts of the wilderness in an effort to draw more visitors to the national parks.

Yosemite was no exception. CCC workers paved over the park's road to Glacier Point and the historical stagecoach route between Wawona and Yosemite Valley. In Sequoia National Park, the CCC extended the Generals Highway from Giant Forest all the way to Grant Grove, built a stone stairway up Moro Rock, and installed the artisanal Spider Gate at Crystal Cave.

As the network of roads increased in the parks, so did tourism, especially once the all-weather highway from Merced into Yosemite Valley was completed in 1926. The next year the famous Ahwahnee hotel opened in Yosemite Valley. This luxurious hotel, another brainstorm from director Mather, attracted VIP visitors to the park, which aided the park's continuing preservation efforts by ensuring popular support from celebrities, high-society movers and shakers, and even U.S. presidents.

During World War II, visitation to the parks dropped, especially as areas of Yosemite came under military control. Security was increased at Hetch Hetchy Reservoir and the grand Ahwahnee served as a military hospital. Nevertheless, after the war, tourism boomed again, thanks to postwar euphoria and a strong U.S. economy. The birth of the classic American driving vacation in the late 1940s and early '50s, during the heyday of Route 66, increased park visitation many times over.

Unfortunately, federal funding for the parks failed to keep pace with increasing tourism. By the early 1950s, the park infrastructure was sadly lacking, having fallen behind the ever bigger crowds who came to visit the parks each year. The buildings constructed by CCC workers in the 1930s became overwhelmed by tourists, and there were not enough NPS rangers to help control the crowds, resulting in widespread damage to some of the country's most-prized national parks.

Midcentury Maneuvers

In 1955, NPS Director Conrad Wirth proposed a solution to the crisis: Mission 66, a federally funded program that aimed to overhaul the parks. Over the next 10 years, the Mission 66 program poured more than $1 billion into rescuing national parks and improving their visitor facilities, most memorably by creating more than 100 new national-park visitor centers. It was during the Mission 66 era that the Tioga Road through Yosemite's high country was realigned and paved, and that Cedar Grove was finally added to Kings Canyon National Park.

The breathtaking, twisting road is still used today by drivers going from Grant Grove to Cedar Grove.

As these Sierra Nevada national parks became increasingly developed and accessible to tourists, Congress wisely passed the Wilderness Preservation Act of 1964, which set aside more than 9 million acres of public lands across the country to remain forever untrammeled by roads or motor vehicles. This important act was passed after the Leopold Report of 1963, which recommended that national parks work to restore the native ecosystems of the areas they protect.

The legislation resulted in widespread NPS policy changes, such as allowing wildfires to burn after decades of fire suppression, and working to hold population levels of wild animals steady. In Yosemite Valley, traffic was curtailed by a system of one-way roads and a shuttle-bus system was implemented. Restoration of the Giant Forest in Sequoia National Park is still an ongoing project.

As national-park visitation increased further after 1970—the year of the Stoneman Meadow riots in Yosemite, when hippies and park rangers clashed on July 4th over public use of fragile meadow areas—the National Park Service limited national-park campsites and placed a quota on the number of people who could use backcountry trails.

The government also sent a strong message about preservation in 1978 when it put the kibosh on the Walt Disney Company's plans for a ski resort in the Mineral King Valley, which was added to Sequoia National Park that same year. Mineral King continues today to be a flashpoint for debate, as many rustic mountain cabins there have been in the same family for generations, and private in-holdings remain inside the national-park boundaries.

⌾ THE PARKS TODAY

Underfunded and overwhelmed is perhaps the rosiest shorthand for the state of many of the national parks, though the effects are quite visible in the Sierra Nevada parks. Bumper-to-bumper vehicles and the pollutants they emit are the unfortunate by-products of popularity, especially at Yosemite, which receives more than 4 million visitors each year.

Sequoia and Kings Canyon national parks also teem with vehicles, especially along the Generals Highway, though in a perverse take on dumping trash in your neighbor's yard, most of the air pollution that hazily obscures viewpoints and mountain peaks of those parks drifts up from California's central valley. Noise from frequent military overflights of these parks is regulated, but still may intrude upon your backcountry experience. More dangerously for the environment, the Sierra Nevada foothills region has become a prime area for illegal marijuana plant cultivation, a harsh mix of terraced landscaping, irrigation pipe systems, and toxic pesticides that seep into the river systems of Sequoia and Kings Canyon national parks.

In response to the underfunding, crowding, and pollution, but more broadly in keeping with the legacy of the Wilderness Act, the National Park Service is trying to restore more parkland to its natural state. Individual parks are doing their best to improve the visitor experience. A free shuttle-bus service has recently started in the Giant Forest area of Sequoia National Park, for example, while in Yosemite Valley a more modern visitor center has been built. And, similar to the Mission 66 project of last century, the NPS's new Centennial Initiative aims to improve park infrastructure, increase outreach to urban youth in public-school classrooms, inventory the incredible

biodiversity of the parks, and freshen up the famous Tunnel View overlook of Yosemite Valley in time for the 100th birthday of the National Park Service in 2016.

A rainbow after a storm arcs over the mountains of Kings Canyon National Park.

Yosemite National Park

The moon casts its glow over North Dome.

No other place in the Sierra Nevada mountains stirs up the soul and can jump-start wild imaginations like Yosemite National Park. For many nature lovers, it's one of the American West's ultimate outdoor destinations, and it's open year-round. You could visit Yosemite in every season for a decade and still not wholly penetrate its wild heart. It's worth fighting the crowds to see this famous place because it's one of those rare things: a wonder of the world that actually lives up to the hype, time and again.

The ethereal beauty of Yosemite, with Half Dome, below right.

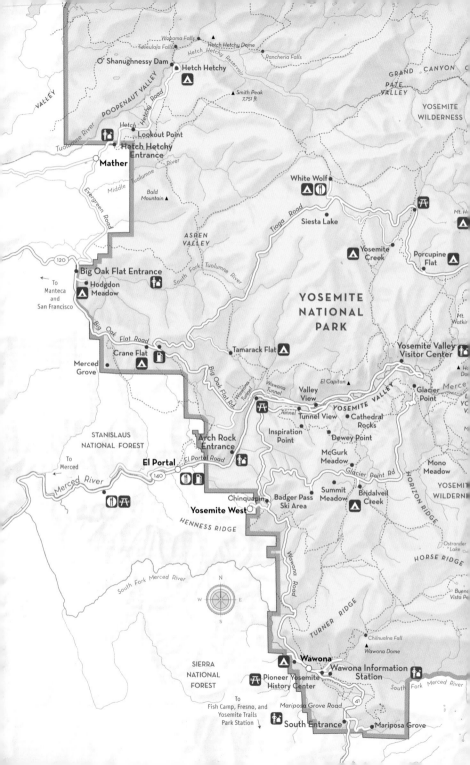

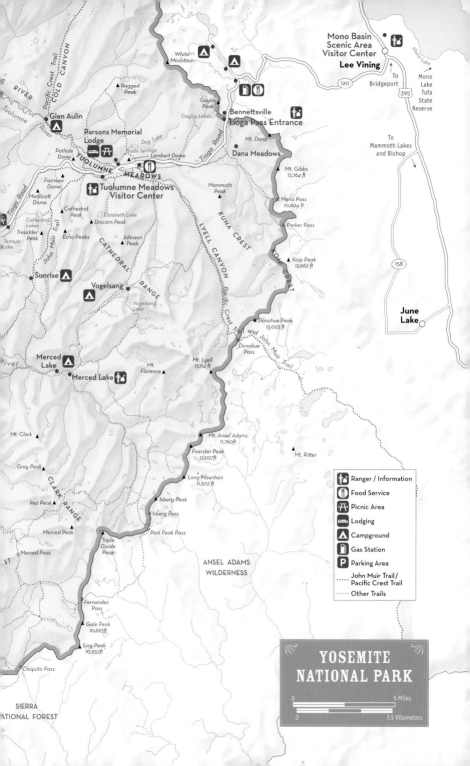

ICONIC ROCKS

**HALF DOME—
ELEVATION:**
8,836 feet

MILES TO HIKE IT:
15-16 round-trip

**EL CAPITAN—
ELEVATION:** 7,569

DAYS TO CLIMB IT:
4-6 days

In early spring, waterfalls burst from sheer granite cliffs as the snow melts off the skyscraping, high-country peaks. As summer arrives, wildflowers fill delicate alpine meadows with a joyful palette of colors, and icy mountain passes become trekable once more. The hottest days of summer invite swimming in the park's lazy rivers and hidden, high-elevation lakes. Summer is also the most active time for the park's wildlife, whether you're eager to photograph delicate hummingbirds or to follow the trails of brawny black bears.

Fall is a more peaceful time, as the wilderness transitions into winter and the crowds begin to thin. However, golden afternoons and snow-free trails tempt plenty of off-season explorers to the park. Winters are cold (regularly dipping below freezing at night) and long (usually lasting from November through April), but there's a freshness in the crisp air and beauty in the powdery layers of snow that blanket the park from peak to valley, beckoning to snowshoers, skiers, and those seeking solitude.

Yosemite National Park comprises almost 1,200 square miles of mountainous terrain. The park has four main tourist areas: Yosemite Valley, Glacier Point, Wawona/Mariposa Grove, and Tuolumne Meadows, and two minor areas, Hetch Hetchy Valley and Crane Flat. The regions are only an hour or two apart by car, so it's theoretically possible to stop at all of them, however briefly, in just one day. But then you would miss out on some of Yosemite's most spectacular moments that justify lingering longer, from walks beside the Merced River and its dew-drenched meadows while dawn breaks over the Yosemite Valley, to watching the moon rise above the Sierra Nevada's jagged peaks as you sit on ancient rocks atop Glacier Point. Make more time to absorb the awesome experiences this singular wilderness offers. Stay overnight in a campground, at an in-park lodge or hotel, or in a gateway town (*see* the Where to Stay and Eat chapter).

Alpine scenery stretches along Tioga Road.

Water flowing through Yosemite Valley. (top left) Catching the view from Glacier Point. (bottom left) A deer wades through the Tuolumne River.

PLANNING YOUR TIME

If you've come for a weekend, spend the first day exploring Yosemite Valley. Free yourself from the confines of your car by leaving it behind in a day-use parking lot. Ride the free shuttle bus from point to point, or rent a bicycle to explore at your own pace. First visit the Yosemite Valley visitor center and museum in Yosemite Village, where at the Ansel Adams Gallery you can see iconic black-and-white photography of the park's well-known landmarks. Then ride out to view the valley's famous waterfalls, especially Yosemite Falls and Vernal Fall near the Happy Isles, where you learn about the park's unique ecology at a family-friendly nature center. Just before sunset, drive up to Glacier Point; you may wish to stay for the excellent stargazing.

On your second day, drive the scenic Tioga Road through the Sierra Nevada high country that John Muir and others worked so hard to preserve. The road is only open during summer, when you can relish sunny walks around Tuolumne Meadows and Tenaya Lake. Or, head south from the valley to Wawona, with its historical sites and the nearby Mariposa Grove of giant sequoias. Anyone with more time to spend in the park can tour at a more leisurely pace, taking time

(bottom) Fern-covered black rocks frame 317-foot-tall Vernal Fall; rainbows often play in the spray at its base. (right) Yosemite Valley has many of the park's most famous sites.

YOSEMITE AND SEQUOIA / KINGS CANYON NATIONAL PARKS

Rising more than 350 stories above
Yosemite Valley, El Capitan (shown
on both pages) is the largest exposed
granite monolith in the world.

out for more day hikes to waterfalls, craggy granite formations, and photo-worthy viewpoints.

⟨•⟩ SIGHTS

YOSEMITE VALLEY

See the Yosemite Valley Floor map.

The wellspring of Yosemite National Park is the grand **Yosemite Valley** (elevation 4,000 feet). Ranchers, tourists, writers, and painters all began trickling into this idyllic valley after Native Americans were forced out in the mid-19th century. One early visitor, part of the Mariposa Battalion, described being moved to tears by the sight of the valley —a response that echoes over the centuries. Most of today's 3 million annual visitors to Yosemite start by visiting the valley, that constant source of awe and wonder.

One way to explore Yosemite Valley and see its key sights is by combining driving with walking—basically enjoying a scenic drive with several stops along the way. By car, there are a few ways to access the valley, but the southern approach provides the most thrills. In the park, Highway 41 becomes Wawona Road as it skirts north along the western edge of the Wawona region.

Once you've emerged from the almost mile-long **v**, which was bored through the mountainside by Civilian Conservation Corps (CCC) workers in the 1930s, pull over at ★**TUNNEL VIEW**. There awaits a framed postcard-perfect view of the entire Yosemite Valley. On your left stands mighty **El Capitan** (elevation 7,569 feet), an iconic formation that issues a siren's call to rock climbers. Rising more than 3,000 feet above the valley floor, it is the world's largest granite mono-lith. The curved tooth of **Half Dome** (elevation 8,836 feet) rises, also more than 3,000 feet, in the central background. And off to the right, Bridalveil Fall plunges off the cliffside into the valley below.

Tunnel View's restoration was unveiled in fall 2008, making this classic stop better than ever. Among the improvements to the over-look was the addition of a large viewing area separated from the parking lot—meaning you can now angle for your photos without dodging cars.

Be forewarned that a confusing system of one-way roads flows through the 7-mile-long valley. A free national-park map handed out to visitors at the entrance stations will help you navigate the spottily

(opposite) Taking in the view of Yosemite Valley near Wawona Tunnel.

Yosemite is a wonder of the world that actually lives up to the hype, time and again.

signposted roads. When in doubt, go with the flow. You'll rarely get lost for too long.

Beyond Tunnel View, Wawona Road continues east deeper into the valley. Your next stop is **Bridalveil Fall**, a lacy waterfall that tumbles off the valley's steep cliffs for 620 feet. From the parking lot, you can walk to the waterfall on a half-mile round-trip trail that ends with a climb up to the fall's base—if you're there during its peak flow in May, be prepared to be sprayed. (The trail to Bridalveil Fall is paved—except for the short climb at the end—so people in strollers and wheelchairs can experience this attraction as well (though it's an uphill trail, so it may still be a small challenge for those in nonmotorized wheelchairs). The fall flows year-round, though it may dry to barely a trickle in drier months. In winter, icy conditions prevail, so the trail may be slippery.

Continue driving east on Wawona Road, which has now become Southside Drive (it switches en route between Tunnel View and here) past the twin **Cathedral Spires**, which jut skyward out of the valley's meadows off to the right. On the Merced River, which flows through the entire valley, **Cathedral Beach** on your left makes a good place to stop for a picnic and provides dead-on views of El Capitan, which towers above the treetops on the north side of the road. To the east of "El Cap," look for the **Three Brothers**, a trio of granite points more than 3,000 feet tall dominated by **Eagle Peak** (elevation 7,779 feet). Two more inviting picnic areas are found farther east along the river at **Sentinel Beach** and the **Swinging Bridge**. If you walk out

YOSEMITE'S INDIAN WARS, NEW AND OLD

The Yosemite Valley was first inhabited by Native American tribes, notably Southern Miwok people from the west side and Paiutes from the Mono Lake region to the east. Despite frequent battles ("Yosemite" is a Miwok word meaning "those who kill"), a rich cultural intermingling also took place between the tribes, resulting in intermarriage and a distinct set of religious rituals, political laws, and habits of everyday life. Descendants of both tribes continue to debate whose heritage is more closely linked to protecting Yosemite's vast parklands and fight for federal recognition accordingly.

At the time of initial contact with Europeans, Chief Tenaya led the mixed band of Native Americans living in Yosemite Valley. They called themselves the Ahwahneechee, or people of the Ahwahnee, which means "wide, gaping mouth," in reference to the valley. As the California Gold Rush began in 1848, miners invaded the Sierra Nevada, stirring up trouble with local tribes. In 1851, the state of California sent the Mariposa Battalion into Yosemite Valley to forcibly remove its indigenous peoples to a reservation outside Fresno. Chief Tenaya and his people were captured, and their village was burned. Today, a reconstructed tribal village with a short self-guided interpretive trail is set up outside the valley's Yosemite Museum.

Come in via Highway 41 and your first marvelous view in the valley is of Bridalveil Fall, a 620-foot filmy fall that is often diverted as much as 20 feet one way by the breeze.

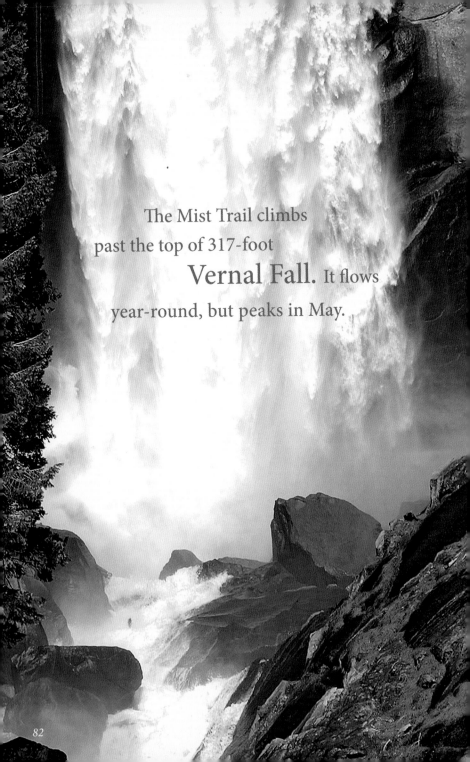

The Mist Trail climbs
past the top of 317-foot
Vernal Fall. It flows
year-round, but peaks in May.

The Merced River plunges out of the high country toward the eastern end of Yosemite Valley, creating 594-foot Nevada Fall.

Composed of three falls, Yosemite Falls form the highest waterfall in North America and the fifth highest in the world. The water from the top descends 2,425 feet. When the falls run hard, you can hear them thunder across the valley.

The LeConte Memorial Lodge is named after University of California geologist and former Sierra Club director Joseph LeConte.

into the middle of Swinging Bridge, you may glimpse Yosemite Falls on the opposite side of the valley.

Southside Drive next passes the white wooden **Yosemite Chapel** (*Southside Dr.; no phone; www.yosemitechapel.org*), with its petite steeple stretching above the pine trees. A popular spot for weddings, the 1879 structure is a serene spot to stop and reflect upon what John Muir described as nature's temple. From the chapel's grassy front lawn you can catch a view of **Yosemite Falls**.

East of the chapel, the drive approaches a heavily trafficked intersection at the **Sentinel Bridge**. You have two choices here. If you continue straight without crossing the Merced River, you'll find yourself on a one-way driving loop that takes you past the Housekeeping Camp and the unusual looking Tudor-style **LeConte Memorial Lodge** (*Southside Dr.; 209/372–4542; www.sierraclub.org*), a National Historic Landmark built of granite and wood. Named after a California geologist and operated by the nonprofit Sierra Club for more than a century, the lodge is open between May and September from 10 AM until 4 PM Wednesday through Saturday. Family-friendly nature programs are offered throughout the day, with natural and cultural history presentations at 8 most evenings.

Next, the one-way loop passes the "tent camp" **Curry Village** (*Southside Dr.; 209/372–8333*), a rustic family-friendly resort with canvas tents, cabins, and casual dining halls started by an enterprising couple, David and Jenny Curry, in 1899. Back then at the village, "a good bed and clean napkin with every meal" cost just $2 a day. Today, Curry Village is a buzzing hub for outdoor activities in all four seasons. At its Mountain Shop, you can rent outdoor-activity gear, including bicycles for pedaling around the valley—a great way to avoid the all-too-common traffic jams.

Before looping around past the valley's main campgrounds—Upper Pines, North Pines, and Lower Pines—and the horse stables, the one-way driving loop passes the **Nature Center at Happy Isles** (*Southside Dr.; 209/372-0631*), where in the summertime, kids can explore the valley's wildlife ecology and its forest, river wetlands, and granite talus environments through hands-on exhibits and interpretive trails. Bubbling brooks and streams bring their sounds to the air outside the center; it's a great place to sit on a cool boulder and simply breathe in the fresh air deeply.

The Mist Trail (*see* "Best Day Hikes" in the Activities section, *below*) climbs past the tops of 317-foot-tall **Vernal Fall** and 594-foot-tall **Nevada Fall**, from where daring hikers can continue to the summit of the park's most famous granite formation, **Half Dome**, perched high above the valley floor. The falls flow year-round but peak in May. From here the road continues looping around the valley past the Happy Isles and the trailhead for the Mirror Lake hike before running into the Yosemite Village area.

Earlier at the Sentinel Bridge fork, if you skip the one-way driving loop and instead choose to turn left to cross over the Sentinel Bridge, you'll be on a small road that approaches **Yosemite Village**. Just across the bridge, signs point out day-use parking lots east of the intersection. Use these lots, as it's easier to leave your car parked while you explore the rest of the valley on foot, bicycle, or the free

AMONG THE LOVERS OF NATURE

"But no temple made with hands can compare with Yosemite. Every rock in its walls seems to glow with life. . . . Awful in stern, immovable majesty, how softly these rocks are adorned, and how fine and reassuring the company they keep: their feet among beautiful groves and meadows, their brows in the sky, a thousand flowers leaning confidingly against their feet, bathed in floods of water, floods of light, while the snow and waterfalls, the winds and avalanches and clouds shine and sing and wreathe about them as the years go by, and myriads of small winged creatures—birds, bees, butterflies—give glad animation and help to make all the air into music. Down through the middle of the Valley flows the crystal Merced, River of Mercy, peacefully quiet, reflecting lilies and trees and the onlooking rocks; things frail and fleeting and types of endurance meeting here and blending in countless forms, as if into this one mountain mansion Nature had gathered her choicest treasures, to draw her lovers into close and confiding communion with her."

—John Muir, *The Yosemite*, 1912.

shuttle buses that loop the valley continuously. It's a short walk from the parking lot to the village area, where you will find a post office, a medical clinic, a mechanics' garage, a supermarket with a sports shop, and a variety of places to eat.

In the village, the nonprofit **Yosemite Association** (*209/379–2646; www.yosemite.org*) runs the worthwhile bookstore inside the impressive **Yosemite Valley Visitor Center** (*off Northside Dr.; 209/372-0200*), where National Park Service (NPS) rangers orient visitors to the park's offerings. Stop by to peruse the exhibits for a quick overview of Yosemite's natural and cultural history, starting with its geological prehistory when glaciers that had slipped down from the uplifted Sierra Nevada mountains and the Merced River worked together to carve this valley, through Native American times and early pioneer days in the wilderness, to the contributions of important contemporary figures in the park. The center's theater presents live performances and shows free films of interest to amateur naturalists, historians, and extreme athletes, too. The lineup of movies keeps changing, but films usually deal with nature, history,

YOSEMITE VALLEY VISITOR CENTER

TELEPHONE:
209/372–0200

ADDRESS: off Northside Drive, Yosemite Valley

The Nature Center at Happy Isles is a great place to sit on a cool boulder and breathe the fresh air.

and/or adrenaline-pumping pursuits in the park, like rock climbing and mountaineering.

Beside the visitor center, the **Yosemite Museum** (*off Northside Dr.; 209-372–0200*) focuses on park history, specifically the Native American cultures that once flourished here. A Native American tribeswoman is often available to demonstrate the craft of basket-weaving and beadwork inside the museum, which is a contemplative place to spend an hour, even in peak summer months. Behind the museum stands an interpretive reconstruction of what the Yosemite Valley's Ahwahneechee village may have looked like in the mid–19th century, before it was destroyed by the Mariposa Battalion. Farther west across the street, you can stroll through the pioneer-era **Yosemite Cemetery**.

Back inside the museum, on summer days an art gallery often displays historic photographs of the park, including priceless prints by Ansel Adams. Best known for his black-and-white photographs of the American West, Adams began visiting Yosemite Valley with his fam-

(top right) Earth Day in Yosemite Valley. (bottom right) A craft demonstration at the Yosemite Museum.

ANSEL ADAMS, AT HOME IN YOSEMITE

"I *knew* my destiny when I first experienced Yosemite," claimed Ansel Adams. One of the most revered photographers of the 20th century, Adams is inextricably linked with the Sierra Nevada, especially, Yosemite National Park. He was Yosemite's most famous portrayer, and he worked tirelessly for its conservation.

Adams was born in San Francisco in 1902. His family lived by the Golden Gate beaches, so they were spared the worst of the Great Quake and fires of 1906. But during an aftershock, Adams fell and bashed his nose sideways, giving him his distinctive "earthquaked" profile.

His first trip to Yosemite was on a family vacation in 1916—and it was a momentous one. When he saw Bridalveil Fall for the first time, he realized that "a new era began." His parents gave him his first camera, a Kodak Box Brownie, and he started a visual diary of the landscape's wonders. For the rest of his life, Adams spent at least part of every year in Yosemite.

By 1919, Adams had joined the Sierra Club and was working for the group in Yosemite Valley. But he was also considering a career as a concert pianist, and in 1921 he began visiting an art and souvenir studio in the park to practice on its piano. There he met the owner's daughter, Virginia Best; they were married in the studio in 1928. (Years later, he and Virginia took over the space, selling special-edition prints and teaching photography workshops. Now the studio is the Ansel Adams Gallery.)

As the Sierra Club's photographer, Adams recorded a relatively pristine Yosemite throughout the late 1920s. One spring day in 1927, he set out to capture one of the park's most dramatic landmarks. During the climb to his vantage point, most of his glass plates were ruined. With just one plate left, he decided to use a red filter to retain the striking contrasts between light and shade. The result was his first iconic image: *Monolith, the Face of Half Dome*.

Monolith signaled a shift to a more personal, emotionally expressive photographic style. It also showed how Adams could use equipment and technique to realize an inner vision. Among photographers, Adams quickly became known for his technical brilliance and for sharing his innovations through writing and teaching. Meanwhile, his inspiring images of Yosemite and the Sierra Nevada sparked the American imagination.

These photos had a major material impact as well. In 1936, as one of the Sierra Club's board of directors, Adams went to Washington as the organization's representative. Lobbying to win Kings Canyon protection as a national park, he showed his photos to conservationist and Secretary of the Interior Harold L. Ickes, who in turn brought some of Adams' influential pictures to President Franklin Delano Roosevelt. In 1940, FDR signed the bill making Kings Canyon a national park.

For decades, Adams championed the importance of wilderness, the caretaking of national parks in general, and the protection of his beloved Yosemite. Although he wanted Yosemite, like other parks, to be accessible to the public, he fought against the "resortism" of concessionaires and other modern developments. He also contributed photos to *This is the American Earth*, a Sierra Club book that became a classic of the conservation movement.

Although he photographed all over the country, Adams always considered Yosemite to be his spiritual home. His luminous black-and-white images have become enduring visions of the American West and the power of nature.

–Jennifer Paull

Photographer Ansel Adams in 1943.

The Ansel Adams Gallery displays and sells original and reproduction prints and posters by Yosemite's most famous photographer.

ily in 1916, and returned for many seasons to take photographs while trekking in the high country of the Sierra Nevada.

Just east of the museum next to the visitor center, the **Ansel Adams Gallery** (*off Northside Dr.; 209/372–4413; www.anseladams.com*) and gift shop regularly exhibits the photographer's masterful prints, along with rotating exhibits of works by contemporary landscape photographers. The gallery, which also organizes print and digital photography workshops for visitors, inhabits Best's Studio, dating from 1902.

If you feel inspired to try your own hands at creating art during your sojourn in the park, stop by the **Yosemite Art and Education Center**, which offers morning and afternoon classes from spring through fall in everything from landscape watercolor painting to travel journaling. The center, just south of the village store, accepts reservations for art classes a day in advance and sells art supplies if you didn't bring your own.

It's a short walk from the main Yosemite Village area to the **Yosemite Lodge at the Falls** (*Northside Dr.; 209/372–1274; www.yosemitepark.com*), which offers an array of services, from bike rentals to a staffed tour-and-activities desk, in addition to a coffee shop, food court, restaurant and bar, and a nature-themed gift shop. In summer, the outdoor amphitheater behind the lodge becomes the happening place. Rangers and naturalists lead evening programs, and movie nights occur regularly (the selection varies; sometimes they're educational, sometimes more entertaining).

Although the lodge's early-20th-century buildings look bland, it's what you can view on the cliffside above that makes it worth a detour. At 2,425 feet high, the namesake **Yosemite Falls** comprises three waterfalls, with the Upper, Middle, and Lower Falls all bouncing off cliffs and plummeting into the valley below. If you hike the mile-long loop trail (which is partially paved for wheelchair access) to the base of the Lower Falls during the peak water flow in May, expect to get soaked. The trio of falls usually thunders from April through June, but typically runs dry between August and October. In winter, an ice cone forms at the base of the Upper Falls, presenting a unique opportunity for photographers. Farther west of the lodge is **Camp 4**, the infamous campground that gets taken over by rock climbers every year. The trailhead for the hike to Upper Yosemite Falls (*see* Best Day Hikes, *below*) is nearby.

Before leaving the valley, take the side road east of Yosemite Village over to **The Ahwahnee** *(Ahwahnee Rd.; 209/372-1407; www.yosemitepark.com)* hotel, now a National Historic Landmark. It was built in 1927 at the request of Stephen T. Mather, then the director of the NPS, who chose this site for its remarkable views, particularly of Half Dome. Unlike many of the rustic park lodges of its day, The Ahwahnee was not built of wood, which would make it vulnerable to fires, but instead of poured concrete that was treated to look like redwood. The interior design boldly mixes Native American, Arts and Crafts, and art-deco stylistic elements, but it's the sheer size of the public areas that impresses most. Peek inside the Mural Room, with its enormous wall painting of Yosemite's flora and fauna, then take a breather in the solarium while you contemplate Glacier Point, or just have a cocktail at the bar beside the Great Lounge, where a fireplace blazes on chilly nights.

After backtracking to pick up your car from the day-use parking lot, join the westbound traffic leaving Yosemite Valley via Northside Drive. You'll pass the Three Brothers again before reaching **El Capitan Meadow**, a favorite viewpoint for staring up in awe at the sheer vertical face of this monolith, which sets the standard for big-wall climbing.

On the east side of El Capitan Meadow, look for 1,000-foot-high **Horsetail Fall**, which usually flows from December through April. In the latter half of February, it famously glows as it reflects the setting sun. This is the only time of

★ Souvenir Alert ★

Here's a place to flex your wallet: The Ahwahnee gift shop has an unmatched selection of artisan crafts, from wood carvings and Native American beadwork to fine-art nature photographs.

Laden with snow in winter and decked with color in the fall, oak trees stand guard at El Capitan Meadow; Middle Cathedral Rock hovers in the background.

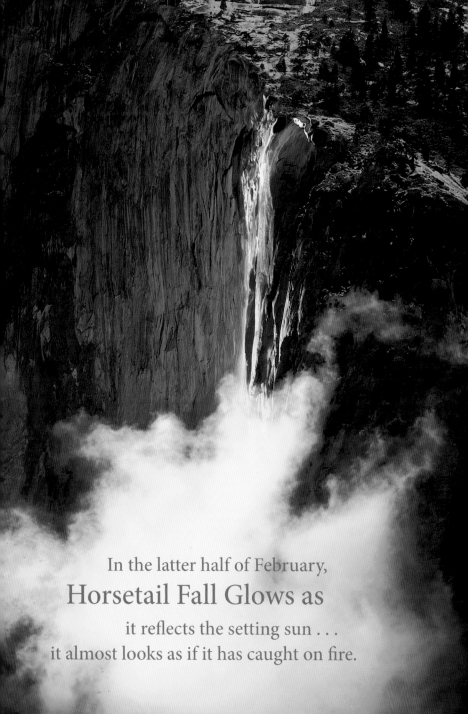

In the latter half of February,
Horsetail Fall Glows as
it reflects the setting sun . . .
it almost looks as if it has caught on fire.

Mist from Horsetail Fall blows over the east side of El Capitan.

At 1,612 feet, Ribbon Fall
is the highest single fall
in North America. The
rainwater and melted snow
that create the slender fall
evaporate quickly at this
height, making it the first of
the valley waterfalls to dry
up in summer.

year when the sun is at the right angle to illuminate the falls, so that it almost looks as if they have caught on fire. To the west of the meadow, the 1,612-feet-high **Ribbon Fall** peaks in May, but usually flows from March through June.

Driving west of El Capitan, pull over just short of the Pohono Bridge at the **Valley View** vista point for one last, lingering look at the Yosemite Valley before reluctantly leaving it behind.

GLACIER POINT ROAD

See the Yosemite Valley Floor map.

Although Yosemite Valley is where visitors spend most of their time, taking the road to Glacier Point is also a must-do. Detouring here will give you an eagle-eyed overview of the entire Yosemite Valley, plus gorgeous views of Half Dome, all from dizzying heights that you won't have to earn the hard way on hiking trails that are like steep granite stairways leading out of the Yosemite Valley.

Here the nature walks are short and pleasurable, and the winding road itself is incredibly scenic. It takes at least an hour to drive the 30 miles south from Yosemite Valley to Glacier Point. You can also access it by driving north from Wawona on Highway 41. Keep in mind that Glacier Point Road is open to vehicle traffic beyond the Badger Pass Ski Area only from May or June until November, weather permitting.

As you drive toward Glacier Point Road, keep a sharp eye out for the Chinquapin intersection. That is where you'll turn east to access Glacier Point Road. Though once a dirt path for wagons, created in 1882 for early tourists to the park, the route is now paved. As it climbs for 16 miles through pine and fir forests from Chinquapin to Glacier Point, the road winds past **Badger Pass Ski Area** (*see* Winter Sports, *below*); **McGurk, Summit and Mono Meadows**, where wildflowers usually bloom in June; and **Bridalveil Creek Campground**, not too far from the trailhead for **Ostrander Lake**, where a rustic hut is open to experienced backcountry skiers and snowshoers in winter. Three miles before reaching Glacier Point, you find the trailhead for **Sentinel Dome**, one of the park's easiest hikes, taking you to the summit of this iconic granite formation (*see* Best Day Hikes, *below*). As you continue driving east on Glacier Point Road, you come to **Washburn Point**, which looks out at Half Dome as well as Nevada and Vernal Falls. It's worth stopping for the view, because it's a different perspective than what you'll get at the road's end.

Glacier Point Road leads you to knockout views of Half Dome.

From Glacier Point, the dead-on views of Half Dome are unmatched by any other roadside viewpoint in Yosemite National Park.

With its sweeping, bird's-eye views, Glacier Point is also a wonderful place to watch a sunset.

Finally, the road reaches its namesake destination, ★GLACIER POINT (elevation 7,214 feet), where you are rewarded with a stunning overlook of Yosemite Valley. To see it, you must pull into the parking lot and then take a short walk. Though the drive up is not bumper to bumper, you'll find that once you reach Glacier Point, the crowds are almost always thick during the day, as people tend to stay awhile. Also, as in the Yosemite Valley, black bears are active in this area, so do not leave any food or scented items in your car. To discourage bear break-ins, either lock everything out of sight in the trunk or better yet, use the bear-proof metal lockers provided around the lot.

From Glacier Point, the dead-on views of Half Dome are unmatched by any other roadside viewpoint in Yosemite National Park. It looks as if you could step right off the edge of the cliff and walk out onto the clouds and over to the dome. Also visible are Yosemite Falls tumbling into the valley below and many of the craggy peaks of the Sierra Nevada high country farther north toward Tioga Road and Tenaya Canyon, which appears to the left of the famous dome. The view from Glacier Point is so iconic that in 2005 it was commemorated on the California state quarter, which depicts John Muir standing atop the point and gazing at Half Dome, while incongruously a California condor flies overhead.

If the crowds are too crushing at Glacier Point, walk down the Panorama Trail to the right for about 20 minutes to have equally gorgeous vistas all to yourself, including better views of Nevada and Vernal Falls. Along the trail, watch for black bears foraging in the forest and ripping up fallen logs to uncover tasty insects beneath the bark. Observe wild bears from a distance and remember never to feed them. (*See* the Health and Safety section in the Practical Information chapter for tips.) If you're feeling hungry yourself, walk back toward Glacier Point, where there is a snack bar, gift shop, and bookstore.

WAWONA

See the Wawona and Mariposa Grove map.

About an hour's drive south of Yosemite Valley is the remarkably peaceful enclave of Wawona (elevation 4,000 feet). In a scenic location nestled beside lush meadows near the South Fork of the Merced River, days pass deliciously slowly. Far less crowded than the valley, Wawona is steeped in the early pioneer history of the Sierra Nevada, and stopping here feels like walking backward in time.

Wawona offers a variety of outdoor activities, from forested and waterfall hikes, horseback rides, and swimming holes to, surprisingly, tennis and even golf. In winter, snowshoeing and cross-country skiing among the giant sequoia trees are hardy adventures for those with backcountry experience.

Just 5 miles north of the park's South Entrance Station, Wawona is a hub of vital visitor services, including an old-fashioned hotel with a restaurant, a gas station, a gift and sundries shop, and a post office. A short distance down Chilnualna Falls Road, east of Highway 41, is a campground

THE FIREFALL

Now discontinued, the old tradition of the Yosemite firefall dates from the late 19th century. An Irishman named James McCauley constructed a 4-mile-long trail from Yosemite Valley to Glacier Point, which hikers paid a toll to use. Soon McCauley also built the Mountain House hotel atop the point. According to legend, one night McCauley shoved a campfire right over the edge of the cliff, some say to entertain his guests while others say out of frustration over lack of tourist business. Whatever the motivation, the firefall became a much-anticipated ritual, occurring whenever enough people were willing to pay for it.

At first, McCauley charged tourists $1.50 to watch the spectacle. When he'd gathered enough interested viewers, he'd send his sons up the steep trail to Glacier Point from the valley below on pack animals to carry out the firefall.

In the early 20th century David Curry, the cofounder of Yosemite's Camp Curry, turned the firefall into a nightly event to attract more business. Crowds would gather in Camp Curry to hear the echoing yell "let the fire fall!" shouted by those standing atop Glacier Point. During World War II, the firefall was suspended when the U.S. military assumed control of areas of the park. By the time the National Park Service stopped the firefall in 1968, due to its destruction of natural resources, uncountable visitors had witnessed the sight of thousands of sparks floating over the cliff.

WAWONA AND MARIPOSA GROVE

0   1 Miles
0   1.5 Kilometers

Chilnualna Fall

Wawona Dome

YOSEMITE

NATIONAL

PARK

Wawona
Campground

Wawona Rd.

Chilnualna Falls Rd.

Ranger Station

Pioneer Yosemite
History Center

Wawona Meadow

Wawona Information
Station

Wawona Hotel
and Golf Course
(summer only)

Wawona

Meadow Circle Rd.

41

Chowchilla Mountain Rd.

Wawona Point
(8,810 ft.)

Mariposa Grove
Museum

Clothes
Tree

California
Tunnel Tree

**Mariposa
Grove**

Griz
Gia

South Entrance

Mariposa Grove Rd.

Fallen Monarch

N

W   E

S

Summerdale
Campground

41

Forest Dr.

Yosemite Mountain Ranch Rd.

Fish Camp

To
Fresno

Jackson Rd.

reservation office, a public library, a small market, and a cluster of private vacation-house rentals.

It is believed that the Wawona Road follows the same path taken by the Mariposa Battalion in 1851, when they ousted Native Americans from Yosemite Valley. The road, which became a stagecoach route for tourists in the 1870s, was paved over by CCC workers during the Great Depression. By that time, what had been merely a stagecoach stop run by pioneer Galen Clark, appointed guardian of the Yosemite Grant from 1866 through 1889, had become a popular mountain resort visited by such dignitaries as U.S. presidents Ulysses S. Grant and Theodore Roosevelt. The name of the place had also been changed, from Clark's Station to Big Trees Station, referring to the nearby Mariposa Grove of giant sequoias. Later it became Wawona, which an early hotelier's wife believed meant "Big Trees" in a local indigenous dialect.

Guests today can unwind on the verandas and manicured lawns of the **Wawona Hotel** (*Forest Dr.; 209/375–6556; www.yosemitepark. com*), a National Historic Landmark dating from 1879. The Victorian-era hotel where Grant and Roosevelt once stayed is a genteel getaway and a convenient enough base for exploring the park. Sitting in an Adirondack chair on the hotel's front porch, you can gaze across the highway at the **Wawona Meadow**, once used as a landing field for airplanes and now the site of a golf course that dates from 1918, making these the oldest greens in the Sierra Nevada mountains. For some old-fashioned fun, stop by the hotel lobby any evening for cocktails and often a performance by longtime resident pianist Tom Bopp.

Built in 1879, the Wawona Hotel is an example of Victorian resort architecture.

Adjacent to the hotel is the **Wawona Information Station** *(Forest Dr.; 209/375–9501)*, where you can get oriented to the park and check schedules of free ranger-guided programs and activities, including morning and twilight strolls and presentations on natural and cultural history at the Wawona Campground Amphitheater. The information station stands inside the historic studio once occupied by late-19th-century landscape painter Thomas Hill, who worked alongside Hudson River School artists before moving to California, where he became closely acquainted with John Muir and photographer Carleton E. Watkins. Today, the information station has small displays about Hill's work.

Inspect the yesteryear trappings of the **Pioneer Yosemite History Center** *(Chilnualna Falls Rd.; 209/372–0200)*, which lies a short walk north of the hotel across a covered bridge that was recently restored using hand-hewed timbers and 19th-century woodworking techniques. The history center, which is especially enjoyed by families with young children, is an amalgamation of buildings from different eras of the park's development, all of which were moved here during the 1950s and '60s. Highlights include the Wells Fargo Office, once used by tourists to send telegrams and make phone calls out of the valley; Degnan's Bakery, which supplied the valley with fresh-baked goods until 1900; a U.S. Calvary office that served Yosemite's first rangers; and some 19th-century pioneer cabins. During summer, park interpreters dressed in period costumes give demonstrations, including blacksmithing and spinning.

Back on the south side of the river near the bridge is the historic Grey Barn, where stagecoaches were repaired and horses rested before making the eight-hour overland journey from Wawona to Yosemite Valley. The horse-drawn stage service was discontinued in 1914, when automobiles began flooding the valley. In the summer, you can try a short but bone-rattling ride on a horse-drawn stagecoach here for a small fee.

In Mariposa Grove, the Grizzly Giant stands 209 feet tall.

What brings most day visitors to the Wawona area of the park is the chance to wander among the giant sequoias of the monumental ★**MARIPOSA GROVE**, the largest of the park's three giant-sequoia groves (the other two are near Crane Flat). Standing beside one of these towering trees is an awe-inducing experience, especially early in the morning, when dew is still glistening, or at sunset as the changing colors of the sky create a painterly background to the trees' massive trunks. Still inside the national-park boundary, a short distance north of the park's South Entrance Station, a side road (usually open from

April through November) heads east to the Mariposa Grove. The parking lot at the road's end is often full. To avoid parking hassles you can take the free seasonal shuttle bus that runs frequently to the grove from the Wawona general store and from near the Mariposa Grove Gift Shop near the South Entrance Station.

From the parking lot, a self-guided interpretive trail leads moderately uphill for three-quarters of a mile to the **California Tunnel Tree**, a still-living sequoia you can walk through—once upon a time carriages even passed through it. Numbered among the other famous giants in the grove are the **Wawona Tunnel Tree**, which toppled onto its side in the winter of 1968–69; the **Clothespin Tree**, which looks exactly like its name suggests, due to its hollowed-out trunk; and the **Grizzly Giant**, the largest giant sequoia tree in the grove, which has been estimated by scientists to be almost 1,800 years old.

About 2 miles from the trailhead you can familiarize yourself

Standing beside one of these towering trees is an awe-inducing experience, especially at sunset as the changing colors of the sky create a painterly background to the trees' massive trunks.

with the lifecycle of these gentle giants inside the **Mariposa Grove Museum**, on the site where pioneer Galen Clark built a small cabin in 1861. Also here, schedules of ranger-guided walks and talks are posted.

If you push onward and upward for another mile past the museum, you'll reach **Wawona Point** (elevation 6,810 feet), from where you can peer out over thick forests, parted by the meandering south fork of the Merced River and the polished top of Wawona Dome (elevation 6,903 feet), to Wawona Meadow, with its conspicuously green golf course. If you'd rather not hike around the grove, buy tickets for a narrated tram tour, which leaves from the gift shop continuously from 10 AM until 5 PM daily, usually from May through October.

CRANE AND BIG OAK FLATS

See the North Yosemite and Hetch Hetchy map.

Heading northwest from Yosemite Valley, Big Oak Flat Road leaves the canyon of the Merced River as it climbs uphill through the thick forest toward the busy **Crane Flat** intersection: although not a point of interest, Crane Flat is a crossroads for visitors driving between Yosemite

A FEAST OF TREES

"And here let me renew my tribute to the marvelous bounty and beauty of the forests of this whole mountain region. The Sierra Nevadas lack the glorious glaciers, the frequent rains, the rich verdure, the abundant cataracts of the Alps; but they far surpass them—they surpass any other mountains I ever saw—in the wealth and grace of their trees. Look down from almost any of their peaks, and your range of vision is filled, bounded, satisfied, by what might be termed a tempest-tossed sea of evergreens, filling every upland valley, covering every hillside, crowning every peak but the highest, with their unfading luxuriance. . . .Steep mountainsides, allowing them to grow, rank above rank, without obstructing each other's sunshine, seem peculiarly favorable to the production of these serviceable giants. . . .Their extremities gracefully bent down by the weight of winter snows, making them. . . the most beautiful trees on earth. . . I never before enjoyed such a tree-feast as on this wearing, difficult ride."

—Horace Greeley, *An Overland Journey from New York to San Francisco in the Summer of 1859*.

Tuolumne Meadows.

Valley and the high country. If you need to refuel, Crane Flat has a small store and a service station with 24-hour gas pumps open year-round. Turning right at this intersection steers you onto Tioga Road (Highway 120), usually open from June through October, to reach White Wolf and Tuolumne Meadows (*see* the following section), eventually coasting by Tioga Pass (elevation 9,943 feet) over to the east side of the Sierra Nevada mountain range and otherworldly Mono Lake.

If you have some spare time and a desire to go hiking among more groves of giant sequoias, you can continue straight ahead on Big Oak Flat Road (Highway 120) to reach the trailhead for mercifully uncrowded **Merced Grove**. It's a moderate 3-mile round-trip hike to this petite grove surrounding a rustic cabin. Alternatively, from the Crane Flat intersection, you can drive east toward Tioga Pass for about a mile before pulling off into the parking lot for the more heavily used trail to **Tuolumne Grove**, which follows Old Big Oak Flat Road (closed to vehicular traffic, but open to cyclists and pedestrians). It's a tough, steep 1-mile walk each way to the Tuolumne Grove, where few can resist the chance to walk through the "Dead Giant," a tunneled-out stump that seems almost as big as a house. Because both of these giant-sequoia groves are less visited than the Mariposa Grove near Wawona, they offer a more serene experience of the giant trees.

From the Merced Grove trailhead parking lot, Big Oak Flat Road (Highway 120) continues northwest to the park's **Big Oak Flat Entrance Station**, which has a small visitor center that can assist with wilderness permits and campground reservations. This entrance is the least-traveled in the entire park. If you want to visit the Hetch Hetchy area (*see below*), you should exit the park here.

Tioga Road and Tuolumne Meadows

See the North Yosemite and Hetch Hetchy map.

Driving north of Yosemite Valley along the curvy Tioga Road is like riding on the rooftop of the planet. Riding so high among the jagged peaks of the Sierra Nevada feels otherworldly, and around almost every twist and turn in the road lies another jaw-dropping viewpoint or a gentle trailhead issuing a sirens' call. Most people visit during July and August, when alpine wildflowers bloom at Tuolumne Meadows, and paddlers and brave swimmers rush to the shores of cool Tenaya Lake.

Unless the most recent winter has been unusually harsh, vehicle traffic is allowed on the Tioga Road (Highway 120) east of Crane Flat between June and October, with most visitor services staying open from late June until early September. It's a 46-mile trip from the

A drive up Tioga Road (Highway 120) to the high country will reward you with gorgeous scenery, including crystal-blue lakes and high-alpine peaks.

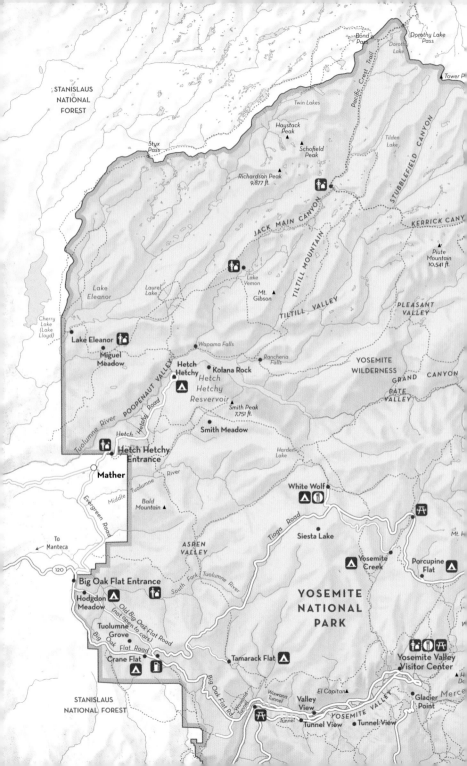

0   5 Miles

0   5 Kilometers

Twin Lakes

To Bridgeport

SAWTOOTH RIDGE

Matterhorn Peak

Slide Mountain

Burro Pass

HUMBOLDT-TOIYABE NATIONAL FOREST

Whorl Mountain

Virginia Pass

167

Virginia Peak

Green Lake

CANYON

MATTERHORN CANYON

VIRGINIA CANYON

McCabe Lakes

Lundy Lake

167

Mono Lake

INYO NATIONAL FOREST

North Peak

Saddlebag Lake

395

COLD CANYON

Pacific Crest Trail

White Mountain

Gaylor Peak

Lee Vining

RIVER

Ragged Peak

Bennettsville
Tioga Pass Entrance

120

To Mammoth Lakes and Bishop

Parsons Memorial Lodge

Glen Aulin

Tuolumne Meadows Wilderness Center

Mt. Dana

Tuolumne River

Dog Lake Trailhead

Dana Meadows

Pothole Dome

TUOLUMNE

Soda Springs
Lembert Dome

Tioga Road

MEADOWS

Mt. Gibbs
12,764 ft.

Fairview Dome

Tuolumne Meadows Visitor Center

Mammoth Peak

Mono Pass
10,604 ft.

Medlicott Dome

Cathedral Peak

Unicorn Peak

Parker Pass

KUNA CREST

158

Cathedral Lakes

Tresidder Peak

Echo Peaks

Johnson Peak

Koip Peak
12,962 ft.

KOIP CREST

Tenaya

John Muir Trail

CATHEDRAL RANGE

N

W   E

S

Sunrise

Vogelsang

LYELL CANYON

Pacific Crest Trail and John Muir Trail

Donohue Peak
12,023 ft.

Merced Lake

Donohue Pass

John Muir Trail

Merced Lake

Mt. Lyell
13,114 ft.

Mt. Florence

Legend

- 🚹 Ranger / Information
- 🍴 Food Service
- ⛩ Picnic Area
- 🛏 Lodging
- ⛺ Campground
- ⛽ Gas Station
- 🅿 Parking Area
- – – John Muir Trail / Pacific Crest Trail
- ····· Other Trails

The moon fades away above Tenaya Lake in northern Yosemite.

Crane Flat intersection with Big Oak Flat Road east to the Tioga Pass, where cars are usually lined up at the park's eastern entrance station. In winter, cross-country skiers and snowshoers may attempt to traverse sections of Tioga Road.

Realigned and paved over in 1961, the Tioga Road follows an old Native American traders' trail and later the Great Sierra Wagon Road, which was built in 1882 to service a short-lived mining district near Tioga Pass. Today, you can still follow sections of the old wagon road, for example, east of White Wolf on the way south to Yosemite Creek Campground or from Tioga Road north to the May Lake trailhead, west of Olmsted Point. The modern highway is more a pleasure, however, simply for its epic scenery, and there are plenty of panoramic viewpoints along the way. The road is also a major point of departure into the backcountry for hikers, backpackers, rock climbers, and equestrians. Before setting out along the Tioga Road, be sure to fill up your gas tank at Crane Flat, because the next gas station doesn't appear until Tuolumne Meadows, almost 40 miles away across the mountains.

East of Crane Flat, the thickly forested road ascends a ridge that divides the basins of the Tuolumne and Merced rivers. Once you rise above 7,000 feet in elevation (markers note this along the road), look for towering stands of red fir trees, which are conifers with blue-green, needlelike leaves. Evergreens like these are commonly sought after as Christmas trees. As the 1940s-era *Yosemite Road*

Guide dryly notes, these national-park specimens "are not, of course, available for home use."

Next, petite Siesta Lake appears on the south side of the road, where the shoreline is bordered by stalky green rushes in summer and golden ferns in autumn. About 15 miles east of Crane Flat is a turnoff for the short side road north to **White Wolf**, which has a campground, a small store, and a lodge with canvas tents, wooden cabins, and a dining room that's open during the summer season (*see* the Where to Stay and Eat chapter). Despite the area's name, wolves are not naturally known to be endemic to Yosemite National Park, although many visitors mistake sightings of coyotes for wolves.

Continuing eastward, the road climbs through windy forests of western juniper and quaking aspen trees. As the road curves around past Porcupine Flat Campground, the often snow-covered summit of **Mount Hoffman** (elevation 10,850 feet), where John Muir once rambled, comes into view. So does iconic Half Dome, overshadowing the Yosemite Valley far below. If you take the 2-mile side road north toward **May Lake**, a moderate 2.4-mile hike brings you to the pretty alpine lake itself, backed by massive Mt. Hoffman. It's an ideal spot for a picnic, with the shores often lined with wildflowers and patchy snow, even in July.

Although the literally breathtaking Tioga Road is full of classic Sierra Nevada high-country scenery, the best roadside viewpoint along Highway 120 is **Olmsted Point**. From this point you can gaze out at Little Yosemite Valley below Half Dome and peer into the rugged canyon of Tenaya Creek. From the Olmsted Point parking lot, it's a short walk down to the point. Interpretive signs examine the distinctive geology of the Yosemite region, from places that show evidence of glacial polish (where glaciers once carried pebbles across the surfaces of rocks, making them smoothed or grooved), to the weathering process of exfoliation, in which massive granite domes like Yosemite's Half Dome and North Dome slough off their concentric outer layers, much like peeling an onion. Just to the east is **Clouds Rest Vista Point**, which also frames views of Half Dome.

A couple of miles farther east, the Tioga Road hugs the shoreline of majestically beautiful **Tenaya Lake** (elevation 8,149 feet). Named for Chief Tenaya, the leader of the Native American band living in the Yosemite Valley who was captured by the Mariposa Battalion in 1851, this is the largest natural lake in all of Yosemite National Park. Its beautiful basin was carved by glaciers; and its waters, which reflect the clouds and the craggy peaks all around, are clear enough that you

Tuolumne Meadows is especially magical after the mountain snowpack melts in early summer, when a watercolorist's palette of alpine wildflowers is in bloom.

Deer frolic in Tuolumne Meadows, the Sierra Nevada's largest subalpine meadow.

can see the rounded granite rocks on the lake bottom. Small ice floes may partially cover the lake's surface in early summer, while later in the season mosquitoes swarm picnickers who follow the hiking path around to the west end of the lake.

All of the beauty that you've witnessed so far still does not prepare you for arriving at ★TUOLUMNE MEADOWS (elevation 8,600 feet). Called "the most . . . delightful high pleasure-ground I have yet seen," by John Muir after his first summer in the Sierra Nevada mountains, Tuolumne Meadows is especially magical after the mountain snow-pack melts in early summer, when a watercolorist's palette of alpine wildflowers is in bloom and deep blue lakes draw day-trippers. Unlike the Yosemite Valley, where the spiring walls of granite can evoke claustrophobic feelings, here the Sierra Nevada high-country is lush, wide-open meadow, fed by the Tuolumne River and several streams. It's so idyllic that all you want to do is just lie on your back in the tall grasses, inhaling the pine-scented fresh mountain air and soaking up the brilliant high-altitude sunshine.

TUOLUMNE MEADOWS VISITOR CENTER
TELEPHONE:
209/372–0263
ADDRESS:
Hwy. 120

Tuolumne Meadows has many visitor services, including a gas station, a post office, a small market, a lodge with canvas-tent cabins, a restaurant, a fast-food grill, and a sport shop selling outdoor-activity gear. Park your car in one of the day-use lots, then hop on the free Tuolumne Meadows shuttle, which loops around the meadows area and over to Olmsted Point and Tenaya Lake, usually operating from mid-June through early September. At the **Tuolumne Meadows Visitor Center** *(Hwy. 120; 209/372–0263),* have your questions answered and learn about glacial geology and the delicate ecology of these meadowlands, which come alive during the high country's all-too-brief summer season. You can buy maps and self-guided interpretive trail brochures here or at the **Tuolumne Meadows Wilderness Center,** farther east on Highway 120, near the Tuolumne Meadows Lodge.

To truly experience the wonder of the meadows, you must explore them without a car. Opposite the visitor center, a short interpretive trail leads across the biggest meadow to **Soda Springs,** named for the naturally carbonated water that bubbles up out of the ground here to form reddish pools that look almost as if they were colored by volcanic cinders. Nearby the springs, which are not necessarily safe to drink from these days, the **Parsons Memorial Lodge** has diverting exhibits about the human history of the Tuolumne Meadows, including when Native American tribes roamed here and the days when John Muir and Robert Underwood Johnson, then-editor of the influential *Century* magazine, plotted out their campaign to protect these mead-

MONO LAKE

East of Tioga Pass, Highway 120 dramatically descends through a forested canyon to the town of Lee Vining on the shores of Mono Lake, which straddles the transition zone between the Sierra Nevada mountains and the Great Basin Desert. The most fascinating thing about the lake is its towering tufa formations, made up of odd spires and knobs of calcium carbonate formed when freshwater springs bubbled up to mix with the alkaline lake water. The tufa grow strikingly close to the south shore, where they look almost like undersea coral castles with their towers poking above the shimmering surface of the lake.

Mono Lake was once threatened with extinction by dropping water levels and increased salinity after the city of Los Angeles diverted most of the water out of Mono Basin. But today, environmental restoration efforts are successfully under way. These efforts include regrowing riparian forests, raising the waters of the lake to a healthy level, and clearing invasive vegetation that blocks tributary streams. That's especially good news for more than 100 species of birds who depend upon the lake as a breeding ground and migratory stopover.

Off U.S. Highway 395, you can walk, canoe, or kayak alongside the alien-looking tufa towers at **Mono Lake Tufa State Reserve**, where interpretive tours and birding walks are offered at least daily from May through October. North of Lee Vining, the **Mono Basin Scenic Area Visitor Center** (off U.S. Hwy. 395; 760/647-6331) offers beautiful views of the lake—including of white Paoha island and black Negrit island—along with interesting natural-history exhibits.

ows as national parklands. The lodge itself was built of granite stone in 1915; for many decades it was a meeting place for the environmental organization Muir founded, the Sierra Club.

There are several well-marked trails that thread through the valley floor along the meadow. We've mentioned the most important ones here. You can't freely roam around the meadows themselves—they are too fragile! So be sure to stay on the trails.

At the west end of the main meadow, a short scramble up **Pothole Dome** will reward you with expansive views over the entire Tuolumne Meadows area. It's especially photo-worthy when the sun sinks over the surrounding peaks and they sometimes blush with alpenglow. At the east end of the main meadow, a more difficult hike ascends **Lembert Dome**, from where you can glimpse the mammoth Sierra Crest poised to the east and the Cathedral Range stretching to the south. The dome is named after John Baptist Lembert, an eccentric pioneer homesteader, butterfly collector, and goat herder who resided here until winter storms drove him out at the same time Yosemite National Park was created in 1890. The dome's summit hike is 2.8 miles round-trip starting from the Dog Lake trailhead, across Tioga Road from the lodge.

Leaving Tuolumne Meadows, Tioga Road heads east for 7 more miles to **Tioga Pass** (elevation 9,945 feet). Along the way it passes forests of lodgepole pine trees and lush **Dana Meadows**, the origin point for the Tuolumne Glacier that flowed westward from here as an ancient river of ice. To the east of the highway, the signature peaks of 13,057-foot-high **Mt. Dana** and 12,764-foot-high **Mt. Gibbs** dominate the horizon. Near Tioga Pass, a gravel side road leads north to the mining ghost town of **Bennettsville**, which spurred construction of the original Tioga Pass road in the late 19th century. There you can wander around the atmospheric town ruins, including some rustic wooden cabins that have withstood more than a century's worth of harsh mountain winters.

HETCH HETCHY

See the North Yosemite and Hetch Hetchy map.

Although John Muir won the war to protect the high country of Yosemite National Park in 1890, he lost the battle to save Hetch Hetchy in 1913, when Congress authorized construction of a dam on the Tuolumne River. Once the O'Shaughnessy Dam was completed in 1923, the resulting reservoir flooded Hetch Hetchy, which Muir described as "one of nature's rarest and most precious mountain temples."

The name Hetch Hetchy comes from a Miwok word for a type of edible food that once grew in the valley and that Native Americans used to harvest when camping there. Although not quite as grand as the Yosemite Valley, Hetch Hetchy is still a beautiful glacier-carved valley that some environmentalists would like to see restored to its natural state. The dam is still in operation. It supplies water and power to the city of San Francisco and the burgeoning Bay Area.

A couple of miles west of the Big Oak Flat Entrance Station on Highway 120, you can turn right onto Evergreen Road, then drive through the thick forest north to Hetch Hetchy Road, which leads east toward the dam. Extra security measures have been implemented since 9/11. All incoming traffic is required to stop at the **Hetch Hetchy Entrance Station** to sign in with the ranger who is normally on duty

The controversial Hetch Hetchy Reservoir supplies water and power to San Francisco. According to the Department of Water Resources, to take the dam down now would cost billions of dollars.

during daylight hours, the only time when you may pick up a day-use permit and parking pass.

The paved drive winds for about 8 miles from the entrance station northeast to the **O'Shaughnessy Dam**. Although 20th-century preservationists could not prevent the dam from being built, similar campaigns to prevent dams in California's Kings Canyon, as well as the Grand Canyon in Arizona, did succeed, in part because of the dramatic example set by Hetch Hetchy. Although debates about whether or not this dam should be removed are ongoing, most critics agree that it is not likely to be torn down anytime soon. You can park off the road above the dam, then walk back downhill and out onto the top of the dam itself, where interpretive signs tell about this controversial project that drowned the valley's once-healthy meadows and drastically changed its ecosystem. Like a watery finger pointing toward the east, the **Hetch Hetchy Reservoir** accounts for about 1% of California's total reservoir-based water supply.

Rising above the north shore of the reservoir is **Hetch Hetchy Dome** (elevation 6,173 feet). Facing off against it on the south shore is **Kolana Rock** (elevation 5,772 feet), an often-photographed granite formation easily recognized by its pyramidal shape. Tumbling off the cliffs on the north side of the reservoir, just west of Hetch Hetchy Dome, is the triple cascade of Wapama Falls (elevation 1,400 feet), which flows year-round but peaks in May.

After walking across the top of the dam to its far side, hikers can continue through an eerie tunnel and onto a moderate 5-mile round-trip trail leading along the north shore past slim **Tueelala Falls**, which appears only in spring, and beyond to the imposing base of Wapama Falls, where the footbridges crossing Falls Creek may be dramatically cut off by rushing water in spring. If the footbridges are passable, it's another challenging 4.2 miles each way to **Rancheria Falls**, a pretty collection of cascades that flows through a narrow canyon and is best viewed in spring.

⌖ BEST DAY HIKES

For day hikers, the wealth of trails inside Yosemite National Park ranges from easy nature walks around the valley floor, to steep descents from Glacier Point past rushing waterfalls, to excursions off Tioga Road and from Tuolumne Meadows into the Sierra Nevada high country, blessed with alpine lakes and meadows where wildflowers bloom. The best of these are detailed below. (For forested hikes to giant sequoia groves in the Crane Flat and Big Oak Flat areas, *see* that section of Sights, *above*.)

Poppies and Indian paintbrush.

Check current schedules of ranger-guided hikes in the free park newspaper *Yosemite Today* or at the main visitor centers in Yosemite Valley and Tuolumne Meadows, where you also can buy hiking maps and self-guided interpretive trail brochures.

YOSEMITE VALLEY

As the most visited part of the park, Yosemite Valley has all sorts of trailheads for day hikers and nature walkers. Most popular in late spring

Catching a view of Yosemite Falls while hiking in Leidig Meadow.

You'll walk through rainbows when you visit Vernal Fall.

Hikers on the John Muir Trail trek near Vernal Fall at Clark Point, with views of Glacier Point and Yosemite Valley. (right) Taking a break in Long Meadow.

and early summer are easy, short strolls to waterfall viewpoints in the area. The gentle **Valley Loop Trail** stops at scenic bridges overlooking the Merced River and wanders beside lush meadows and forests, providing great views of Bridalveil Fall and Yosemite Falls. You can do as much or as little of the 13-mile loop trail as you feel like walking, a refreshing alternative to driving in heavy traffic. Even just a half-mile walk makes for a relaxing amble.

Another easy walk in the Yosemite Valley is the paved 2-mile round-trip trail out to tiny **Mirror Lake**, which fills up in spring and early summer, when it occasionally reflects the peaked cliffs above, including Half Dome. The rest of the year, the lake is more of a meadow alongside Tenaya Creek, which the trail follows for a good distance. You can extend this hike into a moderate 5-mile loop around the lake and into Tenaya Canyon for wildlife watching.

It's the grandeur of Yosemite Valley that inspires even the most casual tourists to attempt more hiking than they've ever done before in their lives. The steep switchbacks required to climb out of the valley don't seem to deter anyone, either. Starting at Happy Isles, the **Mist Trail** climbs steeply upward for 3 miles via a granite staircase of more than 600 steps to the top of **Vernal Fall**, then continues another 2 miles to the brink of **Nevada Fall**. The trail can be treacherous during late spring, when you should expect to get drenched by spray from the thunderous waterfalls.

A route to the falls that is longer but with a more gradual slope follows the **John Muir Trail**, also starting from Happy Isles. Hardy hikers tackle the **Upper Yosemite Falls Trail**, starting near Camp 4. It's

HALF DOME: A SURVIVAL GUIDE

Everyone thinks doing Half Dome is a 100% fun trip, but in reality it's not. It's kind of a pain. The experience is definitely thrilling—it's considered the ultimate Yosemite day hike and once-in-a-lifetime adventure for good reason—but it's not a trip for anyone with a fear of heights or who isn't in top physical shape. Fatal accidents have occurred along the trail, so it's vital to pay careful attention to what you're doing, and to follow the tips here.

First off, consider your clothing and gear. Hiking boots with excellent tread and gloves with good grips are essential. A rock-climbing harness with carabiner clips to attach yourself to the cables—often bottlenecked with climbers that have frozen out of fear or fatigue—are also not a bad idea for safety's sake. That way, if a pole supporting the cable comes loose, or another hiker slips from above, you will not be swept over the cliff's edge. Additionally, wearing sunglasses and a hat will help cut down on the glare of the sun on the rocks. Bring plenty of water, too.

Before your journey begins, get a good night's rest and an early rise. Some attempt this as part of an overnight trek on the John Muir Trail (*see* Backpacking, *below*), but day hikers who want to ascend this most famous of all Yosemite's venerable domes should start out at sunrise.

There are two paths to follow: either the 14-mile round-trip Mist Trail or the 16.4-mile round-trip John Muir Trail. Either route brings you to the 400-foot-long final leg of the ascent of Half Dome, which is only accomplished by cables bolted into the rock—this is where those carabiner clips comes in handy.

In addition to a hiker's skill and stamina, the conditions of the trail and weather need to be taken into account. Like any granite dome, Half Dome should never be climbed when a thunderstorm is approaching or when the trail, rock, and cables are slick with recent rainfall. If you feel static electricity in the air or see lightning flash in the sky, get back down below the tree line immediately. The cables are only up from late May through early October, outside of which you should not attempt this hike.

Once you finally reach the top, you'll suddenly realize why everyone remembers the trip as being nonstop fun and excitement. The challenges of the summit fade with the heart-stopping payoff, standing atop this Sierra Nevada icon and gazing with eagle's eyes into nature's treasure box—meandering streams, meadows, and characterful spires—in the valley below.

a strenuous, 3.6-mile climb to the top of the falls. Many people hike just the first 1.5 miles of the trail to Columbia Rock, which affords gorgeous views of the entire valley. For the **Four-Mile Trail** from Yosemite Valley to Glacier Point, *see below.*

GLACIER POINT ROAD

Starting from Glacier Point, the classic **Four-Mile Trail** (which is actually closer to five miles long these days) follows steep switchbacks down into the valley, with dramatic views along the way that repay all of your knee-trembling efforts. Even more challenging is the 8.5-mile **Panorama Trail**, which visits lacy Illilouette Fall before descending along the **Mist Trail** (*see* the previous section) past Nevada Fall and Vernal Fall from Glacier Point. Both of these one-way hikes require first parking in the valley, then catching the tour bus up to Glacier Point (*see* Getting Around in the Practical Information chapter), for which advance reservations are recommended.

Deer and wild iris in Tuolumne Meadows.

A few miles west of Glacier Point are the signposted trailheads for **Sentinel Dome** and **Taft Point**. Each destination is a moderate 2.2-mile round-trip hike from Glacier Point Road, and the trails are usually not very crowded. The summit of Sentinel Dome (elevation 8,122 feet), which is topped by a photogenic Jeffrey pine, gives 360-degree views of the valley that are even more sweeping than from Glacier Point. This is the perfect alternative hike for those who don't want to hoof (and cable) it to the top of Half Dome (*see* Half Dome: A Survival Guide, *above*). For more vertigo-inducing views without the safety of stone walls that hem in shutterbugs at Glacier Point, the trail to Taft Point passes over fissures, basically deep vertical cracks in the weather-worn cliff—watch your step! Taking children on this hike is not recommended.

Farther back down Glacier Point Road, just west of the turnoff for Bridalveil Creek Campground on the opposite side of the road, a gentle 1.6-mile round-trip stroll leads through woodlands rife with birdsong out to **McGurk Meadow**, which looks prettiest in early summer when wildflowers bloom. From the meadow, you can continue 3 more miles each way to **Dewey Point** (elevation 7,385 feet) to get a dead-on look at El Capitan across Yosemite Valley, and to your right, the Cathedral Rocks and Half Dome.

WAWONA

Many visitors spend time hiking into the impressive Mariposa Grove of giant sequoias (*see* the Wawona sightseeing section, *above*). For a more

challenging day hike in the Wawona area, it's a moderately strenuous 5-mile ascent alongside Chilnualna Creek through a forest of ponderosa pine and incense cedar trees to **Chilnualna Falls** (elevation 2,200 feet). The waterfall trail starts from the east end of Chilnualna Road, past the Pioneer Yosemite History Center, off Wawona Road.

Hiking by lower Cathedral Lake, with Tenaya Lake in the background.

TIOGA ROAD AND TUOLUMNE MEADOWS

It's an easy walk from Tuolumne Meadows to Soda Springs and the **Parsons Memorial Lodge**. Nearby you can easily summit **Pothole Dome** or tackle the moderately difficult hike up Lembert Dome. (*See* the Tioga Road and Tuolumne Meadows section of Sights, *above*). Even more alluring trailheads in the Tuolumne Meadows area lead to pretty alpine lakes, any of which makes a pleasant half-day hike. Don't forget to carry insect repellent, which is an essential item in summer. Recommended meadows-to-lake trails include family-friendly **Dog Lake** (2.8 miles round-trip), with its tree-lined shores and wide-open skies; glacially carved **Elizabeth Lake** (4.8 miles round-trip), which lies beneath horned Unicorn Peak; and **Cathedral Lakes** (6.8 miles round-trip, plus a mile-long spur trail), dramatically surrounded by Sierra Nevada peaks that rise above 10,000 feet in elevation.

Although **Glen Aulin** is primarily a backpacking destination along the High Sierra Camp circuit (*see* Backpacking, *below*), it's also a satisfying 11-mile round-trip day hike of moderate difficulty, following the

Taft Point has a rail so you can get close to the edge—but still be careful!

Gazing down from the
summit of Mt. Hoffman.

canyon of the Tuolumne River and passing pretty cascades, including Tuolumne Fall (at 4 miles in). The Glen Aulin trailhead is on the east side of the main meadow near the Parson Memorial Lodge. Marathon hikers can continue beyond Glen Aulin to **Waterwheel Falls**, but this strenuous 17-mile round-trip excursion is best done as an overnight option.

If sweeping vistas of Yosemite Valley are what you're after, both the challenging 14-mile round-trip hike to **Clouds Rest**, starting from Tenaya Lake west of Tuolumne Meadows, and the difficult up-and-down 10.4-mile round-trip hike to the summit of **North Dome** (elevation 7,540 feet) are unforgettable journeys through the high country. On the latter trail, which starts at the Porcupine Creek trailhead (not to be confused with Porcupine Flat Campground), the Indian Rock spur trail leads to Yosemite National Park's only natural arch. In between these two trailheads, a turnoff onto an old wagon road leads north to the trailhead for **May Lake**, an easy 2.4-mile round-trip hike, where energetic hikers can keep going through a rocky field of granite talus to reach the eroded summit of **Mt. Hoffman** (elevation 10,845 feet). The views back over the lakes and the Sierra Crest are superb from the summit. Mt. Hoffman, which happens to be the geographical center of the park, is a moderately difficult 4.8-mile round-trip trek from the May Lake trailhead.

East of Tuolumne Meadows along Tioga Road are a few more incredible high-altitude day hikes worth mentioning, for example: the 2-mile round-trip journey to incredibly scenic and often forgotten **Gaylor Lakes**; the strenuous 7-mile round-trip ascent of **Mt. Dana** (elevation 13,061 feet); and the 7.4-mile climb up to **Mono Pass** and back, which follows an abandoned Native American trading route. To avoid potential parking hassles, all of these eastern trailheads are accessible via a free shuttle bus that in peak summer season makes four daily round-trip runs between the Tuolumne Meadows Lodge and Tioga Pass.

Keep in mind that all hikes beginning from Tioga Road are much easier when you're already acclimated to high altitudes. If you have symptoms of acute mountain Sickness (*see* the Health and Safety section of the Practical Information chapter), the best remedy is immediate descent—which usually means returning to the trailhead and driving back down Tioga Road toward the valley.

HETCH HETCHY

If you're not up for hiking to the waterfalls that dramatically drop into the dammed valley of Hetch Hetchy (*see* the Hetch Hetchy section in Sights, *above*), take the moderate 3-mile round-trip trail instead to **Lookout Point**, atop which a few lone Jeffrey pines thrive. Photographers are rewarded with excellent views of the valley's falls and of the canyon of the Tuolumne River, with ideal lighting in the early morning.

☞ OTHER ACTIVITIES

Hiking and backpacking are the most popular activities in Yosemite National Park. But there are many more outdoor pursuits here for everyone to try as well, from guided horseback rides through the Sierra Nevada mountains and whitewater-rafting to kayaking trips on the free-flowing Merced River to rock climbing Yosemite's massive granite walls and snowshoeing and skiing off Glacier Point Road in winter. There's even the 18-hole, pesticide-free **Wawona Golf Course** (*Wawona Rd.; 209/375–6572*), which is a certified Audubon Cooperative Sanctuary and is open spring through fall; call to set up a tee time.

Check the free newspaper *Yosemite Today* for seasonal schedules of ranger-led programs and activities happening everywhere around the park, from daytime nature walks and waterfall hikes to old-fashioned campfire sing-alongs and after-dark stargazing programs. Ask at park visitor centers about the Junior Ranger program, which brings together do-your-own arts-and-crafts activities, story time, and nature fun for families.

BACKPACKING

Even if you've scaled peaks in the Rocky Mountains before, or backpacked along long-distance trails in the Pacific Northwest, the sheer number and variety of overnight hikes and multiday backpacking routes in Yosemite cannot fail to impress. Although it takes more time and preparation than a day hike, a backcountry trip will immerse you in the beauty of the wilderness and let you find blissful solitude that Yosemite's roadside viewpoints and valley trails never can.

Although it is possible to take wilderness trips year-round, the ideal time is during summer, especially in the peak months of June and July, when access to the Sierra Nevada high country opens along Tioga Road. For an epic experience, venture forth on the ★JOHN

MUIR TRAIL (JMT), which starts from the Happy Isles in Yosemite Valley and runs over mountain passes for 211 miles through Kings Canyon and Sequoia national parks on its way to a dramatic finish atop Mt. Whitney (elevation 14,505 feet), the highest peak in the contiguous United States. A bit too much? No worries. There are scores of easier choices for weekend backpacking trips.

Starting from Yosemite Valley, the most popular overnight destination is **Little Yosemite Valley**, a moderate 4.7-mile hike up out of the valley along the JMT (*see above*), which gives you a head start for climbing Half Dome (*see* Half Dome: a Survival Guide, *above*) the following day. A less-crowded approach from Glacier Point follows the **Panorama Trail** to the top of Vernal Fall, then joins the main trail past Little Yosemite Valley to Half Dome, a tough 18.4-mile round-trip. Along Tioga Road, there are two dozen wilderness trailheads for backpackers to choose from. Starting from Tenaya Lake, the stunning **Sunrise Lakes Trail** leads over **Clouds Rest** (elevation 9,926 feet), one of the most inspiring viewpoints in the Sierra Nevada mountains, then descends to Sunrise Creek and Little Yosemite Valley campgrounds; it's a moderately difficult 17.3-mile trip from Tenaya Lake to Yosemite Valley.

Other prime high-country destinations lie along the **High Sierra Camp** (*801/559–4909; www.yosemitepark.com*) circuit, where the lucky winners of a lottery held every December get to stay in canvas tents and have all of their meals catered for them (for a cost, of course; the lottery just provides the opportunity to sign up). Otherwise, you'll have to haul all of your own backpacking gear along to visit **Lyell**

Backpackers pass through Yosemite's Tuolumne Meadows.

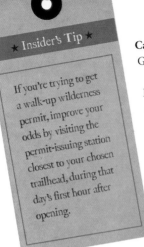

★ Insider's Tip ★

If you're trying to get a walk-up wilderness permit, improve your odds by visiting the permit-issuing station closest to your chosen trailhead, during that day's first hour after opening.

Canyon, **Vogelsang Lake**, **Merced Lake**, or **Glen Aulin** in the Grand Canyon of the Tuolumne River.

Many of the day hikes to alpine lakes described in the Best Day Hikes section, *above*, also make great overnight backpacking destinations. Farther west, the Hetch Hetchy area of the park is the gateway for trips into the remote northern reaches of Yosemite National Park, which is 95% designated wilderness.

PERMITS

All trails inside the national park are subject to a daily trailhead quota. Apply for wilderness permits ($5/person) in advance from the **Yosemite National Park wilderness office** (*P.O. Box 545, Yosemite, CA 95389; 209/372–0740; www.nps.gov/yose*). Applications are accepted by online, telephone, or U.S. mail submission starting 24 weeks in advance of your trip. Check the park's Web site for trailhead quota availability before applying for a permit, and know that summer weekend departure dates fill up months in advance.

If you aren't successful in obtaining a permit, you'll be thankful that about 40% of the trailhead quota remains available for walk-up permits, which are issued on a first-come, first-served basis starting on the day prior to your trip at the Yosemite Valley Wilderness Center in Yosemite Village, the Tuolumne Meadows Wilderness Center on Tioga Road, the Wawona Information Station on Wawona Road, the Big Oak Flat Information Station on Highway 120, and the Hetch Hetchy Entrance Station on Hetch Hetchy Road. Priority is given to those standing at the permit-issuing station closest to the trailhead. All of these stations also rent bear-proof canisters, which are required for backcountry travel. Those who hold valid wilderness permits can camp at designated backpacker campgrounds the night before and after their backcountry trip (no additional reservations are required).

Backcountry trips starting outside the national-park boundaries (that is, on national forest lands) are often subject to trailhead quotas, too; for these trips you may inquire of other federal land-management agencies for wilderness permits and reservations.

FISHING

Good trout fishing is found along the Merced River near the national park boundary at El Portal and along the Tuolumne River near Hetch Hetchy. During summer, fishers also go boating on Tenaya Lake along Tioga Road, west of Tuolumne Meadows.

For half- and full-day guided fly-fishing trips, contact **Yosemite Guides** (*Yosemite View Lodge, Hwy. 140, El Portal; 866/922–9111*) or **Yosemite Fly Fishing** (*209/379–2746; www.yosemiteflyfishing.net*). Trips with the latter are led by conservationist and longtime local resident Tim Hutchins. All anglers aged 16 and older must carry a valid California fishing license, available for purchase at the Yosemite Village Sport Shop and the Curry Village Mountain Shop, as well as at the general stores in Wawona, Crane Flat, and Tuolumne Meadows.

The fishing season for stream and river fishing is open from late April until mid-November, while lakes and reservoirs remain open year-round. Additional restrictions apply inside the national park boundaries; ask at visitor centers for current fishing regulations covering specific bait and hook types, daily limits, and catch-and-release requirements, which vary depending on your location and elevation within the park. The rules are strictest inside the Yosemite Valley. No fishing from bridges is allowed anywhere in the national park.

HORSEBACK RIDING

Scenic trail rides range from two hours to a full day; six-day High Sierra saddle trips also are available.

Far easier than tackling Yosemite's often steep trails on foot, you can saddle up a sure-footed horse or mule and then relax and enjoy the scenery—with your animal hoofing it instead of you—of near-vertical waterfalls and vista points. Most of these trips depart spring through fall, with a shorter summer season at Tuolumne Meadows.

The most popular rides in Yosemite Valley include an easy two-hour trip out to Mirror Lake and longer rides for more experienced riders that clamber out of the valley to waterfalls and vista points. From Wawona, it's a hot half-day ride out to the 2,200-foot-high Chilnualna Falls, where whitewater cascades down the side of granite rocks. At higher-elevation Tuolumne Meadows, you can saddle up for short rides around the meadows or longer half-day trips to nearby waterfalls.

The **Delaware North Companies** (*DNC; www.yosemitepark.com*) is the main concessionaire for mule and horse rides in the park. Half- and full-day trail rides depart from the Yosemite Valley Stables (*209/372–8348*), Wawona Stables (*209/375–6502*), and in the Sierra Nevada high country, the Tuolumne Meadow Stables (*209/372–8427*).

For overnight excursions into the backcountry, fully guided pack trips can be arranged. Multiday saddle trips between the High Sierra Camp (*see* Backpacking, *above*), where riders stay in canvas tents, are extremely popular; call 801/559–4909 for reservations and information.

Established in 1938, the **Yosemite Trails Pack Station** (*P.O. Box 100, Fish Camp; 559/683–7611*) offers half-day guided trail rides into

the Mariposa Grove of giant sequoias, as well as shorter trips along a creekside up to a vista point outside the park. In winter, sleigh rides are available hourly on some weekends and holidays. The stables are in a small town outside the park's South Entrance Station.

Rock Climbing

Yosemite is one of the premier rock-climbing and bouldering destinations in the United States. (*See* the Spotlight on: Rock Climbing in Yosemite.) Big wall climbs in the Yosemite Valley and crack climbs in the canyon of the Merced River present enough challenges for a lifetime. The buzzing center of activity for experienced climbers is **Camp 4**, a walk-in campground on the west side of the valley. During peak summer months, the encampment shifts to Tuolumne Meadows off Tioga Road in the park's high country.

Overshadowing Yosemite Valley, ★EL CAPITAN sets the standard for big wall climbs. El Capitan's "nose" (the prow connecting its two faces) was once considered impossible to climb until modern climbers initially conquered it during a 47-day assault in 1958. Today, the record for speed climbing El Cap is set at under three hours. ★HALF DOME, meanwhile, offers classic slab climbing.

Experienced rock jockeys can free-climb up beside Yosemite Falls and to Glacier Point. Also popular are short- to medium-length dome climbs around Tuolumne Meadows, including several routes up Lembert Dome and **Stately Pleasure Dome** above Tenaya Lake.

For bouldering, head to **The Knobs** near Tuolumne Meadows or around Sentinel Rock and Camp 4, along the **Mirror Lake Trail**, or on the approach to Cathedral Rocks in the Yosemite Valley.

Certified guides from the **Yosemite Mountaineering School** (*P.O. Box 578, Yosemite; 209/372–8344; www.yosemitemountaineering.com*) lead a variety of classes at all skill levels, from introductory "Go Climb a Rock" workshops and basic anchoring for novices, to advanced crack and extreme big-wall climbing techniques for experts, plus self-rescue and snow-and-ice climbing classes. Private lessons and guided climbs for small groups also can be arranged. Based at the Curry Village Mountain Shop from spring through fall, the school temporarily moves up to Tuolumne Meadows for the peak summer season.

Wilderness permits (*see* Backpacking, *above*) are not required for bivouacking overnight on any wall in the park, although climbers are required to follow minimum-impact guidelines, freely available from any wilderness center or permit-issuing station. Wilderness trailhead rangers also can let you know which areas are closed to climbing for

Rock climber Tom Herbert tackles Death Crack, an overhanging climb near Tenaya Lake.

Rafting through Yosemite
Valley, past Yosemite Falls.

safety reasons or to protect nesting peregrine falcons. Camping is not allowed at the base of any granite dome, except Half Dome, for which a wilderness permit is still required.

SWIMMING, BOATING, KAYAKING AND WHITEWATER RAFTING

When the mercury spikes the thermometer above 90 degrees during summer, many park visitors can only think about one thing: where to get wet and cool down. With startlingly clear—but surprisingly cold—streams, rivers, and lakes all around, you'll find plenty of invigorating places to take a quick dip.

In summer, swimming is popular at sandy beaches that appear alongside the Merced River and Tenaya Creek in the Yosemite Valley; on the South Fork of the Merced River in the Wawona area, especially near the Swinging Bridge at the east end of Forest Drive; and along the Tuolumne River and at alpine lakes accessed via Tioga Road through the Sierra Nevada high country, especially near Tuolumne Meadows and at Tenaya Lake.

Keep in mind that winter snowmelt from the Sierra Nevada mountains can turn rivers into a torrent of rapids, especially in late spring (a particularly dangerous time of year for a swim), so always exercise caution. Be prepared for chilly water conditions even during the dog days of August. Swimming is prohibited above all waterfalls, due to the serious risk of drowning, and also at Hetch Hetchy Reservoir.

For a nominal fee, the public is welcome to take a dip in the summer-only swimming pools at Curry Village and the Yosemite Lodge at the falls in the Yosemite Valley. These privately owned pools are open from mid-May through mid-September, weather permitting.

Also in summer (usually during June and July, although the exact times vary from year to year), daytime rafting and kayaking are allowed on the Merced River from the Stoneman Bridge near Curry Village down to the Sentinel Beach Picnic Area. On the main stem and south fork of the Merced River you also can float in an inner tube. You can rent a raft from the Curry Village Mountain Shop or bring your own equipment from home for kayaking and nonmotorized boating on Tenaya Lake. Wherever you swim, boat, kayak, or raft in the national park, be careful to approach the shoreline only from sandy beaches, instead of cutting through grassy meadows and disturbing sensitive riparian areas.

YOSEMITE IN WINTER

Most people don't think of visiting Yosemite in the winter, but independent-minded travelers who do discover that it's a fairy-tale time, when the valley floor is hushed by powdery snowfall and water-falls are partly frozen by ice. Not only is the park less crowded then, but its winter-wonderland attracts families with young children and experienced winter-sports enthusiasts alike. Snowball throwing, ice skating, sledding, and skiing are among the most fun diversions this time of year.

Another big draw is a fizzing calendar of special seasonal events, including food and wine celebrations, old-fashioned holiday parties, and Nordic ski races (*see the Festivals section in the Practical Information chapter*).

Yosemite Valley is generally covered in snow from November to May. The Sierra Nevada high country usually stays snowed in most of the year, typically from late October through early June. Only the park's main roads remain open in winter:

Wawona Road (Highway 41), El Portal Road (Highway 140), Big Oak Flat Road (Highway 120), and Hetch Hetchy Road. Glacier Point Road is only open from the Chinquapin intersection east to Badger Pass. All roads are subject to weather delays and snowplow closures. In the winter, always carry tire chains, which may be required at any time. For road conditions, call 209/372–0200.

Usually open from mid-December until late March, the family-friendly **Badger Pass Ski Area** (*Glacier Point Rd.; 209/372-8430; www.yosemitepark.com*) is one of California's oldest ski resorts. The two terrain parks are tame, so they're excellent places for beginners to learn how to downhill ski or snowboard. Badger Pass, where kids revel in snow tubing and sledding, is also the gateway to groomed cross-country ski trails. The area has a first-aid station, a deli and fast-food cafeteria, and a sport shop renting downhill and cross-country skis, snowshoes, sleds, and limited snow-camping equipment. In winter, there's a free shuttle bus between the Yosemite Valley lodgings and Badger Pass Ski Area.

The **ski school** (*Glacier Point Rd.; 209/372-1000*) offers lessons for all skill levels, and guided cross-country ski tours can be arranged. Plan on taking all day to ski the more than 10 miles from Badger Pass out to the **Glacier Point Ski Hut**, where reservations for overnight stays are required.

For experienced backcountry skiers only, the 10-mile one-way trip off Glacier Point Road out to **Ostrander Ski Hut** (*209/372-0240; www.ostranderhut.com*), a two-story rustic stone building built by Civilian Conservation Corps workers in 1941, is a truly wild adventure; a lottery is held for overnight reservations in early November.

In Yosemite Valley, rangers lead wintertime strolls focusing on the history, geology, and ecology of the park. At Curry Village, an **ice-skating rink** (*Southside Dr.; 209/372-8341*), where skate rental is available, is open from mid-November until mid-March, weather permitting.

Snowshoeing is also a popular activity in the Yosemite Valley and at Crane Flat, the latter of which has a place to rent snowshoes. The moderately difficult 7-mile loop out to Dewey Point is among the most popular snowshoe treks. Rangers lead guided snowshoe walks in both the Crane Flat and Badger Pass areas, including full-moon night walks at Badger Pass only. For an independent adventure, you can cross-country ski along the road (which is closed to vehicle traffic in winter) to the Mariposa Grove of giant sequoias starting near the park's South Entrance Station. You also can snow-camp overnight inside the grove of towering trees, where the stars shine brilliantly in the crisp winter air.

Illilouette Creek in Yosemite National Park.

154

Spotlight on
SUPERSIZED SIGHTS

Central California's trio of national parks—Yosemite, Sequoia, and Kings Canyon—is, simply put, a land of giants. Outdoor playgrounds on a monumental scale, the parks are marked by extraordinary sights: the world's biggest trees, massive granite monoliths, Sierra Nevada mountains soaring above 14,000 feet, and North America's highest waterfall and deepest canyon (yes, even deeper than the Grand Canyon). These tremendous natural wonders are packed into the alpine valleys, rocky river canyons, and jagged mountain passes of the 3,000 square miles of national parklands, including the Giant Sequoia National Monument. Wherever you wander here, you're sure to be awestruck.

◄◄ The sun sets and the moon rises over Yosemite Valley.

BIGGEST TREES

The giant sequoia is the largest living tree on Earth. A rare species, it grows only in scattered groves in the western Sierra Nevada mountains. Among the oldest living flora, these weighty trees are remarkable survivors. Their tannin-rich bark and heartwood, resisting both insects and wildfires, ensures longevity in the forest. The wood is too brittle to be profitably used as lumber, so many trees survived logging attempts in the late 19th and early 20th centuries. Giant sequoias grow at an astounding rate—sometimes adding the equivalent of a 50-foot-tall tree to their own bulk in a single year—and they can live for centuries. Their Achilles heel is a shallow root system, which often topples mature giants in their golden. The world's largest groves of giant sequoias are in Sequoia National Park's Giant Forest.

TIP
To find serenity among these gentle giants, come in late spring, when snow still blankets the forest floor and summer crowds are absent.

Giant Forest

Converse Basin

Grant Grove

KINGS CANYON AND SEQUOIA NATIONAL PARKS

Yosemite's Mariposa Grove of giant trees

200 ►

175 ►

150 ►

125 ►

100 ►

75 ►

50 ►

25 ►

Grizzly Giant
(209 ft.)

Ponderosa
Pine
(100 ft.)

Adult Man
(6 ft.)

Grizzly Bear
(9 ft.)

GROUND LEVEL
(0 ft.)

GIANT SEQUOIAS: WHO'S WHO

When measured by volume, the giant sequoia (*Sequoiadendron giganteum*) is the world's largest living tree. It belongs to the same family as the tallest living tree, the coast redwood (*Sequoia sempervirens*).

Giant sequoias themselves aren't exactly short: the tallest can grow 25 stories high. Despite their life span of well over 1,000 years, they are outlived by the ancient bristlecone pine (*Pinus longaeva and P. aristata*), some of which are 3,000 or more years old.

(opposite page, clockwise from top left) Giant sequoia, coast redwoods, bristlecone pine tree.

HIDDEN GIANT: BOOLE TREE

An old-growth giant cloaked in moss, the Boole Tree in Kings Canyon National Park's Converse Basin was spared by an early-1900s lumber-mill owner. It is now the world's seventh-largest giant sequoia. At the head of the trail leading to the Boole Tree is a field littered with the stumps of giant sequoias that did not share its fate.

Giant sequoias in Grant Grove.

Fallen Monarch log, Grant Grove.

GRIZZLY GIANT

LOCATION: Mariposa Grove, Yosemite National Park

HEIGHT: 209 ft

CIRCUMFERENCE: 92.5 ft

BIT OF TRIVIA: Thought to be the oldest giant sequoia in existence.

GENERAL SHERMAN TREE

LOCATION: Giant Forest, Sequoia National Park

HEIGHT: 274.9 ft

CIRCUMFERENCE: 102.6 ft

BIT OF TRIVIA: Named for Civil War general William Tecumseh Sherman.

WAWONA TUNNEL TREE

LOCATION: Mariposa Grove, Yosemite National Park

HEIGHT: 234 ft

CIRCUMFERENCE: 82 ft

BIT OF TRIVIA: Cut in 1895 for carriages to pass through, this now-fallen beauty toppled during the winter of 1968-69.

GENERAL GRANT TREE

LOCATION: Grant Grove, Kings Canyon National Park

HEIGHT: 268.1 ft

CIRCUMFERENCE: 107.5 ft

BIT OF TRIVIA: Named for Civil War general Ulysses S. Grant.

HOW DID THEY GET SO BIG?

MONOLITHS & MOUNTAINS

Yosemite, Kings Canyon, and Sequoia national parks ride the Sierra Nevada mountain range, which reaches a heady elevation of 14,505 feet atop Mt. Whitney, the highest peak in the lower 48 states. The Sierra Nevada are made of granite, deposited underground by ancient volcanic activity, then tilted and uplifted along fault lines. Some of this subterranean rock has been dramatically exposed to form the parks' granite monoliths, most famously in the Yosemite Valley, with the curved tooth of Half Dome and the sheer wall of El Capitan. These granite icons are the result of weathering after glaciers polished the landscape and shaped the Yosemite Valley and the Kings Canyon thousands of years ago.

TIP

For the best views of Half Dome, drive up to Glacier Point. For a great view of El Capitan, sit beside the Merced River at Cathedral Beach.

El Capitan.

Glacier Point

El Capitan

Half Dome

**YOSEMITE
NATIONAL PARK**

YOSEMITE FALLS

Waterfalls in the Yosemite Valley are especially famous for their heart-stopping drops over sheer granite cliffs. The falls are at their fullest in spring, when snowmelt pours into the river valleys throughout the Sierra Nevada. When the falls' output peaks in May, clouds of mist billow from the base of the plunging chutes, making visitors at the bottom of the falls disappear from view. Stand there yourself and you'll hear the water's roar, as loud as a tornado. Don't forget to bring a rainproof jacket! Yosemite Falls, North America's highest waterfall at 2,425 feet, is especially impressive: at peak times, hydrologists estimate that almost 135,000 gallons of water tumble down its triple cascade every minute.

TIP

Hiking trails climb right up beside some of Yosemite's grandest falls. In spring, these slick footpaths let you feel the full force of nature's power.

Biking past Yosemite Falls.

Yosemite Falls

YOSEMITE NATIONAL PARK

SIZING UP THE WATERFALLS

YOSEMITE FALLS (shown in photo): 2,425 feet tall

VICTORIA FALLS (Zambia/ Zimbabwe): 354 feet tall

IGUAZU FALLS (Brazil/ Argentina): 269 feet tall

NIAGARA FALLS (Ontario, Canada/New York): 176 feet tall

DEEPEST CANYON

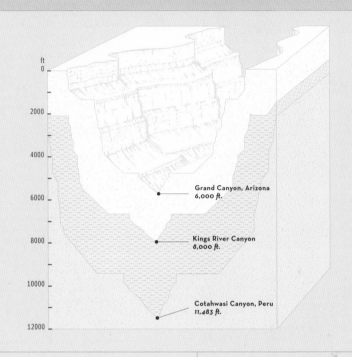

ft
0

2000

4000

6000 — Grand Canyon, Arizona
6,000 ft.

8000 — Kings River Canyon
8,000 ft.

10000

— Cotahwasi Canyon, Peru
11,483 ft.

12000

Kings Canyon

Junction View

Kings Canyon
Scenic Byway

**KINGS CANYON AND SEQUOIA
NATIONAL PARKS**

Reaching a depth of 8,200 fe
when measured from Spanish Pe
(10,051 feet) down to the confl
ence of the North and Middle for
of the Kings River, Kings Canyon
the country's deepest canyon. T
canyon bottom is easily accessib
via a winding, scenic byway. Unli
the Grand Canyon, the Kings Cany
was not cut only by a river. It's al
the work of glaciers, those ancie
rivers of ice, snow, and debris th
flowed through during the last i
age. In 1965 controversial propo
als aimed to dam the Kings River a
flood the canyon in order to supp
water to Los Angeles. We're happy
report that those plans were block

TIP

Drive the Kings Canyon Scenic Byway in early morning or late afternoon, when the pastel color palette is most varied. Stop at Junction View to be awed by the canyon's immensity.

Stretching from the dry, chaparral-covered foothills of the Sierra Nevada to the ferny meadows and groves of the Giant Forest, and even farther up into the glacially carved valley of Mineral King, Sequoia National Park offers a fully-loaded menu of outdoor adventures. Whether you cruise along the Generals Highway through the tall trees to walk the Trail of the Sequoias, or climb Moro Rock for views of the Great Western Divide, then dive underground into jewel-like Crystal Cave, this national park's variety of natural environments and landscapes makes it just as memorable as Yosemite.

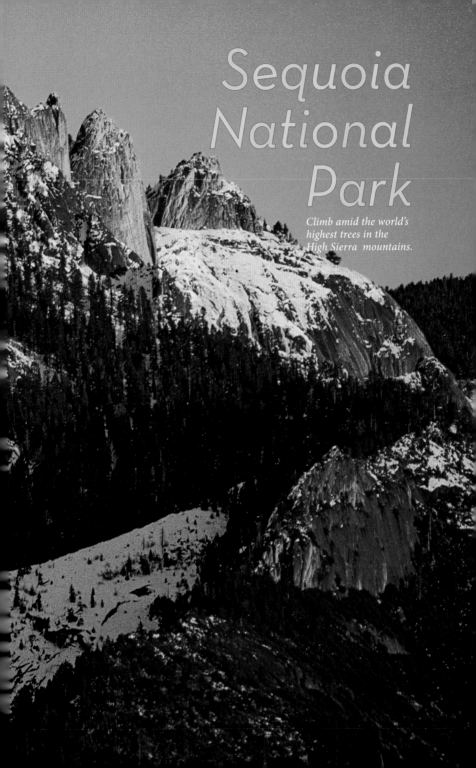

Sequoia
National
Park

*Climb amid the world's
highest trees in the
High Sierra mountains.*

Fires in the park leave burn marks on some of the sequoia trees, like this one. (right) Snow graces the Nation's Christmas Tree, a designation President Coolidge gave the General Grant Tree, a giant sequoia living in the park's Grant Grove.

SEQUOIA TREES

AGE: Can live past 3,000 years.

HEIGHT: Can be greater than 250 feet.

WIDTH: Their diameters can exceed 30 feet.

FUN FACT: They grow faster than any other conifer.

Established by President Benjamin Harrison in 1890, Sequoia was created at the same time as Yosemite National Park, making it a tie for the title of the United States' second-oldest national park. And like Yosemite, Sequoia National Park flourishes with groves of majestic giant sequoias, but the latter park far surpasses the former in this regard. After all, there's a reason Sequoia National Park has this beloved tree in its name: nowhere in the world do giant sequoias grow in such abundance as they do in Sequoia National Park's Giant Forest. So many, in fact, that they can't be counted. Even after all of the 19th-century logging efforts, it's safe to say they still number in the thousands.

Sequoia National Park lies just south of its friendly neighbor, Kings Canyon National Park. Together, these parks comprise even more wilderness territory than Yosemite National Park, which lies farther north a hundred-odd miles in the Sierra Nevada mountain range. Sequoia and Kings Canyon national parks are managed jointly, connected by the lifeline of the Generals Highway, which winds from Grant Grove in Kings Canyon National Park slowly south through the Giant Forest to the Sierra Nevada foothills area of Sequoia National Park. Between Sequoia and Kings Canyon national parks lies the Giant Sequoia National Monument of the Sequoia National Forest, which wraps around the parks. Here, dirt roads lead off into more remote wilderness areas. (Giant Sequoia National Monument is covered in the Kings Canyon National Park chapter.)

In addition to the towering sequoias, the park's top draws include Crystal Cave, where you can go underground to see a wealth of smoothly polished marbled limestone and unusual cave critters that have adapted to a unique subterranean environment found only in this park. Also among the trio of top attractions is Mineral King, once a mining settlement dating from the 1870s and now where the jagged peaks of the Sierra Nevada mountains rise all around you, without your even having to earn the panoramic views by hiking into the backcountry.

PLANNING YOUR TIME

A long day is enough to see many of the park's highlights, but a longer sojourn gives you time to take short hikes through the giant sequoia groves, join a ranger-guided nature walk or talk, and perhaps to take the rugged side road up to Mineral King.

If your time is limited, rise and shine for an early start. Briefly stop at the Foothills or Lodgepole visitor centers to get oriented to the park and to purchase Crystal Cave tour tickets, then drive on the Generals Highway to the Giant Forest Museum, with its educational exhibits for all ages that unlock the ecological mysteries of the giant trees, at the heart of this verdant park. With more time on your hands, you can explore the Native American history of the Foothills area of the park, where riverside walking trails and swimming holes await, which are especially refreshing on hot summer days.

A sequoia's stump reveals the tree's age through its rings. The method of cross-dating trees by their rings points to a potential lifespan for sequoias of more than 3,200 years.

SIGHTS

See the Sequoia National Park map.

This driving tour of the park reflects our suggested itinerary for exploring Sequoia National Park, starting from the South Entrance Station near the Sierra Nevada foothills and climbing into the Giant Forest area, where you can lose yourself among the groves of giant sequoia trees. The southernmost area of the park, which is the Mineral King Valley, also happens to be the most remote and least-visited area of Sequoia National Park, so it appears at the very end of our recommended driving tour.

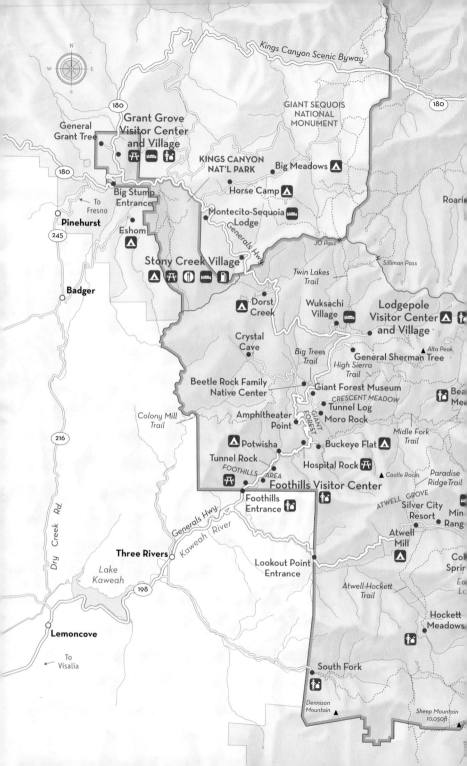

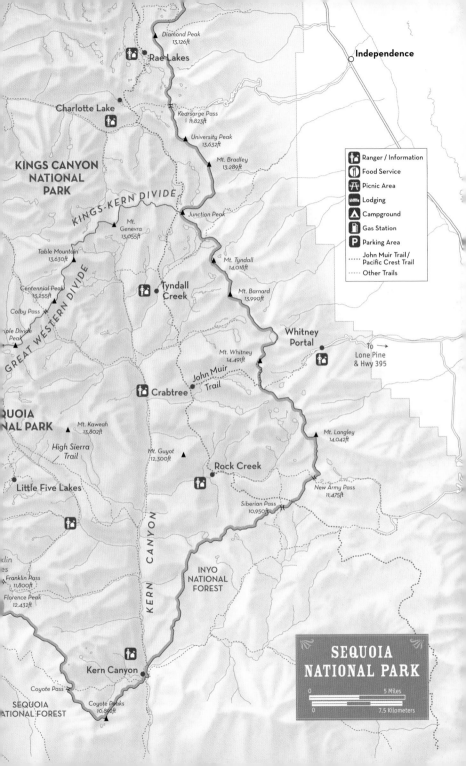

Diamond Peak
13,126ft

Independence

Rae Lakes

Charlotte Lake

Kearsarge Pass
11,823ft

KINGS CANYON
NATIONAL
PARK

University Peak
13,632ft

Mt. Bradley
13,289ft

KINGS-KERN DIVIDE

Mt.
Genevra
13,055ft

Junction Peak

Table Mountain
13,630ft

Mt. Tyndall
14,018ft

Centennial Peak
13,255ft

GREAT WESTERN DIVIDE

Colby Pass

Tyndall
Creek

Mt. Barnard
13,990ft

iple Divide
Peak

Whitney
Portal

Mt. Whitney
14,491ft

To →
Lone Pine
& Hwy 395

John Muir
Trail

Crabtree

QUOIA
NAL PARK

Mt. Kaweah
13,802ft

Mt. Langley
14,042ft

High Sierra
Trail

Mt. Guyot
12,300ft

Rock Creek

Little Five Lakes

New Army Pass
11,475ft

Siberian Pass
10,950ft

KERN CANYON

klin
es

Franklin Pass
11,800ft

INYO
NATIONAL
FOREST

Florence Peak
12,432ft

Kern Canyon

Coyote Pass

Coyote Peaks
10,892ft

SEQUOIA
TIONAL FOREST

Icon	Meaning
	Ranger / Information
	Food Service
	Picnic Area
	Lodging
	Campground
	Gas Station
	Parking Area
- - -	John Muir Trail / Pacific Crest Trail
· · ·	Other Trails

**SEQUOIA
NATIONAL PARK**

0 — 5 Miles
0 — 7.5 Kilometers

FOOTHILLS

At the northern edge of Three Rivers township, Highway 198 memorably crosses the Kaweah River via the **Pumpkin Hollow Bridge,** a distinctive masonry arch structure built in 1922. Migratory swallows return from South America every year, usually around mid-March, to nest in the nooks and crannies of the bridge. You can often observe these twittering birds from the dining room of the town's Gateway Lodge as they glide across the river's banks and hop from tree branch to tree branch in the thick, sweet-smelling forest.

It's less than a mile past the historic bridge to the park's **Foothills Entrance Station**. Just inside the national-park boundary, on the right side of the road, is a hand-carved sign for Sequoia National Park that was created by Civilian Conservation Corps (CCC) artisans in the 1930s. What makes this antique sign notable is its unusual portrait of a Native American man, heralding the area's indigenous history, which is now protected in cooperation by the National Park Service. Until the mid- to late-19th century, these Sierra Nevada foothills were the exclusive territory of the Monachee (Western Mono) tribespeople, with the Patwisha (also called Potwisha or Balwisha) band living south of the Kaweah River divide and the Waksachi band inhabiting the upper valleys to the north. These peoples made seasonal migrations over high mountain passes to trade with the Paiutes living in the Owens Valley on the eastern side of the Great Western Divide.

About a mile past the entrance station, the **Foothills Visitor Center** *(Generals Hwy.; 559/565–3135)* is a good place to stop and stretch your legs. Natural-history exhibits showcase the diversity of flora and fauna inhabiting the park's different ecological zones, which vary in elevation from the foothills to above the tree line. Although the surrounding foothills are hot and dry for much of the year, in spring they're carpeted in wildflowers, especially fields of orange California poppies. Other displays inside the visitor center examine the human history of the park, especially the ways of life of 19th-century conservationists and early Native Americans.

Beyond the visitor center, the Generals Highway starts its long, winding journey up from the foothills to the Giant Forest by following the Kaweah River, which offers scenic canyon views. About 1.5 miles north of the visitor center, **Tunnel Rock** appears on the left side of the road. The tunnel itself was originally dug by CCC workers in the

★ Did You Know? ★

The image of a Native American man on the Foothills Entrance Station sign is most likely modeled after a profile used on early-20th-century U.S. "buffalo nickels," which are now collectors' items.

1930s, which allowed park visitors to drive right through a giant granite rock. Standing here and looking upward at the narrow, twisting highway before you, imagine how much of an adventure it was to visit the national park during the early 1900s, when the road was even narrower and far more of a challenge for touring motorists than it is now, as it lacked many of the guardrails in place today and was more prone to landslides. It was CCC workers who first lined the highway with the rock work that you will see all along the way to the Giant Forest.

After about 3 miles, a side road leads to **Potwisha Campground**. Take it, but instead of turning left into the campground, continue down a paved road to the right until it dead-ends. Once there, it's time to get out of the car again for a little exploration. A short walk takes you to granite slabs where Native American pictographs and *morteros* (mortar holes) used by Monachee tribeswomen for grinding acorns are still visible. Back on the highway, driving north another few miles brings you to **Hospital Rock**. This Native American pictograph and mortero site is easier to access; it's just across the highway from the picnic-area parking lot, standing beside the road to Buckeye Campground.

This Hospital Rock area was once the site of a Monachee village housing up to 500 inhabitants who probably resided here beginning in CF"1350. Archaeologists believe the rock may have been a ceremonial gathering place. In 1860 pioneer John Swanson stayed here for three days while Native Americans treated his broken leg, but the place didn't get the nickname Hospital Rock until 1873, when an early Western pioneer and fur trapper named Alfred Everton lay here waiting while his friend went for help after Everton ironically injured himself with his own bear trap.

FOOTHILLS VISITOR CENTER

TELEPHONE:
559/565–3135

ADDRESS: A mile past Foothills Entrance Station on Generals Highway

Immediately after Hospital Rock, the Generals Highway begins its squiggly ascent out of the gently rolling foothills. Just over 10 miles from the Foothills Visitor Center, look out for **Amphitheater Point** on the west side of the highway, just past a hairpin turn. Pull off to see what lies magnificently spread out before you: not only the Kaweah River as it meanders through the foothills, but also Moro Rock perching over the mixed conifer forests above, signaling the beginning of the giant sequoia's life zone. In the background, the often snow-topped Sierra Nevada high country of the Great Western Divide comes into view. All of this should whet your appetite for what lies just farther ahead up the vertiginous highway.

The Generals Highway climbs upward to **Deer Ridge**, where wide vistas open down into the Kaweah River Canyon and out onto the flat

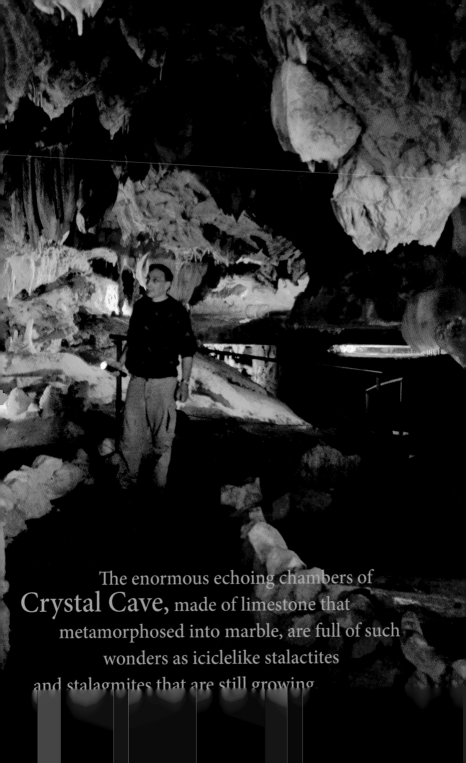

The enormous echoing chambers of
Crystal Cave, made of limestone that
metamorphosed into marble, are full of such
wonders as iciclelike stalactites
and stalagmites that are still growing.

plains of the San Joaquin Valley. The air is often especially fresh and crystal clear after a thunderous storm front moves through. But if all you can see from the highway is haze, blame that drastically reduced visibility on urban air pollution in the form of smog that drifts up from California's central valley. The number of "red alert" days, during which ozone air pollution levels in the park exceed federal environmental standards, is increasing. But when the smog is not as thick, you are well rewarded: the views from here can stretch for more than 100 miles.

CRYSTAL CAVE

Two miles before reaching the Giant Forest Museum, a winding side road (not accessible by RVs or trailers) leads northwest of the Generals Highway for 7 miles to reach the parking lot for ★CRYSTAL CAVE *(Crystal Cave Rd.; 559/565–4251 for information; www.sequoiahistory. org)*, which is open for public tours between May and September. The best-known of more than 240 caves discovered so far in Sequoia and Kings Canyon parks, this underground cavern is made of limestone that was metamorphosed into marble by the uplift of the Sierra Nevada mountain range, then later was polished by running water.

From the parking area, take a pretty half-mile walk along Cascade Creek down to the Spider Web Gate, where guides orient tour groups before leading them inside the enormous echoing chambers full of such wonders as iciclelike stalactites and stalagmites that are still growing, as well as hanging curtains and flowstone formations like the Pipe Organ, which looks just like its name suggests.

The cave is also interesting for its biological diversity, with cave-dwelling bats and creepy-crawly insects like spiders and scorpions living here that exist nowhere else in the world. This is important because the Sierra Nevada has recently been identified as one of the five "hot spots" for cave animal diversity in the United States. The lighted pathways inside Crystal Cave are paved, but they aren't wheelchair-accessible; baby backpacks, strollers, and walking sticks are also not allowed. Because the temperature inside is a chilly 48°F, bring a sweater or jacket.

You'll need to get tour tickets in advance for these explorations. The basic 45-minute tours are a short introduction to the cave's amazing ecosystem, ideal for families with kids and anyone short on time or not really all that keen on stumbling around dark, dank holes in the ground. The 1½-hour Discovery Tour is a more intimate experience that delves into the ecology of the cave environment. First-come, first-served and same-day tickets for either of these two tours are not sold at the cave; you can buy them—in person only—at the Foothills or Lodgepole visitor centers. On Saturdays in the summer, there are also longer, guided Wild Cave Tours. Only available by advance registration, these more adventurous and extensive tours let spelunkers scramble off-trail inside the cave for four to six hours.

Giant Forest

Back on the Generals Highway, the forest canopy points skyward all around you, with encircling lodgepole and ponderosa pines, and white firs and giant sequoias towering above them all. After about an hour's drive uphill from the Foothills Visitor Center, the highway finally enters the **Giant Forest** (elevation 6,400 feet). This precious ecosystem harbors some of the world's largest groves of giant sequoia trees, which exist only on the western slope of the Sierra Nevada mountains. In the late 19th century, timber loggers tried to turn a profit by cutting down giant sequoias, but their brittle aged wood proved too soft and fragile to be economically profitable for logging. These gentle giants fortunately came to be protected in a national park in 1890.

Nowhere in the world do giant sequoias grow in such abundance as they do in Sequoia National Park's Giant Forest.

Ironically, the national park's tourist development in turn stressed the natural ecosystem of the giant sequoia trees. Visitation rapidly increased after 1900, once tourist camps and cabins were constructed in the Giant Forest, with traffic jams and congestion after the Generals Highway opened in 1926. By the end of the 20th century, this development had damaged the giant trees' root systems and a massive restoration project was under way in the park.

All commercial activity has been moved from the Giant Forest into the nearby Lodgepole and Wuksachi village areas. Nearly 300 buildings that once stood cluttered among the trees have been demolished, and more than 200 acres of forested land are now being restored. One way in which this precious land has been restored further is via prescribed wildfire burns. Giant sequoia seeds can only germinate on bare mineral soil that has been scarred by fire. So after so many decades of total fire suppression, these deliberate fires are necessary to keep the trees reproducing.

Often visitors keep their voices hushed, as though the groves of giant sequoias were open-air cathedrals.

A park visitor sizes up a giant sequoia. (top right) Sequoias, like these in the Giant Forest, are thought to have once grown throughout the Northern Hemisphere until glaciers decimated their population. Today groves of these giant trees flourish only in the Sierra Nevada. (bottom right) Carpenter ants can build nests in the bark of sequoias, though fires can evict them from their homes.

(top right)
*Hiking trails fan
across and out of
Crescent Meadow;
the most popular
leads to Tharp's
Log, a fallen giant
sequoia. (bottom
right) But by car
you can access
Tunnel Log, a
giant sequoia that
stretches across
the road with a
tunnel—hence the
name—you can
drive through.*

As it returns to robust health, the Giant Forest remains open to the public as a surprisingly tranquil day-use area. There is just something about these majestic living things, which can live to be more than 2,000 years old, that often inspires visitors to keep their voices hushed, as though the groves of giant sequoias were open-air cathedrals.

By the side of the highway, a historic wooden market building dating from the 1920s has been converted into the **Giant Forest Museum** *(Generals Hwy.; 559/565–4480),* which is open year-round. Interactive exhibits here consider the human factor and the important role of wildfire in the natural history of the giant sequoias, while also illustrating the trees' size, age, and grandeur. Embedded in the pavement outside the museum, a tiled ruler demonstrates the enormous height and girth of the nearby **Sentinel Tree** as it runs alongside the building, outdistancing it by a noticeable measure.

On the opposite side of the road, a short walk from the main museum parking lot, **Beetle Rock Family Nature Center** *(Generals Hwy.; 559/565–4480)* offers family-friendly educational programs during summer. The flat rock is named for the discovery of a new species of beetle here by amateur entomologist Edward Hopping in 1905.

The Giant Forest is strewn with a network of hiking trails *(see Best Day Hikes, below).* If you're short on time and can't visit the museum or take a refreshing hike, at least drive down the busy side road signposted for Moro Rock and Crescent Meadow on the south side of the museum (it's closed to vehicle traffic in winter), so that you can see the **Auto Log**, which is less than a mile along this road. Until the log began to rot, park visitors were allowed to drive across the top of this fallen giant sequoia, which had a roadway notched into its top side.

It's another mile farther along the same side road to iconic ★**MORO ROCK.** A huff-and-puff quarter-mile ascent of 400 stone steps takes you from the parking lot to the top of the granite dome 300 feet up—don't attempt it when lightning is visible in the sky. The view from the top is often diminished by pollution from the valley below. Even so, the sweeping vistas of the Great Western Divide, which separates the watersheds of the Kaweah River to the west and the Kern River to the east, are impressive. Because the mighty peaks that form the spine of the Sierra Nevada that you can see from here rise in elevation more than 12,000

★ Did You Know? ★

Giant sequoia trees are thought to have been named for Sequoyah, who invented a Cherokee syllabary in 1821.

A huff-and-puff ascent up
400 steps takes you from parking
lot to the top of Mono Rock,
a granite dome 300 feet up,

feet, Mt. Whitney (elevation 14,505 feet), the tallest mountain in the contiguous United States, remains hidden from view.

Continue just over a mile along the road to **Crescent Meadow**, where black bears are often seen foraging for berries and acorns from spring through fall. Starting from the meadow's parking lot, a confusing number of trailheads call to day hikers and backpackers. The most popular trail leads 1.3 miles out to **Tharp's Log**, another fallen giant sequoia. This hollowed-out tree once served as a summer cabin for Hale Tharp, the first European resident of the Three Rivers area, who grazed his cattle in the meadow from 1861 until the area was established as a national park in 1890. Today, standing outside Tharp's Log, you can peer in at the treehouse's restored furnishings, which include an unusual rock fireplace.

On the drive back toward the Generals Highway, you will come across the drive-through **Tunnel Log**, a giant sequoia that fell across the road here in 1937. Afterward, CCC workers cut a tunnel through it, but the opening only measures 8 feet high by 17 feet wide, so not all vehicles will fit through. Don't get stuck!

Nothing can compare with the ★GENERAL SHERMAN TREE, which is the biggest tree in the park. It's also the largest giant sequoia tree in the world. Having survived not only the threat of the late-19th-century logging era, but also centuries of snowstorms and wildfires that have left its reddish-brown bark scarred, the General Sherman Tree today stands nearly 275 feet tall and measures more than 100 feet in circumference around its base—and it's still growing.

This estimated 2,000-year-old giant was named in 1879 by pioneer trapper and cattleman James Wolverton, who had served as a Civil War soldier under General William Tecumseh Sherman in the Union Army. Interestingly, the tree was briefly renamed the Karl Marx Tree in the late 1880s by the utopian Kaweah Colony that embarked on an experimental way of life in the Three Rivers area. As the colony labored to build roads and a timber-logging operation into the Giant Forest, conservationists who favored saving the giant sequoia trees from cutting only intensified their efforts, leading to the creation of the national park, which spelled the end of the colony's dreams. Visitors with limited mobility may park off the Generals Highway in front of the General Sherman Tree in the ADA-accessible lot. Everyone else should turn right off the Generals Highway onto the side road leading to the cool, forested **Wolverton Picnic Area** and park in the main lot instead, from where a paved trail visits the tree.

About 2 miles' drive north on the Generals Highway, during which you may be able to catch a glimpse of Marble Fork Canyon through the trees, you come to the busy Lodgepole village (elevation 6,720 feet) area, complete with a market, deli, snack bar, campground, and shower house. Step inside the **Lodgepole Visitor Center** (*Generals Hwy.; 559/565-4436*) to find out more about the geology of the Sierra Nevada mountain range and its endemic wildlife, as well as the region's varied human history, which brims with stories of indigenous Western Mono peoples and early pioneers as well as past and modern conservationists and tourists; video presentations are available upon request. The visitor center and all services in the Lodgepole village area are usually open from May through October. Two miles farther north along the Generals Highway is the **Wuksachi Lodge** (*Generals Hwy.; 866/807-3598*), which has a hotel, restaurant, bar, and snack and gift shop that are open year-round.

Beyond Wuksachi, the Generals Highway passes by Halsted Meadow, another grassy, tree-shaded picnic area; the trailhead for hiking up Little Baldy (*see* Best Day Hikes *below*); and the park's Dorst Creek Campground. The highway continues through the Giant Sequoia National Monument of the Sequoia National Forest north into Kings Canyon National Park.

MINERAL KING

It's an adventure just getting to **Mineral King** (elevation 7,500 feet), one of the oldest settled communities in the Sierra Nevada mountains. Today, it's the least-visited corner of Sequoia National Park. Before the arrival of Europeans, this pristine subalpine valley was a summer hunting camp for Native American tribes. By the 1860s, fur trappers and cattlemen began following the trails that Native Americans had trod up the Kaweah River canyon. The next decade brought hardscrabble miners looking to harvest the riches of the hills. They built a boomtown here called Beulah, and the name was later changed to Mineral King.

Although the mines turned out to be a bust, the road to Mineral King that the miners had built brought logging, hydroelectric development, and, later, tourists into the valley, which soon became a recreational summer resort made up of privately owned cabins, some of which still stand today. In the mid–20th century, the Walt Disney Company planned to build a ski resort here but was stopped by a political coalition that included the National Park Service, USDA Forest Service, and the Sierra Club. In 1978, Mineral King was controversially annexed to Sequoia National Park, ending a protracted battle

LODGEPOLE VISITOR CENTER

TELEPHONE:
559/565-4436

ADDRESS:
Generals Highway

THE BIGGEST LIVING THING IN THE WORLD

What's the largest thing in the world? The verdict is still out, but here's a look at a few of nature's contenders.

Giant sequoia trees *(Sequoiadendron giganteum)* are members of the redwood family, which also includes coast redwoods *(Sequoia sempervirens)* growing on the Pacific Coast of Northern California, and dawn redwoods *(Metasequoia glyptostroboides)* native to southwestern China. The coast redwoods are the tallest trees on Earth. The very tallest among them is a tree known as Hyperion, which stands 379 feet high in an undisclosed location in California's Redwood National Park.

While giant sequoia trees may not be taller than coast redwoods, they are more massive. The largest known giant sequoia is the General Sherman Tree, boasting an ever-increasing volume that is currently 52,500 cubic feet. This Giant Forest icon grows each year by a volume approximately equal in size to a 50-foot-high-tree that is 1 foot in diameter.

But is this Sequoia National Park stalwart the world's largest living thing? Scientists say no. Also staking claims to that title are other gigantic spectacles of nature—from the 1,250-mile-long Great Barrier Reef off the east coast of Australia and an underground fungi that spreads across 2,200 acres in Oregon to an enormous grove of genetically identical quaking aspen trees in Utah whose roots are interconnected and together weigh 6,600 tons!

GENERAL SHERMAN

over private versus public land rights to this highly valued piece of Sierra Nevada wilderness. It took another 35 years for this historical community to be listed on the National Register of Historic Places.

To get to Mineral King, turn off Highway 198 just east of the town of Three Rivers and west of the national park's Foothills Entrance Station. The 25-mile **Mineral King Road** is usually open only from late May through late October. It's an incredibly scenic road, with its sheer, head-spinning drop-offs into the dramatic river valley below and luxuriant mixed-conifer forests growing precipitously on the sides of granite mountains, but also a narrow and winding route requiring you to make almost 700 right-hand turns. In some places, the road is barely wide enough for two cars to pass each other safely (RVs and trailers are not recommended), so take it easy and go slow. The drive takes at least 1½ hours each way.

If you're not going to stay overnight in a national-park campground at Mineral King or in a rustic cabin at Silver City Resort, before venturing up this road, do two things. One, get a very early start, and two, make sure your car's gas tank is full, because there is no place to fuel up after leaving Three Rivers.

The epic drive to Mineral King starts outside the national park boundary and follows the canyon of the East Fork of the Kaweah River. Don't rush the trip, because the scenic drive is the whole point—there aren't any major sights to see along the way, so just enjoy the views.

About 11 miles after leaving Highway 198, Mineral King Road passes the national park's **Lookout Point Entrance Station**. The road continues to climb for another 7 miles onto the spectacular Hockett Plateau to reach **Atwell Mill**, where some relics of 19th-century logging operations, notably a big steam engine, remain for casual inspection. One hiking trail here leads down to a small waterfall on the Kaweah River that usually appears in late spring and early summer. Although petite, the waterfall is surrounded by moss-covered rocks and thick vegetation, making it a surprisingly scenic spot.

On the opposite side of the road, another pleasant trail leads up through Atwell Grove, the park's highest-elevation grove of giant sequoias, where chances are you'll finally have the forest all to yourself, and to lofty Paradise Ridge, where you'll enjoy fine views of the mighty Great Western Divide of the Sierra Nevada range. Two miles farther east along the Mineral King Road is **Silver City Resort** (*Mineral King Rd.; 559/561–3223 in summer, 559/734–4109 in winter*), with a basic restaurant, a store, and rustic cabins and alpine cha-

WARNING: MARMOTS AHEAD

A word of warning before you make the long drive to Mineral King: your car is in danger of becoming a snack for marmots.

Marmots, the largest members of the squirrel family, resemble groundhogs and prairie dogs and are the size of a small poodle. They live in the high mountainous regions of North America and Europe, typically at elevations above 6,000 feet. In most of the Sierra Nevada, you encounter them along high-elevation backcountry trails. The Mineral King Valley has an especially large population.

You'll usually hear marmots before you see them, as they communicate using high-pierced whistles. Don't be alarmed if a marmot runs right up to meet you; they're curious and fearless creatures. But these pesky rodents are known to chew on car hoses and wires. Why? Even though the antifreeze coolant found inside cars is poisonous to humans, it tastes addictively sweet to marmots.

If you leave your car parked for any length of time at Mineral King, you may return to find it seriously damaged, perhaps even undrivable. Occasionally, the determined critters get trapped inside engine compartments, so always check under the hood for stowaways before driving away. Locals recommend placing chicken wire around your vehicle to discourage marmots. You can buy some rolls of chicken wire in the town of Three Rivers before starting the journey up to Mineral King. Sometimes you can also find it at the Silver City Mountain Resort general store.

Backpackers need to pay attention to marmots, too, because your equipment just might be lunch. Marmots like to gnaw on hiking boots, pole grips, and backpack straps once they get a bit salty from sweat. Try to keep your gear safely with you at all times, and hope for the best.

THE BIG TREES

"Descending the precipitous divide between the King's River and Kaweah you enter the grand forests. . . . Advancing southward, the giants become more and more irrepressibly exuberant, heaving their massive crowns into the sky from every ridge and slope, and waving onward in graceful compliance with the complicated topography of the region . . . [which] extends from the granite headlands overlooking the hot plains to within a few miles of the cool glacial fountains of the summit peaks. . . . [H]ere for every old, storm-stricken giant there are many in all the glory of prime vigor, and for each of these a crowd of eager, hopeful young trees and saplings grows heartily on moraines, rocky ledges, along watercourses, and in the moist alluvium of meadows, seemingly in hot pursuit of eternal life."

–John Muir,
The Mountains of California, 1894

lets for rent. It's just 5 more miles to reach **Mineral King Ranger Station** (*Mineral King Rd.; 559/565–3768*), a small outpost providing essential visitor information and issuing wilderness permits. It's opposite Cold Springs Campground.

The road at last ends a couple of miles farther up the gorgeous but windswept and avalanche-prone **Mineral King Valley**. Reminiscent of the Rocky Mountains, the valley is most remarkable for its variety of rocks, including speckled granite, white marble, and black shale. Get out of the car to stretch your legs, and perhaps try out one the valley's many hiking trails (*see* Best Day Hikes, *below*) to gain more spectacular views of the jagged mountains rising all around you.

The vistas from the valley floor are dominated by glacier-carved **Sawtooth Peak** (elevation 12,343 feet). Also scattered around the valley are a few cabins built in the late 19th and early 20th centuries, some of which are now painstakingly restored, and all of which may be of interest to history hounds. Although you can't enter them, walking around the outside of these small cabins lets you imagine what life was like for the early settlers of the valley, and the pleasure-seekers who later made it their prized summer retreat in the late 1800s and early 1900s.

⟿ BEST DAY HIKES

For day hikers, plentiful paths inside Sequoia National Park range from easy nature walks to mountain goat-style climbs. Check the current schedules of ranger-guided hikes at the Giant Forest Museum and the Lodgepole and Foothills visitor centers, where you can buy hiking maps and interpretive trail brochures. The following sections are arranged geographically, with the easiest and most popular family-friendly trails listed first, followed by descriptions of more challenging and off-the-beaten trails for hiking enthusiasts.

GIANT FOREST

Many hikes in the Giant Forest area intersect, which means you could walk all day with hardly any backtracking. The 2-mile **Congress Trail** loop starts from the paved path leading to the General Sherman Tree, naturally making it one of the most heavily-trodden trails in the park, then loses many of the crowds as it heads over wooden footbridges

In Crescent Meadow, you may get a chance to spy on black bears foraging for berries or munching peacefully on wildflowers.

deeper into the serene forest. For even more solitude, the moderately difficult 6-mile **Trail of the Sequoias**, which starts along the Congress Trail, passes stately groves of giant sequoias before ascending a ridge, then continues out toward the High Sierra Trail for dizzying vistas, and returns via verdant **Crescent Meadow,** where you may get a chance to spy on black bears foraging for berries or munching peacefully on wildflowers.

Starting outside the Giant Forest Museum, the paved **Big Trees Trail**, which is graded for easy accessibility, loops for just over a mile around Round Meadow, with interesting interpretive signs illustrating giant-sequoia ecology all along the way. Also starting outside the museum, the gentle half-mile-long **Hazelwood Nature Trail** illustrates the importance of wildfire to the life cycle of the giant sequoias.

It's possible to walk about 1.5 miles from the museum along a sign-posted trail out to **Moro Rock**, or you can drive over for the brief, yet heart-pounding ascent via stone steps to the top of the granite dome, where the Great Western Divide stands spread out before you. Farther

On following pages (top left) Head into the woods on the Congress Trail, which passes by the General Sherman Tree. (bottom left) The walk to the summit and back on the Little Baldy Trail takes about four hours. (top right) Take in the High Sierra views from atop Moro Rock. (bottom right) Clamber across the Auto Log, over which vehicles used to drive.

A fawn pauses near the
Little Baldy Trail.

Breathe in the scent of nature in Crescent Meadow, where wildflowers are in abundance come summertime.

along the same road, Crescent Meadow has many inviting trailheads, but not all are signposted clearly. Take the fairly flat 2.2-mile **Crescent Meadow Loop**, which looks prettiest in the early morning or when wildflowers bloom in early summer. Along the way, you can detour to inspect historic Tharp's Log, a hollowed-out trunk that was converted to a rustic mountain cabin. Starting from the meadow, the first rolling stretch of the challenging **High Sierra Trail** takes you three quarters of a mile to head-spinning Eagle View, perched above the gorge of the Middle Fork of the Kaweah River, where an epic background shows off the peaks of the Great Western Divide.

From Wolverton Road, a short distance north along the Generals Highway, the difficult 13.4-mile round-trip **Alta Peak Trail** is a serious proposition but rewards properly acclimatized hikers with deep views of the Kaweah River gorge and of the craggy Great Western Divide jutting up in front of you. Some of the other lakes-and-meadows trails off Wolverton Road can be done as day hikes, though most hikers prefer to camp in the wilderness overnight (*see* the Foothills section, *below*).

Farther north along the Generals Highway, the Lodgepole village turnoff leads to the trailhead for the moderate 3.4-mile round trip to **Tokopah Falls**, which Sierra Nevada snowmelt turns into a torrent in late spring and early summer. About 6 miles north of Lodgepole along the Generals Highway, a moderate 1.75-mile round-trip ascent of **Little Baldy**, a rounded granite dome once used as a fire lookout, provides 360-degree views from the summit. Starting from Dorst Creek Campground farther north along the highway, the easy 2.1-mile round-trip **Muir Grove Trail** out toward Pine Ridge is a walk through an almost undisturbed grove of giant sequoias. Although the trail has deteriorated somewhat, it's still a small amount of effort to be rewarded with such peacefulness among the giant trees, something John Muir often wrote about in his journals during his early explorations of the Sierra Nevada mountains.

Foothills

In the southern Foothills area of the park, the trails are usually much less traveled than those in the must-see Giant Forest. As you explore here, watch out for poison oak, ticks, and rattlesnakes. Also, don't venture too far off-trail, because if you do, there is a small chance that you just might find yourself in an illegal marijuana garden, which are often guarded by potentially armed growers. Although it's rare that a casual day hiker would run into a marijuana-growing operation, as they're usually well-hidden in the backcountry of the park, it's always good to stay aware of the potential issue.

From Potwisha Campground, an easy half-mile loop trail leads past Native American pictographs to summertime swimming holes along the Kaweah River. Off the same access road, it's a 3.9-mile moderate hike each way to **Marble Falls,** best visited in late spring when the waterfall is at its fullest, fed by melting mountain snows.

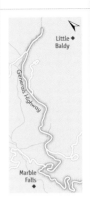

Starting from the Buckeye Flat Campground access road, a long and strenuously uphill 6-mile round-trip hike follows the **Middle Fork Trail** along the Kaweah River for excellent views of Moro Rock, Castle Rocks, and the Great Western Divide before ending with a short but steep climb to Panther Creek. If it's too snowy to drive into the Giant Forest, you can hike in by setting out on one of the trails that begin in the remote South Fork Campground and lead you through the park's lowest-elevation giant sequoia groves; one such trail is a challenging (read: long and strenuous) 5-mile climb to Garfield Creek, past which you can wander through some of the park's most isolated and remote groves of giant sequoia trees.

MINERAL KING

During the adventurous side trip to Mineral King, even short hikes will help you absorb the singular beauty of this subalpine valley. Starting from Cold Springs Campground, the tame, 2.4-mile round-trip **Cold Springs Nature Trail** winds past historic cabins that predate the national park.

Before attempting longer day hikes that ascend to higher-altitude lakes and meadows, stop by the Mineral King Ranger Station for advice and to check on trail conditions. The most popular day hikes include the 6.8-mile round-trip to gorgeous **Eagle Lake** and the 7.5-mile round-trip trek to **White Chief Canyon,** which passes a wildflower meadow, historic miners' cabins, and marble caverns for expert spelunkers. The well-traveled 8.4-mile round-trip trail to **Monarch Lakes** also offers spectacular views back over the entire valley. Before leaving your car at the trailhead for any length of time (that is, longer than a short hike), protect it from those pesky marmots (*see* Warning: Marmots Ahead, *above*).

☀ OTHER ACTIVITIES

While most visitors to Sequoia National Park take time for a short day hike among the giant sequoia trees, there are plenty of other sports to try, all year round. Although the pack station at Mineral King is currently closed, horseback rides are still available nearby (*see* the Kings Canyon National Park chapter).

Besides what's described below, you may want to look into the **Sequoia Field Institute** (*47050 Generals Hwy. #10; 559/565–3759 or 559/565–4251; www.sequoiahistory.org*), which offers educational trips in the national park between April and October. Their options range from photo safaris where camera-toting hikers ascend into wildflower-filled mountain meadows, and art-based tours for avid painters and nature sketchers, or overnight backpacking trips led by entertaining local experts and focused on various topics of interest in natural and cultural history, anything from black-bear ecology to early pioneer-era experiences in the park. The in-depth knowledge shared by these trips' leaders makes them worth the extra effort of signing up for weeks or even months in advance of your trip.

Backpacking—the greatest escape you can make in the park—lets you avoid the traffic noise and summer crowds that flood many day-hiking trails.

BACKPACKING AND MOUNTAINEERING

Wilderness trails beckon to backpackers and mountain climbers on both sides of the Great Western Divide. While you do need hiking experience and plenty of preparation to embark on any of these adventurous overnight trips, you'll be infinitely rewarded by the backcountry's amazing scenery—alpine lakes, profusely blooming wildflower meadows, dense forests where black bears and marmots freely roam, and high above it all, arid Sierra Nevada peaks down which cacophonous waterfalls rush in early summer. In short, backpacking is the greatest escape you can make in the park; you can avoid the traffic noise and the incessant summer crowds that flood many day-hiking trails.

The Giant Forest area, Lodgepole village, and the Mineral King valley are the busiest gateways for backpacking trips into the Sierra Nevada high country. The most well-trammeled route is the epic **High**

A backpacker drinks in the view on the High Sierra Trail.

Sierra Trail, which starts from shady Crescent Meadow and leads for more than 70 miles over the Great Western Divide to Mt. Whitney, at least a week's endeavor even for those in good physical shape. The first 11.5 miles to and back from **Bearpaw Meadow** (elevation 7,800 feet), part of the High Sierra Trail, make an excellent two- or three-day backpacking trip, with time for detours to pretty alpine lakes above the meadow.

Prime scenery also makes weekends trips to **Emerald and Pear lakes**, a moderately challenging 6.1-mile hike each way from the Wolverton Road trailhead, which is very heavily traveled. Also starting from Wolverton Road, a tougher 11.8-mile round-trip trail climbs steadily to **Alta Meadow**, where you can kick back among the wildflowers in early summer. From Lodgepole, a steep and difficult 14-mile round-trip trail to wildly contrasting **Twin Lakes** (the smaller one is completely surrounded by thick forest, while the larger of the pair backs up against granite talus and cliffs) passes fresh Cahoon Meadow.

Several rugged wilderness trails rise out of the Mineral King valley, creating endurance-testing challenges even for experienced backpackers. Many of the day hikes to alpine lakes described in the previous section make great overnight backpacking destinations, too. The most well-traveled backpacking trail leads to **Franklin Lakes**, a difficult 10.8-mile round trip. The **Sawtooth Trail** passes over Timber Gap to reach **Little Five Lakes** and **Big Five Lakes,** beyond which experienced off-trail hikers can make their way over Sawtooth Pass and then loop back to the valley via **Monarch Lakes**. From Atwell Mill Campground, the tough **Atwell-Hockett Trail** passes streams and through verdant forests for 10 miles to reach lush Hockett Meadow.

PERMITS

All wilderness trails inside the national park are subject to a daily quota for overnight backpacking trips. Apply for wilderness permits ($15) in advance from the **Sequoia & Kings Canyon National Park Wilderness Office** *(47050 Generals Hwy., Three Rivers, CA 93271; 559/565–3766; www.nps.gov/seki).* Applications are accepted by fax or U.S. mail starting on March 1 every year.

A limited number of walk-up permits are also issued on a first-come, first-served basis on the afternoon prior to or the same day as your trip only at the permit-issuing station closest to your proposed trailhead. Permit-issuing stations are at the following locations: the **Lodgepole Visitor Center** *(Generals Hwy.; 559/565–4408),* the **Foothills Visitor Center** *(Generals Hwy.; 559/565–3135),* and the **Mineral King Ranger Station** *(Mineral King Rd.; 559/565–3768).*

Each of these facilities rent bear-proof canisters, which are required for all backcountry travel. Reserved permits are not available for the Emerald and Pear Lake trails (for which first-come, first-served permits only are available on the day of your trip or the afternoon prior), and are not necessary for hikers who already have reservations for the Bearpaw and Sequoia High Sierra Camps (*see* the Where to Stay and Eat chapter).

Backcountry trips starting in nearby national forest lands are often subject to quotas, and reservations for wilderness permits are sometimes accepted. For overnight backpacking trips into the Jennie Lakes Wilderness of the Sequoia National Forest, *see* the Kings Canyon National Park chapter.

HIKING MT. WHITNEY

At an eyewatering 14,505 feet, **Mt. Whitney** is the highest peak in the contiguous United States. This soaring peak punctuates the eastern side of the Sierra Nevada, and it has the most popular backpacking trail in the entire region.

Though it's a popular challenge, it's definitely not something to be taken lightly. (If you finish it, you'll have serious bragging rights.) The 22-mile round-trip ascent is for fit, experienced alpinists.

Wilderness permits are required for the Mt. Whitney Zone between May and October. Those starting from Whitney Portal on the east side of the Sierra Nevada mountains must enter the competitive Mt. Whitney permit lottery, normally held in February each year. Contact the **Inyo National Forest** *(351 Pacu Lane, Suite 200, Bishop; 760/873-2485 for information, 760/873-2483 for reservations; www.fs.fed. us/r5/inyo)* for info on trips beginning on the east side. Hikers approaching from the west (starting in Sequoia or Kings Canyon national parks) are subject only to the normal national-park trailhead quotas.

SEQUOIA NATIONAL PARK IN WINTER

Snow usually blankets Sequoia National Park between November and April, which keeps away the crowds and adds an element of magical mystery to your experience of the parks, especially with the towering trees peacefully blanketed by snow. If you do choose to visit in winter, you will be rewarded by peaceful snowshoe walks through groves of giant sequoias, while more adventurous types can lash on cross-country skis.

Although much of the park's wildlife takes a long winter's nap at this time, you may still glimpse birds flying overhead and mule deer bounding through the thick forests, especially in the warmer Sierra Nevada foothills of the park, where a few stubborn black bears lumber about even during the coldest months. The fresh layers of snow also provide an excellent way to study animal tracks, which may go unnoticed or easily trampled underfoot by hundreds of visitors during the summer months. For independent, self-sufficient tourists, the special effort it takes to visit Sequoia National Park during winter is well rewarded by both the scenery and the unusual opportunities for snow sports.

Only a few park roads remain open during winter; which ones are can vary, but the predominant one among them is the Generals Highway. The upper section of the highway through the Giant Forest and the Sequoia National Forest leading to Kings Canyon National Park is especially subject to weather delays and snow-plow closures after heavy storms. Always carry tire chains, which may be required at any time during winter. For current road conditions, call 559/565–3341.

Snowballs fly and children rush about in the **Wolverton** area. This spot off the Generals Highway, about 2 miles north of the General Sherman Tree, is where kids come to play in the snow and leap onto their sleds for a quick flight downhill.

If snowshoeing and cross-country skiing through silent groves of giant sequoias are more to your liking, head to the **Giant Forest** for ungroomed trails, including out to Moro Rock and Crescent Meadow on a side road that's closed to vehicle traffic in winter. Rent cross-country skis and snowshoes at the **Wuksachi Lodge** (Generals Hwy.; 866/807–3598), which also sells basic winter clothing and snow-play equipment like children's plastic sleds. Staff at the lodge groom cross-country skiing trails for beginner to experienced skiers.

If you'd like to join a ranger-guided snowshoe walk, call the **Giant Forest Museum** (Generals Hwy.; 559/565–4480) for reservations. The 1-mile, two-hour trek is usually scheduled on Saturdays and holidays. Equipment is provided for a small donation. For many visitors, this relatively short walk is certainly a lot of exercise (if you've ever tried snowshoeing before, you know it's more tiring than it might at first look), but it's also perhaps the most special experience you can have in the park during winter without venturing into the backcountry. The slow pace of the guided trek lets you savor the experience of the forest during the stillness of winter. The crisp, clear air means that the views are even more impressive than in summer.

For expert backcountry skiers well versed in survival skills, you can find rest at the end of a 6-mile, 2,000-foot ascent from Wolverton Meadow at the **Pear Lake Ski Hut** (elevation 9,200 feet). The hut, which sleeps 10 people, is usually open from mid-December through April. Allow all day to get there. It's heated by a wood-pellet stove, but bring your own bedding, which means subzero-rated winter-weight sleeping bags, to stay warm in the sleeping loft equipped only with basic bunk beds. For reservations, contact the **Sequoia Natural History Association** (47050 Generals Hwy. #10; 559/565–3759; www.sequoiahistory.org).

For more winter recreation areas, including in the Giant Sequoia National Monument of the Sequoia National Forest, see the Kings Canyon chapter.

Fishing

Fishing is more of a pleasurable pastime than a sport inside the park. The catch is almost guaranteed to be of the trout variety—rainbow, brown, golden, and eastern brook. The season is usually from late April until mid-November, except in the Kaweah River drainage, where anglers drop their lines year-round.

You'll need to lace up your boots and hit a trail to reach some of the park's best fishing holes.

Many of the best fishing spots are only accessible via hiking trails—for example, from the Lodgepole village area to Twin Lakes or from Mineral King to Big and Little Five lakes. A few more convenient fishing holes, often requiring only a short walk along a well-trodden trail to reach, are found along the Kaweah River in the southern Sierra Nevada foothills area of the park. Multiday backcountry pack trips undertaken with the aid of an outdoor outfitter that wrangles horses and mules explore the Golden Trout Wilderness of the **Sequoia National Forest** *(Tule Ranger District office: 32588 Hwy. 190, Springville; 559/539–2607; www.fs.fed.us/r5/ sequoia)* south of the Sequoia National Park boundary.

LICENSES

Anglers aged 16 and older must carry a valid California fishing license, which are usually sold at the Lodgepole village market. The general limit is five trout per day, with 10 fish in possession. Additional restrictions apply inside the national park boundaries, so ask at one of the park's visitor centers for current fishing regulations covering specific bait and hook types, daily limits, and catch-and-release requirements, which vary depending on your location and elevation within the park.

Swimming and White-Water Rafting

When thermometers in the foothills top 100°F during summer, a dip in the **Kaweah River** is enticing, as the water's chilly temperatures feel just right. Look for swimming holes in the river along the **Marble Fork**, accessed via a hiking trail north of Potwisha Campground, and on the **Middle Fork** east of Buckeye Flat Campground.

There's a secret swimming hole near the **Lodgepole Village Picnic Area**, too. To find it, ask any of the campground rangers or Lodgepole visitor center staff for directions. If it's a hot summer day, though, probably all you will have to do is follow the sounds of children's happy shouts.

Swimming anywhere in the park can be extremely dangerous in early summer, when mountain snowmelt can turn rivers into a torrent of rapids. As water levels drop later in the summer, sandy and rocky beaches appear. Ask rangers for advice about current conditions and the best swimming spots when you visit, and always exercise caution, as drowning is the number-one cause of visitor fatalities in the park. None of these swimming holes in the parks have any sort of lifeguard or posted ranger lookout, so it's important to look out for not only yourself but everyone else if you choose to swim here. If you see a swimmer get into trouble, immediately call a ranger or dial 911 from any pay phone to contact park dispatch for help with swift-water rescue.

All white-water rafting on the Kaweah River (with Class III–V rapids) happens outside the national park boundaries; the usual take-out point is Lake Kaweah reservoir, southwest of the town of Three Rivers. **Whitewater Voyages** (*5255 San Pablo Dam Rd., El Sobrante; 510/222-5994, 800/400-7238*) and **Kaweah Whitewater Adventures** (*P.O. Box 1059, Three Rivers; 800/229-8658*) offer one- and two-day rafting adventures on the Kaweah River. The white-water-rafting season usually runs from late spring into early summer.

Spotlight on
ROCK
CLIMBING
in Yosemite

It's no exaggeration to say that Yosemite National Park is not only the birthplace of American rock climbing but one of the best places to climb in the world. The breathtaking scale, beauty, and concentration of the rock formations here have inspired generations of climbers to develop new techniques, to invent equipment, and to set eye-popping records. The granite itself is polished by glaciers, fissured with vertical cracks, and often extremely steep. Most Yosemite routes involve traditional or "trad" climbing, which means finding routes and placing protective gear—a mental *and* physical challenge. Whether you're a veteran climber, starting out with an introductory class, or just watching from the ground, you're sure to be awestruck.

—Jennifer Paull

◀◀ On the West Ridge of Mt. Conness.

EPIC CLIMBS

Two of Yosemite's icons are also iconic rock-climbing locations: Half Dome and El Capitan. The breakthrough year was 1957, when each was tackled by a pioneering climber. Royal Robbins managed the first technical climbing route of Half Dome, up its northwest face. Meanwhile, Warren Harding, Wayne Merry, and George Whitmore started a fixed-rope route up the prow, or "Nose" of El Capitan. It took Harding's group more than a year of successive aid climbs before they summited in November, 1958. In so doing, they established "seige" climbing, hauling up supplies and spending days at a time on the rock. Their feat also ushered in the era of climbing publicity by attracting hordes of reporters and wide-eyed tourists. There are now dozens of climbing routes up these monoliths. El Capitan's Nose has become a top route for speed-climbing.

ROUTE RATINGS

The American rating system used to gauge the difficulty of hikes and climbs is named for Yosemite: the Yosemite Decimal System. Routes get a numerical grade, from a flat trail (Class 1) to rock climbing using protective gear (Class 5). Class 5 climbs are then divided into more than a dozen subsets, from the relatively easy 5.0 on up.

Tackling a multiday climb up El Capitan.

El Capitan

Half Dome

YOSEMITE NATIONAL PARK

EL CAPITAN

HEIGHT: 3,593 feet from the valley floor

NICKNAME: the Big Stone

WHERE TO WATCH CLIMBERS: Bring binoculars to Swan Slab across from the Yosemite Lodge or to the El Capitan Meadow.

HALF DOME

HEIGHT: 4,733 feet from the valley floor

WHERE TO WATCH CLIMBERS:
Bring binoculars to Mirror Lake or hike up to North Dome, which faces Half Dome.

OTHER BIG WALLS

"Big wall climbing," or multiday aid climbs up huge rock faces, was literally invented here in Yosemite, when John Salathé and Ax Nelson spent five thirsty days on Lost Arrow Chimney in 1947. Beyond El Cap and Half Dome, other big walls include Leaning Tower (the steepest), Washington Column, Liberty Cap, Sentinel Rock, and Mt. Watkins.

Big walls are a serious undertaking—you need significant climbing experience, stamina, and advance planning. Not to mention the mental toughness to handle the nonstop work and exposure. The payoff? An indescribable climbing euphoria. If this kind of endurance test is for you, Yosemite's a goldmine of historic, world-renowned routes.

Lost Arrow Spire isn't a big wall, but the pinnacle is a unique draw.

BIVOUACKING

Don't panic if you see the specks of climbers staying put on a big wall for hours. They're (hopefully) not stuck but instead bivouacking, spending the night in midair. On multiday ascents, climbers sleep in a waterproof "bivy"sack on rock or portable ledges, affixed to the cliff hundreds or thousands of feet up.

Bivouacking: time to count birds instead of sheep.

EASIER ROUTES

When it comes to gauging easier climbs in Yosemite, remember that it's all relative. The nature of the rock here—smooth, steep, few handholds since the cracks run vertically instead of horizontally—means that there aren't a heck of a lot of introductory climbs rated 5.7 or less. Beginners usually start around Swan Slab in Yosemite Valley or at Tuolumne Meadows. Both areas are easy to access and usually have plenty of spectators cheering on new climbers. When considering the difficulty of a climb, don't forget to take into account how you'll get to the climbing site (for instance, whether there's a long hike).

GREAT INTRODUCTORY CLIMBS

After Six, in Yosemite Valley

Munginella, in Yosemite Valley

Oak Tree Flake or Claude's Delight, both on Swan Slab

Regular Route or Jamcrack, both on Sunnyside Bench

A freshly hooked climber on the summit of Cathedral Peak.

Tuolumne Meadows is a favorite for all levels of climbers.

Using friction on Zee Tree in Tuolumne Meadows.

BOULDERING

Not all Yosemite climbs are on a huge physical scale—the park is also a great place for bouldering. This form of climbing is usually done on large freestanding rocks, staying about 15 or fewer feet above the ground. Rather than using ropes and a harness, climbers put down a mat or crash pad and use a spotter in case of a fall. Otherwise, the only necessary tools are climbing shoes and hand chalk. Yosemite's bouldering routes, or "problems," were long used for training, but they've now become extremely popular in their own right. The granite boulders around Yosemite Valley's Camp 4 have some of the world's classic problems. Tuolumne Meadows is another boulder-rich area, and new favorites, like Candyland, emerge every summer.

Bouldering among giants in Yosemite Valley.

Going for the "Slap Shot" problem.

On the "Reach for a Peach" problem in Tuolumne Meadows.

WHERE TO LEARN

The Yosemite Mountaineering School (*209/372-8344; www.yosemitemountaineering.com*) is the only in-park climbing school. There's a daily introductory "Go Climb a Rock" beginners' session, plus specialized classes like crack climbing, big-wall techniques, and even a women-only "Girls on Granite" weekend. YMS guides will also take you out for private lessons or guided climbs. The school is based in Curry Village between April and October, with a temporary branch in Tuolumne Meadows during the hottest part of summer. Costs start around $120 for a one-day class.

Southern Yosemite Mountain Guides (*800/231-4575; www.symg.com*) offers private guides for classes at all levels April through November and several weekend-long, small-group trips. Their routes are outside the national park, often in less-trammeled backcountry. Costs start at $255 for a half-day private class.

WHEN TO GO

Late April through June and September through October are generally best in Yosemite Valley. The valley heat gets intense in July and August, with temperatures over 100°F on sunlit rock faces, so a better bet is Tuolumne Meadows. At a higher elevation, Tuolumne is much cooler. Be prepared for the occasional thunderstorm.

A Yosemite Mountaineering School instructor demonstrates knots.

Tuolumne Meadows

YOSEMITE NATIONAL PARK

QUICKDRAW
Used to attach ropes to bolt anchors or other protective gear in the rock.

HELMET
Protects during falls and deflects objects falling from above.

CARABINER
Aluminum loop with a spring-loaded opening. Locking carabiners are used for connections or belays.

HARNESS
Attaches rope to the climber and has loops to hold gear.

CLIMBING SHOES
Thin, tight-fitting shoes with a sticky rubber sole.

221

CLIMBING GUIDEBOOKS

Falcon Guide: Rock Climbing Tuolumne Meadows, 4th ed. by Don Reid and Chris Falkenstein.

Falcon Guide: Yosemite Free Climbs by Don Reid.

Yosemite Big Walls: SuperTopos by Chris McNamara

Yosemite Valley Free Climbs: SuperTopos by Chris McNamara and Steve Roper.

IN THE BEGINNING

Dick Leonard, Jules Eichorn, and Bestor Robinson at their first ascent of Higher Cathedral Spire in 1934.

Early rock climbing in Yosemite was an under-the-radar and seat-of-your-pants experience. In 1875, George Anderson ascended Half Dome by creating a sort of ladder, drilling iron bolts into the granite and threading the bolts with rope. In 1934, three Bay Area Sierra Club members conquered Yosemite's Lower and Higher Cathedral Spires, using pitons and newly acquired alpine rope techniques to belay and rappel—opening a fresh world of possibilities. After World War II, a few climbers returned to Yosemite and tested out new equipment, the result of wartime technological advances. Most importantly, hemp ropes were traded for sturdier nylon. Two more firsts occurred in the 1940s: the invention of hard steel pitons (handmade from a car axle!) and the first multiday, bivouacked climb.

...opelling on Lower Cathedral Spire in 1935.

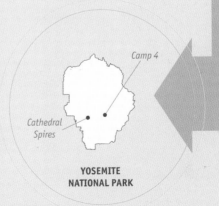

Camp 4

Cathedral Spires

YOSEMITE NATIONAL PARK

CAMP 4 AND THE CLIMBING BOOM

In the 1950s, a handful of eager rock climbers began gravitating to Yosemite Valley's Camp 4 campground. Mostly university students from the San Francisco area, they found ways to stay and climb daily from April to October. By the early 1960s, Camp 4 was the epicenter of American rock climbing. The site became legendary for its scruffy camaraderie, its parties, and increasingly, a touchy hierarchy between hard-core, local climbers and weekenders. The campfire debates about technique and new equipment shaped the future of the sport. The first era of Camp 4 ended with the campground's renovation in 1970; the NPS renamed it Sunnyside. By then, the top climbers were winning international recognition and the sport began to boom. The site quickly became one of the world's most famous climbing destinations. In 2003, it was added to the National Register of Historic Places, and the Camp 4 name was reinstated. Rock rats still flock to it as the ultimate "community center."

Sorting gear at Camp 4.

CLIMBING TERMS AND SLANG

Beta: Information about a climb, like a route's difficulty, length, and advice on holds.

Belay monkey: Someone who patiently belays for a long time (ensuring a cricked neck).

Crux: The toughest, most challenging part of a climb.

Elvis leg: When your leg quivers uncontrollably during a climb, usually due to nervousness plus taxed muscles. Also called sewing-machine leg.

Free climbing: When a climber moves up the rock using only his or her body (as opposed to **aid climbing**, in which climbers rely on equipment like pitons or nuts to advance). Free climbers use ropes and other protective equipment in case of falls.

Jamming: Wedging a body part, like your fingers, into a crack in the rock.

Smearing: Pushing the rubber soles of climbing shoes onto the rock to create friction.

CLIMBING WITH CARE

Climb clean by using nondamaging, removable gear.

Alongside the surge in rock climbing is a rising awareness of climbing's impact on the rocks themselves and the surrounding environment. Below are a few basic conservation rules.

Don't litter anywhere, whether on the rock or in a base area. That goes for "human waste," too. Pick up any litter you see and clean up your chalk marks.

Don't disturb any animals you might encounter. During peregrine falcon nesting season (January through July), certain rock-climbing locations will be closed. Check the kiosk at Camp 4 or the Yosemite Mountain Shop for closure dates.

Be careful of any vegetation. Avoid walking on plants at the bases of climbing areas. Don't clear away plants from the rock (pulling up plants in Yosemite is illegal). Use established trails to reach and descend from your climbing area to reduce soil erosion.

Be careful not to crush or tear up vegetation on trails or rock faces.

Gathering trash at Camp 4.

Kings Canyon
National Park

The Kings Canyon Scenic Byway has stunning views at every one of its many turns.

The grandeur of Yosemite and the towering trees of Sequoia tend to overshadow the splendors of Kings Canyon, making it the least visited of the three Sierra Nevada national parks. But the secrets of Kings Canyon are fiercely guarded by its frequent visitors. It's known and loved best by those who have wandered all over the Sierra Nevada first, only to at last find in this remote canyon the serenity that John Muir sought—and then fought so hard for—in these lofty mountains.

Look, Mom, a treehouse! A couple of aspiring explorers walking through the hollowed-out Fallen Monarch in Grant Grove, (left) where wildflowers cluster among the giant seqouias.

The General Grant Tree was proclaimed a national shrine by President Dwight D. Eisenhower in 1956.

While not spotlighted in its name, Kings Canyon National Park has hidden delights. Among them are many imposing stands of the giant trees—including Redwood Mountain Grove, the largest known grove of sequoias in the world—along with the full spread of what the Sierra Nevada mountains are famous for: treacherously beautiful alpine peaks, painterly wildflower meadows, cascading waterfalls, craggy granite formations, and icy-cool lakes.

What you'll remember best from your visit are the General Grant Tree, first protected on its own as a tiny national park in 1890; the mist-cloaked rocky beaches and gushing waterfalls alongside the Kings River, which rushes through the canyon's amazingly deep gorge; and blissful Zumwalt Meadow, where the strikingly colored western tanager makes its migratory stopover.

Because the park is seldom crowded, you can breathe a little more easily here as you enjoy a measure of solitude that's often absent in Sequoia and especially Yosemite, which receives close to 4 million visitors each year.

Most tourists visit Kings Canyon between Memorial Day and Labor Day, when summer melts snow in the Sierra Nevada high country, opening up jaw-dropping backcountry trails; the chill is taken off the Kings River, which fills with swimmers, mostly shrieking children; and the Kings Canyon Scenic Byway is thrown open from Grant

The giant sequoias in
Grant Grove are between
1,800 and 2,700 years old.

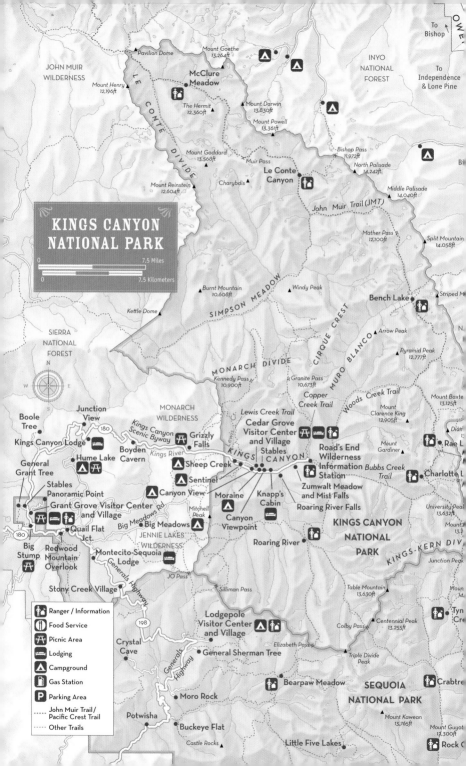

Grove past Hume Lake and Boyden Cavern all the way to Cedar Grove.

If you want to avoid the biggest crowds, plan your sojourn for early June or just after Labor Day, while the weather holds steady and hiking trails through the giant sequoia groves and the canyon remain open. You might even have some of those thickly forest trails to yourself—that is, unless you spot a galumphing black bear in search of berries.

More than half the size of Yosemite National Park to the north, Kings Canyon National Park covers over 700 square miles, making is a little larger than its southern neighbor, Sequoia National Park. Although separated by geography, these two southern Sierra Nevada parks are administered together by the National Park Service, and most tourists usually don't visit one without getting at least a taste of the other.

The main tourist hub in Kings Canyon National Park isn't inside the canyon at all; it's Grant Grove, sitting at the top of the Generals Highway among tall stands of giant sequoia trees to compete with the Giant Forest of Sequoia National Park. Cedar Grove, the park's secondary tourist hub, is nestled deep inside the canyon that John Muir once called "a rival to the Yosemite."

You might even have some of those thickly forested trails to yourself—that is, unless you spot a galumphing black bear in search of berries.

Wrapped around the park and between Grant Grove and Cedar Grove is the Giant Sequoia National Monument of the Sequoia National Forest, which is loved for its hiking trails through primeval forests, idyllic lakes for summer recreation, and a fascinating marble cavern that you can tour.

No matter which road you take into Kings Canyon—whether you choose to travel Highway 180, which twists up the mountain from the farmlands of California's central valley just outside Fresno, or the Generals Highway, an equally winding route connecting Kings Canyon National Park to Sequoia National Park—the journey here is at high altitudes, so it quite literally takes your breath away. The Kings Canyon Scenic Byway, another twisted route with hairpin turns and heart-racing drop-offs, connects the park's tourist centers of Grant

The wild back-country of Cedar Grove varies in its terrain, with rocky outcrops and cliffs as well as forested areas and waterfalls.

Grove and Cedar Grove. The latter is where Highway 180 finally rolls to a stop and the wild backcountry of the Sierra Nevada begins.

PLANNING YOUR TIME

If your main intent is to hit the highlights, you could easily do Kings Canyon in a day. But if you want to soak in the serenity Muir encountered here, stay awhile. A stretch of even just a few days gives you time to take some short hikes around the tall trees of Grant Grove, to visit lesser-known wonders like the Boole Tree, and to try a ranger-guided activity such as a wildflower walk or a campfire talk under the stars.

If your time is limited and you'll just be here a day, then get an early start. Stop briefly in Grant Grove to see the famous tree and to get oriented to the park, and then head down to Road's End, about an hour's drive northeast along the canyon's byway. Try to arrive in Cedar Grove before lunchtime to get ahead of the worst day-tripper crowds. Time your return trip up the canyon to catch a tour of Boyden Cave and to make photo-safari stops at scenic overlooks of the vast canyon, which look most idyllic around sunset.

If you've got two or more days to spend, take a day each in Grant Grove and Cedar Grove, then explore the Giant Sequoia National Monument, with its thickly forested trails and alpine lakes with any extra time you've got to spare. With a week or longer, make reserva-ions well in advance for a backpacking or fishing and horseback-riding pack trip into the high-country wilderness.

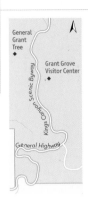

SIGHTS

See the Kings Canyon National Park map.

This section starts at the most popular spot in Kings Canyon National Park, which is Grant Grove. It then follows the Kings Canyon Scenic Byway, which links Grant Grove with Cedar Grove, the park's other tourist hub, via a stunning wild backcountry corridor through the Giant Sequoia National Monument of the Sequoia National Forest. Cedar Grove is located at the end of the road, where Highway 180 comes to an abrupt stop alongside the Kings River at the very bottom of the Kings Canyon. Finally, it travels along the Generals Highway, which connects Grant Grove with Sequoia National Park to the south, via even more forest lands now also protected as part of the Giant Sequoia National Monument.

GRANT GROVE

A few miles beyond the Big Stump Entrance Station, Highway 180 slows as it enters **Grant Grove village** (elevation 6,600 feet). The busiest section of Kings Canyon National Park, the village offers the most visitor services in the park, including a post office, convenience market, gift shop, lodging, and a basic restaurant. At the hopping **Grant Grove Visitor Center** (*Highway 180; 559/565–4307*), a cooperative venture between the National Park Service, USDA Forest Service, and nonprofit Sequoia National History Association, you can peruse natural history exhibits, then watch a 15-minute orientation film that gives you a bird's-eye view of the park, from its mellow groves of giant sequoias to the near-vertical high country of the Sierra Nevada. Also at the center you can learn about hiking options, including overnight backpacking, and horse-riding trips up these mountains, which rank among California's highest (*see Best Hikes, below*).

Just north of the visitor center on Highway 180, a well-signposted turnoff leads downhill to the ★**GENERAL GRANT TREE**, a towering giant named after Civil War general and President Ulysses S. Grant. It's the third-largest tree in the world, measuring 268 feet high and more than 40 feet wide at its base of its gnarly, thick trunk. Designated a National Shrine, the historic landmark is also the United States's official Christmas tree (ordained so by President Calvin Coolidge in

GRANT GROVE VISITOR CENTER

TELEPHONE:
559/565–4307

ADDRESS: Near the Big Stump Entrance, Highway 180

GENERAL GRANT
THE NATION'S CHRISTMAS TREE

GENERAL GRANT TREE
THE NATION'S CHRISTMAS TREE
A LIVING SHRINE

Dominating its forest neighbors, the General Grant Tree is considered by many to have the most beautiful "classic" giant sequoia form. The fossil record indicates this ancient species first appeared in the western U.S. about 50 million years ago. Changing climatic conditions reduced its range to isolated groves along the western slope of the Sierra Nevada. Congress created General Grant National Park in 1890, a 4 square mile area to protect the Big Trees from the lumberman's axe. In 1926, this tree was proclaimed the Nation's Christmas Tree, and annual celebrations are held at its base each December. More recently the Tree was dedicated as America's only living National Shrine in memory of those who died defending this country.

	GENERAL GRANT	GENERAL SHERMAN
Estimated Age	1800-2000 years	2300-2700 years
Height Above Base	267.4 ft. (81.5m)	274.9 ft. (83.8m)
Circumference at Base	107.6 ft. (32.8m)	102.6 ft. (31.1m)
Maximum Basal Diameter	40.3 ft. (12.3m)	36.5 ft. (11.1m)

1926). Because every park visitor is eager to see this famous sequoia, the parking lot here is usually overflowing. It's worth the wait and crowds, though. As you stand beside the General Grant Tree, peering up at its lofty green branches that climb like a ladder toward the sky, it's impossible not to feel awed, especially if you visit early on a peaceful summer morning when dew droplets shine in the sun or if you snowshoe around the imperial grove after a winter storm blankets it in a mantle of silence.

Surrounding this star attraction are multiple sequoias, some scarred by fire and others numbering among the loftiest, greenest and most impressive of their kind still standing. Inside the enormous grove is the historic **Gamlin Cabin**, built by a 19th-century homesteader; it eventually became the national park's first ranger station. Also amid the grove you can scramble inside the impressive **Fallen Monarch**, a hoary, hollowed-out remnant of a giant sequoia carved by fire. During the late 19th century, this natural treehouse variously served as a hotel, saloon, and U.S. cavalry stables.

On the opposite side of Highway 180, a side road (which is closed to traffic during winter) leads steeply for more than 2.3 miles to truthfully named **Panoramic Point**. An easy paved trail leads from the parking lot to the lookout itself, where a sign identifies noteworthy peaks in the

A GRANDER CANYON

"In the vast Sierra wilderness far to the southward of the famous Yosemite Valley, there is a yet grander valley of the same kind. It is situated on the south fork of Kings River, above the most extensive groves and forests of the giant sequoia, and beneath the shadows [of] the highest mountains in the range, where the cañons [sic] are deepest....

"From this long, flowery, forested, well-watered park the walls rise abruptly in plain precipices or richly sculptured masses.... The so-called war of the elements has done them no harm. There is no unsightly defacement as yet; deep in the sky, inviting the onset of storms through unnumbered centuries, they still stand firm and seemingly as fresh and unworn as new-born flowers.

"I fancy the time is not distant when...a road will be built up the South Fork of Kings River through the sequoia groves, into the great cañon.... Let our law-givers then make haste before it is too late to set apart this surpassingly glorious region for the recreation and well-being of humanity, and all the world will rise up and call them blessed."

–John Muir, "A Rival of the Yosemite: The Cañon of the South Fork of the Kings River, California," *The Century Illustrated Monthly Magazine*, November 1891.

Sierra Crest, a hugging-the-clouds ridge that parallels the Great Western Divide, where water on the west flows to the Pacific Ocean and water on the east runs into the Great Basin Desert. The peaks visible here are so enormous that they hide from view even Mt. Whitney, the highest point in the contiguous United States, which sits behind them at an elevation of 14,505 feet.

KINGS CANYON SCENIC BYWAY

To get from Grant Grove to Cedar Grove, the one and only route to take is the ★KINGS CANYON SCENIC BYWAY (Highway 180), which passes through the Giant Sequoia National Monument inside the Sequoia National Forest. This remarkably scenic highway, with its series of heart-in-your-throat twists and turns, is the only road leading down from any direction into Cedar Grove. This means that after you've successfully made the white-knuckle trip deep into the canyon and you're ready to explore elsewhere, backtracking is your only option. But the Kings Canyon Scenic Byway has such memorably scenic Sierra

Kings Canyon's maximum depth of 8,200 feet makes the Grand Canyon's vertical drop of 5,300 feet look small in comparison.

Nevada views that most people don't mind driving it twice.

Highway 180 is open year-round on the portion from Grant Grove to Hume Lake, in Sequoia National Forest, but beyond Hume Lake the road is usually open only from mid-April until early November. Both portions are equally scenic, though the sheer canyon drop-offs only appear past Hume Lake. This section covers the highway all through Giant Sequoia National Monument from Kings Canyon National Park boundary near Grant Grove to Kings Canyon National Park boundary near Cedar Grove.

The road pierces the glacially carved **Kings Canyon**, one of North America's deepest canyons when measured from Spanish Peak (elevation 10,051 feet), located just west of the national park in the Sequoia National Forest down to the confluence of the North and Middle forks of the Kings River. Its maximum depth of 8,200 feet makes the Grand Canyon's vertical drop of 5,300 feet look small in comparison.

For much of the 20th century, this canyon was under threat, first from the timber industry, which cut down hundreds of sequoias, then by developers who wanted to dam the Kings River to supple-

You'll get to see Kings Canyon Scenic Byway in both directions, since it's the only road to Cedar Grove.

ment the water supply to the city of Los Angeles, just as the damming of Yosemite's Hetch Hetchy Valley had attempted to slake San Francisco's thirst. The timber industry shut down when the national park expanded in 1940, but even before this logging of the sequoias was proving unprofitable. As these giants age, their wood becomes softer and more brittle, and they often splintered apart upon impact after being felled. As for the dam plan, after much political wrangling, it was dropped in 1965.

A few miles north of Grant Grove, beyond the McGee Overlook (which is a great place to pull over for vistas of the pastoral San Joaquin Valley), a signposted dirt road leads off to north through shadowy forest into **Converse Basin**, one of the strangest and perhaps saddest places in the national monument. Here a thriving meadow lies starkly littered with the stumps of giant sequoias cut down by 19th-century loggers, and the naked sight can be a shock to those who have come to the park seeking pristine wilderness. The only old-growth survivor still standing is the magnificent **Boole Tree**, named after the lumber mill owner who spared it. Cloaked by deep and buggy forest, you can discover the giant for yourself via a relatively short hiking trail.

Back on Highway 180 and east of Princess Campground, another detour, this time to the south, off Highway 180, leads to **Hume Lake**, found in one of the most handsome parts of the Giant Sequoia National Monument. Formed in 1908 by a multiple-arch dam, this lake once supplied water for the world's longest lumber flume that reached the mill town of Sanger, almost 75 miles away. Shrouded by evergreen trees, this sparklingly clear, chilly lake is fed by Tenmile Creek, which flows into the Kings River. The lake is popular with campers and swimmers (*see* Other Activities, *below*). Open year-round, a lakeshore **Christian family camp** (*64144 Hume Lake Rd; 559/335–2000; www.humelake.org*) offers limited accommodations, a take-out burger shop, a small market, and a gas station with 24-hour pumps.

Beyond Hume Lake, Highway 180 tackles more challenging switchbacks as it drops into the canyon proper. Although there are more than a few viewpoints to choose from, be sure to pull off at **Junction View**, where jagged peaks rub shoulders at the confluence of the Middle and South forks of the Kings River. The highway levels a few miles later as it passes the **Kings Canyon Lodge**, with its working vintage gas pumps, cabins, and a

★ Prime Pumps ★

The gas pumps at Kings Canyon Lodge have been operating since the 1920s. These cool relics are also the country's oldest gravity pumps still in use. Too bad the gas prices aren't vintage as well!

small shop selling snacks, then plunges downward again as it twists and turns by Yucca Point and Convict Flat, named for the prisoners who hazardously labored to build this road during the 1930s.

Finally, Highway 180 plunges downhill to meet the rushing Kings River. You'll come to several bridges before you hit Road's End, but only one before you've crossed over into the national park boundaries.

Just before (and beside) that first bridge, you'll be at **Boyden Cavern** (*Hwy. 180; 209/736–2708 for information; www.caverntours.com*). Although it's not as large as Crystal Cave (*see* the Sequoia National Park chapter), it's still impressive. Composed of marble and volcanic rock, it's filled with stalactites and stalagmites, which respectively grow from the ceiling and the floor of the cavern. Just as intriguing are ribbon draperies, nicknamed "cave bacon" for their rusty color and the translucency of the minerals, and also the spaghetti-like helictites that appear to defy gravity.

The gift shop sells tickets for the family-friendly, easily trekable tours of the cavern, which usually last 45 minutes and are available hourly throughout the day. It's only 53°F inside the cave, so bring a jacket and wear sturdy shoes to grip the paved lighted pathways.

After Boyden Cavern, Highway 180 gently curves alongside the Kings River for 5 more miles to the **Grizzly Falls picnic area**, another good place to stop and stretch your legs. It's only a short walk from the car to glimpse the 75-foot-high waterfall, which often mists over the footpath in late spring and early summer. Nobody knows for sure how the waterfall got this name, but it's a certainty that you won't see any grizzly bears here, because they were hunted to death in California by the early 1920s, although the park does have black bears aplenty.

CEDAR GROVE

The least-visited area of Kings Canyon, **Cedar Grove** (elevation 4,600 feet) is named after its scattered stands of fragrant incense-cedar trees, the aroma of which can only be detected if you stand close enough to practically embrace them. More than 30 miles and about an hour's

---

TOO BIG TO BE TRUE?

In Sequoia National Monument's Converse Basin you just might be stumped. That is to say, you'll see before you a field of stumps, with the largest of them named the Chicago Stump. The tree itself, a giant sequoia, was shipped east by train to Chicago and reassembled for the 1893 World's Columbian Exposition, where skeptical crowds derided it as the "California Hoax" because they found it hard to believe a real tree could grow this big.

Deep in Kings Canyon National Park, the Cedar Grove area is often only reachable from late spring through early fall.

drive from Grant Grove, this secluded area of the park feels wonderfully remote. The canyon walls here comfortably widen beside the Kings River, which in early spring blasts with such force that white-water sprays onto the highway.

You could spend many a long summer's afternoon swimming in the river, walking in the woods past waterfalls and around lush meadows, or tackling hiking trails that ascend to scenic overlooks of the canyon. However you choose to spend your time here, it's well worth the detour. Note, though, that from late fall through early spring, the public can't get to Cedar Grove at all (not even by hiking or snowshoeing).

As described in the section above, the only way to get into and out of Cedar Grove by car is via the Kings Canyon Scenic Byway (Highway 180). After crossing over the park boundary from the Sequoia National Forest on Highway 180, a series of bridges hovering beside summer-only beaches brings you into the main **Cedar Grove village** (elevation 4,635 feet) area. Here, you can step inside a rustic log cabin, home to the **Cedar Grove Visitor Center** (*Hwy. 180; 559/565–3793*). Browse its book collection, and examine animal pelts, sugar-pine cones, and Native American arrowheads. On the opposite side of the road is a motel-style lodge, which has a small market, a public shower house for beachgoers, and a take-out grill with picnic tables on a balcony overlooking the Kings River.

Beyond the village turn-off, Highway 180 pushes another 6 miles deeper into the canyon. About a mile east of the village, look for the small roadside pull-out for **Canyon Viewpoint**. The mighty work of glaciers that carved this canyon, now filled by grassy meadows with healthy groves of trees climbing the cliff sides, is evidenced by the distinct U-shaped sides of the valley. Unlike the sharper V-shaped valleys cut by rivers, the glacially carved canyons of the Sierra Nevada have a softer U-shape: a flat valley floor with gently curving talus slopes on both sides leading upward to sheer vertical walls of granite.

Another mile farther east along the highway, **Knapp's Cabin** is just a short scramble from the roadside pull-off. During the 1920s, wealthy Santa Barbara outdoorsman George Knapp used this scenically set cabin to stores supplies for deluxe fishing and camping expeditions with family and friends. The cabin is one of the only places in Cedar Grove to enjoy a long vista of the canyon floor spreading westward, best viewed around sunset.

Halfway between the village and Road's End, leave your car behind to take the short walk to **Roaring River Falls**. This pint-sized cata-

CEDAR GROVE VISITOR CENTER

TELEPHONE:
559/565–3793

ADDRESS:
Highway 180

ract plunges into a deep pool, which roils turbulently in early spring. Although it's tempting to jump into the pool below the waterfall later in summer when things calm down, that's still a downright dangerous idea, and rangers don't advise it.

From the waterfall pull-off, it's less than 2 miles east along Highway 180 to idyllic ★ZUMWALT MEADOW, named after early preservationist D.K. Zumwalt. In early spring, this lush meadow backed by high granite cliffs is often flooded, appearing more like a swamp. Later in spring and early summer, as the waters recede to small streams running off from beside the river, a profusion of wildflowers bloom, including purple lupines and pinkish pussy paws. For wildlife watchers, the chance to observe birds and black bears with their

> The chance to observe birds and black bears with their cubs lumbering alongside the river is a huge draw.

Black-chinned hummingbird and black bear. (right) Roaring River Falls, midway between Cedar Grove Village and Road's End.

cubs lumbering alongside the river is a huge draw. Walk out to the wooden suspension bridge for a grand view of the river, then continue east toward the boardwalk, which has the best views of the meadow, including of mule deer that frequently graze here.

After passing North Dome (elevation 8,717 feet), where adventurous rock climbers can occasionally be spotted, Highway 180 rolls to a halt at **Road's End**. Due to a land deal with the Zumwalt family, a proposed trans-Sierra highway was never built here. Road's End today is the gateway to the dramatic high country of the Sierra Nevada (*see* Backpacking and Climbing, *below*). For an idea of the sheer size of the peaks encountered up there, just crane your neck upward from the parking lot at the Grand Sentinel, which rises a dizzying 3,500 feet above the canyon floor on the south side of the river.

A short walk toward the river from the parking lot along a dirt footpath brings you to **Muir Rock**, a flat elevated slab that served as an informal pulpit for conservationist John Muir when he would escort groups of friends here on pleasure outings to talk about environmental ethics—only natural in such an inspiring setting.

From the **Road's End Wilderness Information Station** (*Hwy. 180; no phone*), in summer rangers lead guided walks to the site of an early-20th-century tent camp run by the intrepid Kanawyer family, who briefly tried their hands at copper mining here.

Kings River was possibly named by explorers in 1805 who reached the river on Feast of Epiphany, a day noting the three kings' arrival to the birthplace of Christ.

Those looking to see wildlife, such as black bears and birds, are drawn to Zumwalt Meadow.

A 1.5-mile trail winds through Zumwalt Meadow in Kings Canyon National Park's Cedar Grove.

An alternate return route to Cedar Grove from Road's End leaves Highway 180, just east of Roaring River Falls. The pavement quickly turns to gravel along the one-way, 3-mile-long River Road, also known as the "Motor Nature Trail," which heads westward past prime fishing holes to the horse corrals.

ALONG THE GENERALS HIGHWAY

Connecting the Grant Grove area of Kings Canyon National Park to Sequoia National Park, the high-elevation Generals Highway winds through a less heavily touristed section of the Giant Sequoia National Monument of the Sequoia National Forest. Escaping the crowds here is thankfully not much more difficult than turning off the highway onto a roughshod dirt forest-service road, all of which are normally open from late spring until early fall. The Generals Highway itself is subject to road closures after snowstorms (*see* Kings Canyon National Park in Winter, *below*).

About 3.5 miles south of the busy junction with Highway 180, the Generals Highway passes **Redwood Mountain Overlook**. Pull off the road and peer out at a sea of trees hiding one of the world's largest old-growth groves of giant sequoias, where hiking trails lead deeper into the forest (*see* Best Day Hikes, *below*). A bit farther south along the highway, past the Quail Flat junction (where you can pick up the scenic back road to Hume Lake), is the **Kings Canyon Overlook**, which honestly offers the best vistas of the canyon of any roadside viewpoint along the highway.

The next signposted turnoff is at **Big Meadows Road**, which leads off-road to trailheads for backcountry trips into the pretty Jennie Lakes Wilderness (*see* Backpacking and Climbing, *below*). If you're feeling adventurous, follow Forest Road (FR) 14S11 for about 15 miles (a high-clearance 4WD vehicle is recommended) northeast to Summit Meadow, where energetic hikers can tackle the 0.5-mile trail up **Lookout Peak**, which offers even more all-encompassing views of the entire canyon.

En route back to the highway along the same road, turn right at Horse Camp to uncover **Buck Rock Lookout** (elevation 8,500 feet), a 1920s-era fire observation station with unmatched views of the Great Western Divide of the Sierra Nevada. The lookout is staffed in summer and open to the public; access is via steep flights of 172 nerve-wracking metal stairs hair-raisingly suspended from the side of the rock.

Back on the Generals Highway, you will pass old-fashioned **Montecito Sequoia Lodge**, which stays open year-round for outdoor family fun, from swimming and crafts and outdoor activity camps in summer to sledding, ice skating, and skiing in winter, quickly followed by **Stony Creek Village**, a pit stop with a small motel, restaurant, market, and gas station that are usually open from May through October. The Generals Highway continues southward into Sequoia National Park.

Youngsters enjoy a ranger-led hike through the park.

⊶ BEST DAY HIKES

For day hikers, plentiful paths inside Kings Canyon National Park and the Sequoia National Forest next door range from easy nature walks to mountain goat–style climbs. You can get information about ranger-guided hikes and purchase hiking maps and interpretive trail guides at the visitor centers in Grant Grove and Cedar Grove.

GRANT GROVE

Many hiking trails in the Grant Grove village area interconnect, so you can walk almost all day without backtracking. Everyone walks the easy 0.35-mile paved interpretive **General Grant Tree Trail** to touch

A splashy finale
awaits hikers and
horseback riders on
the Mist Falls trail.

the giant sequoias and stand beneath their mighty branches. You can escape some of the crowds and still walk among the giant sequoias on the moderate 1.5-mile **North Grove Loop**, which heads downhill through the forest, then scrambles back uphill to the parking lot.

Hikers with more energy and time take the challenging 6-mile **Sunset Loop Trail** toward pretty Sequoia Lake, starting from the Grant Grove visitor center and passing springtime waterfalls. Back near the park entrance station at the Big Stump Picnic Area, it's a relaxing 0.5-mile stroll past the stumps of giant sequoias that were logged in the 19th century down to stream-fed **Hitchcock Meadow**, where wildflowers bloom.

North of Grant Grove, off the Kings Canyon Scenic Byway, you can visit the gigantic old-growth **Boole Tree** on a moderate, rolling 2-mile round-trip hike through shady Converse Basin. A shorter, easier nature trail that shows off some of the region's most distinctive flora and fauna begins at Princess Campground, near the level 3-mile recreational loop trail around **Hume Lake**.

CEDAR GROVE

The Cedar Grove area offers a variety of day hikes. Start with the easy 1.5-mile interpretive loop around **Zumwalt Meadow**, which is particularly lovely in late spring and early summer. Mule deer and black bears often forage here. Self-guiding interpretive trail brochures may be available at the trailhead for a small donation; if not, you can pick them up at the visitor center.

A short trail off the Kings Canyon Scenic Byway leads to Roaring River Falls in Cedar Grove.

The moderate 3-mile **River Trail** along the South Fork of the Kings River is a peaceful way to trek from Roaring River Falls to Road's End via Zumwalt Meadow, and even walking along it for a short way will take you through forests shared with black bears and along small granite staircases that climb a short way up the canyon's wall. Starting from Road's End, it's a moderately challenging 3.8 miles across the forested floor of the canyon and up a series of granite staircases, which grant panoramic views of the canyon and glimpses of the Sierra Nevada high country, to ★**MIST FALLS**, which pours thunderously in late spring and early summer. An alternate 4.3-mile return route from the falls crosses the Bailey Bridge to the shadier south side of the river. That bridge also lets you access the difficult **Bubbs Creek Trail**, where a steep set of switchbacks leads approximately 3.5 miles each way from Road's End to views of The Sphinx rock formation.

For seasoned hikers, the challenging 8-mile **Hotel Creek–Lewis Creek Loop**, which reaches head-spinning views of the Sierra Nevada peaks and wanders through meadows flush with birdlife, ascends laboriously from the trailhead near the pack station turnoff from the Cedar Grove village area. After the first 2 miles, be sure to take the side trail to windy **Cedar Grove Overlook** (elevation 6,000 feet) for the best scenic view of the canyon that you can access without an overnight backcountry permit.

Along the Generals Highway

Along the Generals Highway south of Grant Grove you can uncover less-trampled trailheads. Inside the national park boundaries, loop trails of varying lengths lead deep into peaceful and solitary **Redwood Mountain Grove**, where black bears can often be spotted ripping up giant sequoia tree logs to feed on the insects swarming around inside. Farther south along the Generals Highway are two trailheads offering 360 degree views of the Central Valley and the Sierra Nevada crest. The moderate 1-mile ascent of **Buena Vista Peak**, which begins just south of the unmissable Kings Canyon Scenic Overlook, is often crowded, but leads to a 360-degree view overlooking Redwood Canyon and gazing out past the Buck Rock fire lookout toward the crest of the Sierra Nevada divide.

More energetic trails of varying lengths lead into the **Jennie Lakes Wilderness**. Starting mostly off Big Meadows Road, they all climb challengingly through mixed forests of pine and fir trees and amble alongside alpine lakes. For mountaintop views and more solitude, it's a difficult 6.5-mile round trip up **Mitchell Peak**, where the sky-piercing mountains of the Monarch and Great Western Divides will spread out before you.

★ Black Bear Stats ★

Average weight for males: 300–600 pounds

Active times: dawn and dusk

On their menu: berries, nuts, grasses, insects

⊶ OTHER ACTIVITIES

While day hiking is the most popular activity for visitors to Kings Canyon National Park, backpacking trips into the Sierra high country are also favorite journeys for those with more time and energy. Swimming and fishing are great ways to spend a lazy summer afternoon, or horseback rides into the mountains can be arranged. During winter, snowshoeing and cross-country skiing engage park visitors.

BACKPACKING AND CLIMBING

Kings Canyon is a major gateway for backcountry treks into the Sierra Nevada high country, including in the northern section of Kings Canyon National Park that is usually visited only by hard-core backpackers on their way to or from Yosemite National Park. The busiest departure point for backpackers of all abilities, from beginner Boy Scouts to accomplished alpine mountaineers, is Road's End, where Highway 180 finishes in Cedar Grove.

For the ultimate taste of the backcountry, the amazing four-day **★RAE LAKES LOOP** climbs beyond Mist Falls to the north of Road's End and the stream-fed Paradise Valley past the skyscraping Castle Domes, then follows the epic **John Muir Trail (JMT)**, which travels from Yosemite all the way to Mt. Whitney, into the Rae Lakes basin, before toppling over Glen Pass (elevation 11,978 feet). The loop returns to Road's End via Junction Meadow, a favorite haunt of black bears and where you can detour to East Lake and Lake Reflection. Then it follows along the Bubbs Creek Trail, which passes Charlotte Dome, offering multi pitch hauls for rock climbers.

A tougher trail, **Copper Creek**, steeply ascends from Road's End into the rocky wonderland of Granite Basin, where experienced backpackers can venture to alpine lakes. More trails lead over the Sierra Nevada crest, including from the JMT crossing near Charlotte Lake to Onion Valley outside the town of Independence, off U.S. Highway 395, on the east side of the Sierra Nevada mountains. Off the Generals Highway, the Jennie Lakes Wilderness is also prime backpacking territory and offers endless overnight trip destinations; ask at the Grant Grove Visitor Center for recommendations.

PERMITS

All trails inside the national park are subject to a daily quota. Apply for wilderness permits ($15) in advance from the **Sequoia & Kings Canyon National Park Wilderness Office** (*47050 Generals Hwy., Three Rivers, CA 93271; 559/565–3766*). A limited number of walk-up permits are issued on a first-come, first-served basis on the afternoon prior to, or the same day as, your trip. They are issued at the Grant Grove Visitor Center and the Road's End Wilderness Information Station, but you can only get them at whichever of the two is closest to your trailhead. Both rent bear-proof canisters, which are required for backcountry travel.

Backcountry trips entirely within national forest boundaries do not require wilderness permits, although a free campfire/campstove

Exploring the park like Theodore Roosevelt and John Muir once did—on horseback—these riders head toward Mist Falls.

Kings Canyon National Park has one stable (in Grant Grove) and one pack station (in Cedar Grove). At either place, in season, you can get outfitted to see the park by horseback.

permit is required. Pick one up at the Grant Grove Visitor Center or at the Hume Lake Ranger District office (*35860 E. Kings Canyon Rd./ Hwy. 180, Dunlap; 559/338–2251; www.fs.fed.us/r5/sequoia*).

Horseback Riding

Both of the national park's horse-riding outfits are owned by the Loverin family, who are long time area residents. **Grant Grove Stables** (*off Hwy. 180; 559/335–9292 in summer, 559/337–2314 in the off-season*) offers short trail rides into the giant sequoia forest daily in summer. The **Cedar Grove Pack Station** (*off Hwy. 180; 559/565–3464 in summer, 559/337–2314 in the off-season*) arranges longer trips into the Sierra Nevada high country during summer, including multiday guided trail rides for fishing enthusiasts.

In the Sequoia National Forest, **Horse Corral Pack Station** (*Big Meadows Rd.; 559/565–3404 in summer, 559/564–6429 in the off-season*) has half- and full-day rides appropriate for beginners as well as all-inclusive multiday guided rides into the backcountry for experienced riders. The full-day excursion up Mitchell Peak is an unforgettable trip—just imagine riding a sure footed mule picking its way alongside granite precipices that you might hesitate to traverse alone on foot—that's well worth reserving in advance.

Swimming, Boating, Kayaking and White-water Rafting

The most popular place for swimming, and one of the safest places to swim in early summer, is at the easily accessible **Hume Lake** in the Sequoia National Forest, not far from Grant Grove and just off the

Kings Canyon Scenic Byway leading to Cedar Grove. Rowboats and kayaks are rented from a Christian family camp. Families flock to Hume Lake, not only for its friendly atmosphere but also because lakes are calmer places to swim than mountain streams or the Kings River, which rush with thunderous snowmelt in early spring. Even so, note that lifeguards are not always on duty here.

Although the **Kings River** can be chilly—water temperatures only climb to about 62°F in summer—that can feel refreshing during the dog days of August. And when water levels drop later in the summer, sandy and rocky beaches appear alongside the Kings River as it often runs closely alongside Highway 180 between Boyden Cavern and Road's End. Among the prettiest beaches on the river are the busy **Lewis Creek** and **Muir Rock**, both in the Cedar Grove area. For more privacy, the **Red Bridge** beach is a 10-minute walk from the Road's End parking lot up the trail signposted for Bubbs Creek and Zumwalt Meadow. Flotation devices (e.g., inner tubes) and watercraft are prohibited on the South Fork of the Kings River in the Cedar Grove area.

Ask rangers for advice about current conditions and the best swimming spots when you visit, **and always exercise caution when swimming—especially in the river, where swift currents naturally occur and are not always visible from the surface**—because drowning is the number-one cause of visitor fatalities in the park. Swimming can be extremely dangerous in early summer, when mountain snowmelt turns the river into a torrent of rapids. Almost none of these swimming holes in the park or national forest have any sort of lifeguard, so it's important to look out for not only yourself but everyone else if you choose to swim here. If you see a swimmer get into trouble, immediately call a ranger or dial 911 from any pay phone to contact park dispatch for help with swift-water rescue.

If you want to brave some of those violent rapids outside the park, don a life jacket and hop in a raft for a guided excursion. **Kings River Expeditions** (*211 N. Van Ness, Fresno; 559/233–4881, 800/846–3674*) offers one- and two-day white-water rafting trips on Class III rapids along the Middle Fork of the Kings River near Pine Flat reservoir, west of Kings Canyon National Park. **Whitewater Voyages** (*5255 San Pablo Dam Rd., El Sobrante; 510/222–5994, 800/400–7238*) also offers Kings River rafting trips outside Fresno. The white-water-rafting season usually runs from late spring into early summer. Although no previous experience is generally required, and the trips are open to both adults and children who meet the minimum-age requirements,

The South Fork of Kings River in the park's Cedar Grove area is a terrific place to drop a line for a relaxing morning of fishing.

they're not trips to be taken lightly. Come prepared for a fun workout in the hot summer sun; trips are usually offered only when water levels are high enough, generally from May through August.

FISHING

Although you're not going to catch anything big enough to boast about, the South Fork of the Kings River in the Cedar Grove area of the park offers wonderfully lazy and, more importantly, shady fishing holes, especially near Road's End and along the one-way River Road heading back west toward the main village area. It's easy to catch fish here, and the fishing holes are easy to find. Fishing is allowed in both the national park and the Sequoia National Forest, including at Hume Lake, which is stocked with trout periodically throughout the summer by the California Department of Fish and Game.

LICENSES AND RULES

Anglers aged 16 and older must carry a valid California fishing license, sold at Hume Lake and the Grant Grove village market. The fishing season for rainbow, brown, golden, and eastern brook trout is from late April through mid-November. The general limit is five trout per day, with a maximum of 10 fish in possession at any one time. Additional restrictions apply inside the national park boundaries; ask at visitor centers for current fishing regulations covering specific bait and hook types, daily limits, and catch-and-release requirements, which vary depending on your location and elevation inside the park.

KINGS CANYON NATIONAL PARK IN WINTER

When Kings Canyon National Park is blanketed by snow from November through April, it attracts experienced winter-sports enthusiasts as well as beginners. Winter is not a common season to visit the park, which makes it the least crowded time of year to experience the magic of the giant sequoia groves.

Wherever you go in the park once it's covered in snow, you'll hear the excited shouts of children fresh up from California's parched central valley, who are eager to get their first taste of the cool, white stuff. Sledding and snow-play are popular in Grant Grove, especially around the Big Stump and Columbine picnic areas. The Columbine area, near the General Grant Tree, is also where carolers sing a few Christmas favorites the second Sunday of December for the annual Trek to the Tree (*see* Festivals and Seasonal Events in the Practical Information chapter).

Though closed to vehicle traffic in the winter, Panoramic Point is among the ungroomed trails leading through the giant sequoia groves that are open to cross-country skis and snowshoes. You can rent cross-country skis and snowshoes at the Grant Grove Ski Center (*Hwy. 180; 559/335-5500 ext. 309*). If you want to trek through the snow with others, call the Grant Grove Visitor Center (*559/565-4307*) to reserve a spot on a ranger-guided snowshoe walk (all equipment is provided for a small do-

nation). This 1-mile, two-hour tour is usually scheduled on Saturdays and holidays.

Four more winter recreation areas are located on national forest land inside the Giant Sequoia National Monument: Cherry Gap, north of Grant Grove along Highway 180; and three areas off the Generals Highway near Quail Flat and Big Meadow. Farther south along the Generals Highway, the Montecito Sequoia Lodge (*63410 Generals Hwy.; 559/565-3388, 800/227-9900; www.mslodge.com*) grooms up to 50 kilometers of cross-country ski trails. The lodge particularly draws families thanks to its fun winter activities like downhill tubing with a handle tow, ice-skating on a lighted rink, snow biking, snowshoeing, and guided dogsled trips. Equipment rentals and lessons are available at the lodge's winter sports center.

Come winter, only a few roads remain open in Kings Canyon National Park and the Sequoia National Forest: Highway 180 to Grant Grove and Hume Lake, and the Generals Highway to Sequoia National Park. The latter especially is subject to weather delays and snowplow closures after heavy storms. Always carry tire chains, which may be required at any time from late fall through early spring. For road conditions, call 559/565-3341.

In winter, inner tubes get put to work on the slopes instead of the river.

Where to Stay
and Eat

Sunset over Tuolumne River.

Up high in the mountains, in the Vogelsang High Sierra Camp, you'll be surrounded by peaks and lakes.

☞ THE LOWDOWN ON LODGING

The camaderie of outdoor adventurers sparks over a campfire, shown here at Tuolumne Meadows Lodge.

After dark, when day-trippers have gone home and serenity settles over the national parks, the sights and sounds of the outdoors take on new wonder. Staying overnight inside the parks is a trip highlight for many. The choices vary, from sleeping alfresco, where you can watch the moonrise and stargaze into the wee hours, to hiding away inside a romantic, rustic pioneer-style cabin or a historic hotel room with nature stretched out before you courtesy of panoramic windows. Whichever option you go with, you'll wake up the next morning with no worries of dealing with traffic. You're already right in the park, primed to beat the crowds to the next trailhead or viewpoint.

Lodgings in and around the national parks have higher rates during the peak summer months of June, July, and August. Almost all accommodations drop their rates during the off-season (October through March in Yosemite, early September through late May in Sequoia and Kings Canyon). Sometimes the rates dip by more than 50 percent. If budget-saving is a priority, accommodations outside the park still put you near the action and can be less expensive—though you need to factor in the price of gas for commuting. To make sure you get a room or site in the park, or as close by as possible, **book your lodgings as** far in advance as you can, especially for stays in the Yosemite Valley or the Sierra Nevada high country.

National park lodge rooms, cabins, cottages, and canvas-tent villages are all entirely nonsmoking, as are the lodges' sociable public areas, including lobby bars and restaurants. **Air-conditioning is a rare commodity** at in-park accommodations, which are typically either fan-cooled or have windows to let in the breezes. This isn't always enough to make all travelers comfortable during the dog days of July and August.

If the following recommended lodgings are fully booked, you can try one of the many chain motels and hotels found in gateway towns just outside the parks. In California, these accommodations generally are also nonsmoking, and that applies whether you're staying at a hotel, bed-and-breakfast, or hostel. Lodgings outside the park usually offer more perks, such as telephones, satellite TV, and Wi-Fi access. These properties sometimes allow pets, which are usually not welcome at in-park accommodations, unless they're on a short leash and accompanied by their owner inside the national parks' campgrounds. Inquire of each property individually about whether there are any restrictions on children as guests. It's not necessarily true that children can stay for free in the same room as their parents. Policies vary by property.

All properties are open year-round unless stated otherwise. Also, in California, many B&Bs do not offer breakfast. However, any B&Bs included in this chapter do offer a full breakfast unless the review notes otherwise.

Credit cards are accepted at most accommodations inside the parks (except for campgrounds, as described in the next section) and at most motels, hotels, and lodges outside the parks (but often not at B&Bs). Ask when booking about any and all payment policies.

☞ THE LOWDOWN ON CAMPING

Campgrounds in the national parks book up almost as quickly as hotels and lodges, especially on summer weekends and holidays. **If you arrive in the parks without a reservation, time your arrival between 10 AM and noon,** the time period during which last night's campers are vacating their sites. To find which campgrounds have first-come, first-served sites, check the park newspaper (you'll be given a free copy at the entrance gate when you pay your admission

★ Shutterbug's Tip ★

If you're a keen photographer, there's extra incentive to stay inside the parks: catching the best light at dawn and sunset.

fee). You'll also see them listed in the chart later in this chapter.

Many campgrounds in the park accommodate both tents and RVs, although RV dump stations are rare and there are usually no electricity or garbage hook-ups for RVs at any public (e.g., national park or national forest) campgrounds. Limited pull-through sites are available, and restrictions on the length of RVs allowed vary from place to place within the parks. Private campgrounds located far outside the park boundaries may offer sites with full hookups and amenities including swimming pools and Internet access. Permits are required for backcountry camping.

You also can camp in national forests; the public campgrounds there are a good place to check for campsites when national park

*"More, please."
These young
campers enjoy
dinner alfresco.*

campgrounds are full. Information for national forest campgrounds near the parks is listed in the camping chart later in this chapter.

While camping in the Sierra Nevada, **proper storage of all food and scented items is essential**. Feeding any wildlife is prohibited by law. Habituation to human food causes black bears to become aggressive, and eventually they must be destroyed. Avoid bear break-ins by removing all food and scented items from your vehicle at night and placing them in the bear-proof lockers provided at national-park campgrounds and at many parking lots, or at least lock everything out of sight in the trunk.

Campfires are normally allowed in the parks, but only at designated picnic areas and developed campsites that have preexisting fire pits and grills. Occasionally during summer, when fire conditions in the parks are dangerously high and the forests are like dry tinder, additional restrictions may be imposed; ask at visitor centers. Depending on where your backpacking trip takes you, campfires may not be allowed in the wilderness areas you camp in; ask the wilderness ranger issuing your backcountry permit about current fire restrictions. Camping in national forest lands may require a special campfire permit, available at visitor centers. It's more convenient to carry a camp stove instead of relying on building campfires in the wilderness, which can be a risky proposition if you don't know how to do it correctly, keeping it as small as possible.

Credit cards are only accepted to guarantee campground reservations, not for on-the-spot payments. If you're grabbing a first-come, first-served site, be sure to pay for it within 30 minutes of arrival at the campground by depositing the nightly fee in an envelope provided at the campground entrance, where you'll also find a locked "iron ranger" to deposit the fee envelopes into. Change is normally not available, so **bring lots of $5 and $1 bills**—or consider any small overpayment for your campsite as a donation to the national parks, which can always use the extra funds.

⊕ THE LOWDOWN ON PLACES TO EAT

Dining in the restaurants in and around the parks may whip up nostalgia of eating in the dining lodge at summer camp or your college cafeteria. That is to say, eating in these national parks is usually more about convenience, not culinary fireworks. Food served by park concessionaire services at cafeterias, snack bars, and most lodge restaurants is predictably standard, both in quality and selection—quesadillas are about as exotic as menus get. But hey, after a day of hiking through giant sequoia groves or tackling granite domes, just about anything tastes good, right?

Culinary lovers, take note: a couple of exceptions to this dreary gastronomic outlook are found at some of the Yosemite lodges. These **select lodges, like The Ahwahnee, have restaurants that are consistent standouts,** not only for their seasonal menus and fine-dining atmosphere but also for their historic surroundings and gorgeous views.

Outside the national parks, the cuisine varies a lot; the only reliable rule of thumb is that the farther from the parks you go, the more affordable and tastier the food becomes.

Are you thinking about brown-bagging it? Compared to many of the parks' vistas and other spots capturing the surrounding beauty, designated picnic areas in Yosemite, Kings Canyon, and Sequoia can be unexciting. There's often not much to distinguish them and they're usually situated along busy park roads that endure heavy traffic noise, tucked into a shady spot without much of a view. Also, because so many visitors illegally feed the parks' wildlife, you may be hounded to death for food by noisy Steller's jays or encounter a curious black bear, patiently waiting for you to forgetfully turn your back on your picnic cooler for just a few seconds.

The best places to picnic in the parks are often at scenic vistas, such as Glacier Point in Yosemite, or hiking trailheads, for example the Mineral King Valley in Sequoia National Park or Roads End in Cedar Grove, deep inside Kings Canyon. The Yosemite Valley and Tuolumne Meadows areas are also memorable places for a picnic. Almost any place in the park is fair game, save one: picnicking inside a national-park campground that you aren't staying at is a no-no.

In addition to the restaurants recommended in this chapter, many casual places to eat, such as grills, delis, cafeterias, markets, and snack bars, are briefly mentioned in each of the individual national park chapters earlier in the book.

DINING
The following price categories apply for the average price of most main course dishes:

$ = under $10	$$ = $10–$20	$$$ = $20–$40	$$$$ = over $40

LODGING
The following price categories apply for the average price of a single night's peak-season rate for a standard double room:

$ = under $100	$$ = $100–$200	$$$ = $200–$400	$$$$ = over $400

Picnicking at Glacier Point in
Yosemite National Park.

⊙→ YOSEMITE NATIONAL PARK

Although places in the valley are far from quiet in summer, there's nothing like rolling out of bed to see the early-morning sun lighting up the steep granite walls rising all around you, or to hear the babbling Merced River running right by your campsite and watching the moon rise over Glacier Point.

If you'll be spending more than a day at Yosemite, then ideally, you'll want to stay right in the park. Park lodging is operated by Delaware North Companies (DNC) Parks & Resorts. If cost is your main concern, **gateway town accommodations are often a better value than in-park lodgings, but they're not nearly as convenient** and the headache of commuting to and from the park is usually not worth it for first-time visitors. In fact, if you stay in Yosemite Valley, you can opt not to drive at all once you're ensconced in your in-park accommodations. Just walk or take the shuttle from your nightly resting place.

There's no one particular gateway city for Yosemite that's preferred, just certain recommended properties in various towns; these places are reviewed below. Also, if you're willing to make the drive, the town of Mariposa, about an hour west of the park via Highway 140, has a pleasant collection of bed-and-breakfast inns. Since they're outside the region, they're not reviewed here, but you can learn about them at www.yosemitebnbs.com or 209/742–7666.

Whether you're staying in the park or just outside it, **it's essential for you to make reservations—and make them well in advance—** for any stays May through September and on weekends and holidays year-round. For reservations with DNC, which can be made up to a year or more in advance, call 801/559–4884 or reserve online at www.yosemitepark.com. Individual property contact information is also given with each review below.

HOTELS AND LODGES INSIDE YOSEMITE

★**THE AHWAHNEE.** In the grand tradition of the historic national park lodges, The Ahwahnee offers an unexpected dose of refinement in the midst of Yosemite Valley, starting from when you pull up to the valet parking stand to when you hear the tinkling of ivories issuing out of the hotel's grand dining room. As you amble through the hotel's impressive public areas and hallways, inspect the gorgeous architectural detail—from Native American–inspired art-deco mosaic floors and murals to California-style Arts and Crafts woodworking and stained

Following page: The Ahwahnee hotel is acclaimed for its architecture, which blends with nature, as seen by its floor-to-ceiling windows in its Great Lodge and Solarium Room. Its dining options include the Ahwahnee Dining Hall, where food is artfully presented.

glass. Converse in one of the fireside lounges or sip a cocktail as you view Half Dome from the back patio (watch out for falling acorns!). The swanky-meets-rustic theme continues into the 99 guest rooms inside the three-story hotel. Top-floor parlors and suites have floor-to-ceiling windows overlooking the valley. Much more plain are the 24 fan-cooled cottages tucked away from the hotel in shady groves of dogwoods and pines. Each cottage room comes with an outdoor patio, some with postcard views over the valley. Hotel guests can play on the tennis courts and swim year-round in The Ahwahnee's heated outdoor pool, which is slightly removed from the hubbub of the hotel lobby. *Ahwahnee Rd., Yosemite Village; 209/372–1407, reservations 801/559–4884; www.yosemitepark.com.* **$$$$**

Yosemite's Four Seasons. For location, variety, and size, these rental units close to Yosemite Valley are hard to beat. Sitting just outside the national park boundary, off Wawona Road and south of Glacier Point Road, the Yosemite West private housing development is an ideal base for exploring the park. More than 50 rental units are available. Types of rentals range from log cabins and chalets to apartments and condominiums. Generous floor plans can accommodate groups, sometimes up to eight people, making these rentals an excellent choice for families. Compared to other vacation rentals in or near the park, most of these units have more modern furnishings as well as more amenities, such as full kitchens, satellite TV, central air-conditioning, and heating. *7519 Henness Circle; 209/372–9000, 800/669–9300; www.yosemitelodging.com.* **$$$–$$$$**

Yosemite Lodge at the Falls. When Yosemite Valley's waterfalls peak in May, there is no place closer to the action than this lodge with standard, no-frills rooms. It's a short walk from here to the heart of Yosemite Village, too. Another perk is the lodge's tours and activities desk, which can arrange everything from bicycle rentals to guided horseback rides. Staying here also lets you beat the crowds that line up nightly outside the extraordinary Mountain Room restaurant (*see* Where to Eat in Yosemite National Park, *below*). Of the 249 rooms at this centrally located lodge there are three types: Basic, Lodge, and Family. A step up from the basic, motel-style rooms, the lodge rooms are more ample, and sometimes have French doors opening onto a small balcony with views of the falls. Family rooms, which are essentially large lodge rooms, are the best bet for groups traveling together, as they sleep six comfortably. There's no air-conditioning, but fans are provided and you can cool off in an outdoor swimming pool, which is open only in summer (exact dates vary year to year, depending on

There's nothing like rolling out of bed
to see the **early-morning sun**
    lighting up the steep granite walls
  rising all around you.

Perfecting a putt on the grounds of the Wawona Hotel.

weather conditions). *Northside Dr., Yosemite Village; 209/372–1274, reservations 801/559–4884; www.yosemitepark.com.* **$$**

Wawona Hotel. With its spacious and shady verandas, antique light fixtures, and old-style concrete swimming tank outside, the Wawona Hotel transports guests to another time—the Victorian era, to be precise. This National Historic Landmark near Yosemite's south entrance was built in 1879 using a wood-frame construction. It is the largest Victorian-era hotel inside a national park. Stop in the hotel's piano parlor to view the historical photographs of pioneers and early tourists in the park. (The parlor is also a good place to relax, thanks to its cozy overstuffed sofas and a fireplace that's toasty on chilly mornings and cool evenings). Given that the lodgings come with a heaping dose of yesteryear, don't expect anything too terribly fancy. About half of the 104 spartan guest rooms, both in the main hotel and in nearby cottages, have private baths; others share public bathhouses (bring a warm robe and shower sandals). There are no phones or TVs, the lack of which enhances the hotel's restful, unhurried atmosphere (which is possibly disturbed only by the thin walls between rooms). They may be furnished too elementally for some, but others appreciate them precisely for their back-to-basics, time-warped appeal. *Forest Dr., off Wawona Rd.; 209/375–6556, reservations 801/559–4884; www.yosemite park.com.* **$$**

Generations of families have slept in these canvas tents and rustic wooden cabins near the Happy Isles, where a bubbling brook darts around granite rocks that make perfect sunbathing perches.

Curry Village & Housekeeping Camp. Opened in 1899, this historic tourist camp and the housekeeping camp just down the road, beside the river, combine to form a beloved Yosemite Valley institution. Some people return here every summer, and even newcomers will feel swept up in the infectiously rambunctious atmosphere, where adults can act like kids at summer camp again, playing flashlight games late into the night and parking bicycles right outside their own front door. Generations of families have slept in these canvas tents and rustic wooden cabins near the Happy Isles, where a bubbling brook darts around granite rocks that make perfect sunbathing perches. Curry Village is tent camping without having to pitch your own tent and with a real bed to sleep in. You can choose unheated or

Studio cabins come with solid walls, a step up from the canvas cabins.

heated canvas tents with a shared bathhouse nearby, or studio cabins with solid walls (and therefore more privacy) and shared or private baths. Larger, en-suite cabins also have electrical wall heaters and outlets. None of the cabins have campfire or kitchen facilities. With room for more than 1,000 guests, Curry Village can get very crowded, especially on summer weekends. The nearby Housekeeping Camp rents more basic, semi-enclosed sleeping platforms—essentially wooden-floor tents without four walls—that can accommodate up to six people apiece. Units come with beds and picnic tables, as well as Merced River beach access, making getting out of bed, stretching and then dashing out for a morning swim about a 30-second endeavor, perfect for those always-impatient kids. Curry Village is often closed midweek during winter; the Housekeeping Camp is only open from mid-May until mid-October. *Southside Dr., Curry Village; 209/372-8333, reservations 801/559–4884; www.yosemitepark.com. $–$$*

Tuolumne Meadows Lodge & White Wolf Lodge. During the brief summer of the Sierra Nevada high country, these seasonal canvas tents are your only overnight option in Tuolumne Meadows other than pitching your own tent. Less rambunctious than Curry Village in Yosemite Valley, the Tuolumne Meadows Lodge and the White Wolf Lodge are both pleasant places to bed down and to do some stargazing after the day-trippers leave. The wood-framed and -floored canvas platform tents have beds but are not equipped with electricity. Instead, you must rely on candles and an old-fashioned wood-burning stove (for heat only; no cooking), with shared bathhouses. Tuolumne Meadows has 69 of these cabin-like tents that come with bedding for up to four. In addition to 24 soft-sided cabins, White Wolf Lodge also rents four simple wooden cabins with a few more creature comforts, including limited electricity and heat. All of these cabins are usually open from June or July through mid-September, weather permitting. Rustic breakfasts and dinners (the latter by advance reservation only) are served in communal outdoor tents at both lodges. Guests can also order boxed lunches to take on the trail with them from the lodges the night before. *Tioga Road; reservations 801/559–4884; www.yosemite park.com.* $

Lodging Outside Yosemite

Château du Sureau. Incredible personalized attention from the staff sets this polished property apart from other lodging options near Yosemite. A 10-room inn and a two-bedroom villa decorated in exquisite Provençal style, with canopied bedchambers, wall tapestries, and sun-soaked-color butter-yellow and sky-blue schemes, as well as authentic 19th-century artwork comprise this small, self-styled estate. Canopied beds, antique soaking tubs, and gas fireplaces are among the amenities in many of the château's 10 rooms. Guests have access to an intimate spa and an outdoor swimming pool. Little touches like tea and snacks upon arrival add to the romantic nature of the place, with its cozy nooks and very private bedroom retreats. The restaurant's a

James Overbaugh is the head chef at Château du Sureau's posh restaurant, Erna's Elderberry House.

THE LURE OF THE LODGES

"If you build it, they will come" could apply easily to the railroad companies who laid track in the early 1900s to draw wealthy Easterners westward. These shrewd rail companies took the idea an inspired step further when many of them thought to also build luxury hotels at the end of the line to accommodate the weary riders. When these top-notch properties were set in the beautiful natural surroundings of a national park, travelers had the best of both worlds.

The railroads were not the only ones who profited. NPS director Stephen Mather believed that attracting wealthy, influential visitors to the national parks would lend support and congressional funding to the national parks system. He wanted Yosemite to have one of these grand lodges that incorporated the environment, and so he persuaded the concessionaire Yosemite Park & Curry Company to undertake the building of the park's stunning masterpiece, The Ahwahnee hotel.

Architect Gilbert Stanley Underwood won the commission for the project in 1925. He had previously designed lodges at the Grand Canyon and in Bryce and Zion national parks. For Yosemite, Underwood was asked to build a first-class hotel that was fireproof (a necessity in a forested area), that blended in with the granite cliff landscape of the site, and that showcased the park's iconic Half Dome.

Constructing the hotel was a tough undertaking. The roads to and from the remote site were challenging, making the trucking of materials difficult. In order to make the structure fire-resistant, Underwood used hidden steel framing and concrete. To make it seem more natural, concrete was made to resemble redwood by being poured into timber shells, giving it a grained texture, and then getting a dye job.

The valley's indigenous heritage is captured in some of the hotel's architectural detail: the motifs and patterns found in the basketry of the local Indian tribes were used on ceiling beams, stained-glass windows, and concrete floors. Other elements, like mosaics, reflect the 1920s art-deco style.

In its early days, the elegant Ahwahnee saw many a wealthy patron, as well as the U.S. Navy, which seized the hotel in the early 1940s for a hospital for wounded soldiers. Four decades later, Queen Elizabeth II rested her royal head here. Other noteworthy visitors have included the Shah of Iran, Walt Disney, Will Rogers, Lucille Ball, and Presidents Dwight D. Eisenhower, Herbert Hoover, John F. Kennedy, and Ronald Reagan. Luxury cars and even limousines are still frequently seen today in front of the National Historic Landmark. They built it, and they still come.

–Debbie Harmsen and Marge Peterson

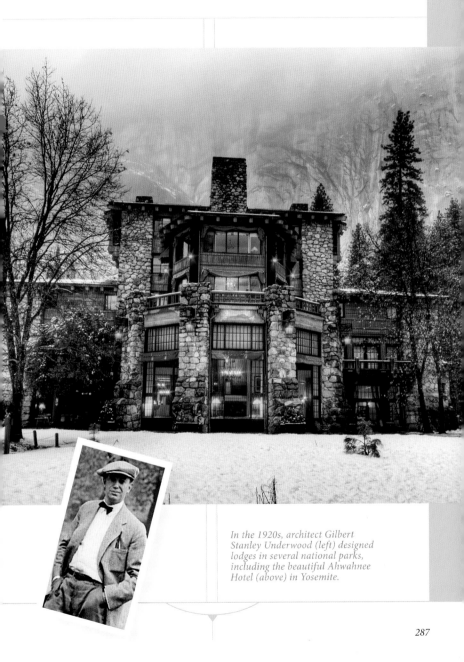

In the 1920s, architect Gilbert Stanley Underwood (left) designed lodges in several national parks, including the beautiful Ahwahnee Hotel (above) in Yosemite.

standout as well (*see* Erna's Elderberry House, *below*). The inn is farther from the park than many other places to stay—it's about 15 miles south of Yosemite's south entrance station, off Highway 41—but if a luxurious hideaway is what you're after, it's worth the drive. Just don't expect to drive up to the grand porte cochere out front and then step into the gracious lobby in your muddy hiking boots. *48688 Victoria Lane, Oakhurst; 559/683–6860; www.chateaudusureau.com.* **$$$–$$$$**

Tenaya Lodge at Yosemite. With its perfect-for-cold-weather perks, this might be the place you want to stay when the snow is falling. A short drive south of the park on Highway 41, the upscale Tenaya Lodge offers more hotel-style amenities than most in-park lodgings, including indoor and outdoor heated swimming pools, an outdoor ice-skating rink (seasonal), a hot tub, a fitness center, and a for-guests-only spa. The 244 hotel rooms have fairly bland earth-toned decor, but they have down bedding and personal climate controls, helping visitors stay nice and toasty come wintertime. Pet friendly and ADA-accessible accommodations are available. *1122 Hwy. 41, Fish Camp; 559/683–6555, reservations 888/514–2167; www tenayalodge.com.* **$$$**

Big Creek Inn Bed & Breakfast. Popping out along the roadside like a fairy-tale cabin in the woods, this romantic bed-and-breakfast inn south of the park, off Highway 41, offers an array of perks that put it ahead of the competition. Private balconies with creek and meadow views? Check. An outdoor hot tub and a sundeck? Check, check. Guest rooms equipped with satellite TV, DVD player, and Wi-Fi access? Check, check, check. The inn has three rooms; if you're visiting on a snowy winter's night, pick the one with a gas fireplace. An expanded Continental breakfast, sometimes with warm pastries or hot country-style oatmeal, is served in the wooden-floored dining room. *1221 Hwy. 41, Fish Camp; 559/641–2828; www.bigcreekinn. com.* **$$–$$$**

Evergreen Lodge. A short drive from the Big Oak Flat Entrance Station and Hetch Hetchy, this classic 1920s mountain resort amid tall pine trees provides a rejuvenating stay for romantic couples or active families. It's the professionalism of the staff that makes staying in one of the many individualized units here a stress-free experience. Beautifully well-kept duplex cabins and private stand-alone cottages come with private baths and decks, heating and fan cooling, and even stereos with satellite radio. The woodsy decor makes it look a lot like a ski resort, with plush beds and kitchenettes in some units. Relax in the family-friendly recreation hall, equipped with board games, tourist information, and free Wi-Fi access. Mountain bikes and snowshoes can be rented. For a modest day-use fee, guests also have access to neighboring Camp Mather, which has a natural lake (can be used for swimming), tennis courts, and an outdoor swimming pool. *33160 Evergreen Rd., Groveland; 209/379–2606, 800/935–6343; www.ever-greenlodge.com.* **$$–$$$**

Hotel Charlotte. Run by a convivial couple, this hotel listed on the National Register of Historic Places can give you a taste of pioneer life during the California Gold Rush era. Though you're not going to find anything as eccentric as gold-pan-shaped sinks, it's the helter-skelter architecture of the place, with its snug rooms and creaky narrow hallways, along with historic photographs hanging in the public spaces, that let you imagine the speculative scene in the mid–19th century. All guests rooms have air-conditioning, satellite TV, and private bathrooms (some with antique claw-foot tubs). A better value for families are the adjoining rooms that share a bathroom and can sleep four people. Most of the 10 rooms come with shabby-chic country furnishings and are on the upper story of this busy hotel, which has a popular café downstairs. Ask about private vacation-rental condos and houses, too. *18736 Main St. (Hwy. 120), Groveland; 209/962–6455; www.hotel charlotte.com.* **$$**

Sierra Sky Ranch. Off Highway 41 just 10 miles south of the park, this 19th-century cattle ranch located near a hidden grove of giant sequoia trees provides a restful, rustic retreat. Expect to find tidy rooms with simple country-style decor, like log-framed beds and checkered comforters and French doors that open out onto airy porches for unwinding on a summer's evening. Stay connected to the modern world with cable TV and free Wi-Fi access. A heated swimming pool and a steak house (*see* The Branding Iron Steakhouse & Saloon, *below*) are on-site. Individual heating and air-conditioning in the 24 rooms make the ranch a four-season getaway, while the stone fireplace in the honeymoon suite is a wintertime bonus. Well-behaved dogs are welcome for a surcharge. *50552 Road 632, Oakhurst; 559/683–8040; www.sierraskyranch.com.* **$$**

Yosemite Rose Bed & Breakfast. Twenty miles west of the park's Big Oak Flat Entrance Station via Highway 120, this modern inn on a working horse and cattle ranch has a charming hostess—ask her in advance about opportunities for formal horseback riding lessons and overnight pack trips, as well as the chance to watch the ranch's workhorses being shoed. Each of the seven rooms is done up in elegant style, with solid wood furnishings, gauzy draperies, and boudoir lamps. Those on upper floors may have views of oak trees and meadows. A fetching private one-bedroom cottage with a stone chimney, whitewashed exterior walls, and exposed cedar beams inside has a full kitchen and an extra bedroom upstairs with its own private bath—ideal if you're bringing along the kids. Relax on the sunny verandahs of the main house, a replica of a 19th-century Italianate revival building from the San Francisco Bay Area, or inside the library and billiards room, which has free Wi-Fi access. A hearty country breakfast is included in the room rates for those in the main inn, but not for cottage guests. A two-night minimum may apply on summer weekends; call to inquire. *22830 Ferretti Rd., Groveland; 866/962–6548; www.yosemiterose.com.* **$$**

Yosemite Bug Rustic Mountain Resort. An alternative-minded, overgrown youth hostel in the woods with an ever-increasing galaxy of accommodation options, the sociable "Bug" is a Yosemite institution. With raucous dormitory lodge rooms, peaceful, but basic wood-framed tent cabins with beds, and more solid private rooms in wooden duplexes with private or shared baths, the rustic Bug's got something for everyone traveling on a budget. All guests have access to a common kitchen for cooking meals, where you can share any tasty, leftover backpacking supplies with other travelers, who are often happy to pitch in and make budget feasts together. There's also a simple omnivorous café on site, as well as a health spa with herbal soaking tubs and yoga classes. Thanks to its wandering hiking trails and seasonal summer swimming holes, the Bug's thickly forested property feels almost like being in Yosemite, even though it's a 30-minute drive west of the park along Highway 140. The YARTS bus (*see* the Getting Around section of the Practical Information chapter) stops here, too. *6979 Hwy. 140, Midpines; 209/966–6666, 866/826–7108; www.yosemitebug.com.* **$–$$**

Campgrounds Around Yosemite

See the price chart on p. 275. Also see the campground chart on pp.305-307

Yosemite National Park offers over a dozen campgrounds totaling more than 1,400 campsites (some of which are seasonal), with more camping available in national forest lands surrounding the park (again, with many being seasonal, varying year to year). All campgrounds regularly fill by noon from April through September, especially on weekends and holidays. Only about half of National Park Service (NPS) campgrounds accept reservations—however, reservations are required year-round for most Yosemite Valley campgrounds, and from spring through fall for campsites in Wawona, Crane Flat, Hodgdon Meadow, and certain sections of Tuolumne Meadows. You can reserve NPS and USDA Forest Service campsites five months or more in advance online at www. recreation.gov or by calling 877/444–6777. All reservable sites between May and September typically sell out on the first day they become available. For an overview, *see* the chart at the end of this chapter.

If you arrive in the park without reservations, stop by the year-round **Yosemite Valley Campground Office** (*Southside Dr., near Curry Village; 209/372–8502*) to inquire about last-minute availability. Other seasonal campground offices are found at Wawona and Big Oak Flat (open late spring through early fall) and Tuolumne Meadows (open in summer only). Your best chances of finding an available first-come, first-served campsite are in more remote areas of the parks (for example, off Tioga Road). Pay showers are available to campers at Curry Village and the Housekeeping Camp in Yosemite Valley and also at Tuolumne Meadows Lodge on summer afternoons.

If you'd rather not pitch your own tent or carry a camp stove and food into the wilderness, the **High Sierra Camps** (*www.yosemitepark. com*) are a popular circuit of backcountry canvas-tent dormitories in the beautiful Sierra Nevada high country off Tioga Road. Each camp—Merced Lake, Vogelsang, Glen Aulin, May Lake, and Sunrise Camp—is located within a day's hike of another. Hot showers and restrooms are available, and all meals are catered. All you need to carry on the trail are your own sheets and towels. These camps are usually open from mid-June until mid-September, weather permitting. For reservations, a special lottery is held in early December, with the deadline for application requests in late November; to check last-minute availability, call 801/559–4909 anytime after April 1. The rates are about $150 for one night's accommodation, which includes dinner, breakfast, and a sack lunch.

At Yosemite Valley campgrounds, such as Lower Pines, North Pines, and Upper Pines, don't expect much privacy; the sites are small and crowded close together. Nevertheless these campgrounds are always the most sought-after, mostly for their prime positions near the park's main attractions, as well as for their proximity to perks like hot showers at Curry Village and nearby grocery and laundry facilities.

Tuolumne Meadows is another desirable campground, with its easy access to its namesake area; it offers many of the same amenities as Yosemite Valley. For more peace and (possibly) quiet—and stunning stargazing opportunities—pick lesser-known, more remote campgrounds off Tioga Road or Glacier Point Road. Or choose to camp outside the park entirely in less-developed national forest campgrounds that surround Yosemite.

WHERE TO EAT IN YOSEMITE NATIONAL PARK

See the price chart on p. 275.

In addition to the places recommended here, the Yosemite Valley has snack bars, a grocery market, a food court, delis, and grills for fast, easy meals. Along Tioga Road, which is open in summer, a small market at Tuolumne Meadows supplies picnickers and campers, while the Tuolumne Meadows Lodge serves family-style breakfasts and dinners and the White Wolf Lodge offers hearty lunches. There are small convenience stores in Wawona and Crane Flat for buying snacks and drinks. All of these are open year-round unless otherwise noted.

The Ahwahnee Dining Room. With its beautifully arranged tables, formally outfitted wait staff, and ambient piano music, this restaurant set in Yosemite Valley's landmark Ahwahnee hotel presents itself as a sumptuous affair. But looks can be deceiving. The menu does not consistently deliver the artfully balanced seasonal tastes it promises, with such dinner mains as braised rabbit with wild-mushroom polenta and grass-fed prime rib with winter spinach and Yorkshire pudding not living up to the expectations that the price point sets. For some people, the high-beamed ceilings and rustic beauty of the dining room makes up for the kitchen's shortcomings. Rather than dinner or the overly hyped (but unfortunately quite disappointing) Sunday brunch, come for lunch instead and order a market-fresh salad or club sandwich on herbed foccacia bread. Truly outstanding are special holiday dinners and other seasonal food-and-wine celebrations (*see* Festivals and Seasonal Events in the Practical Information chapter). The wine list offers standard Napa vintages by the glass and more unusual bottled selections from lesser-known California wine countries such as the Alexander Valley and Amador County. At dinner, a collared shirt and slacks are preferred for men, and the dress code for women is upscale (no hiking boots, outdoor wear, jeans, etc.). Make dinner reservations as far in advance as possible—to be on the safe side, aim for at least a month ahead of time during summer; during less busy times of year, a couple of weeks prior is probably sufficient. *Ahwahnee Rd., Yosemite Village; 209/372–1489.* $$$–$$$$

★MOUNTAIN ROOM RESTAURANT. If you're commemorating a wedding anniversary or high-fiving a successful summit of Half Dome, this is the place where you can celebrate in style. From the

While away the time with a classy cocktail in the Mountain Room's rough-hewn bar, where rock climbers down microbrews as they brag about the day's accomplishments.

welcoming smile of the hostess at the front desk to the attentiveness of your server, this classic national-park lodge restaurant always feels like a special occasion. Open only for dinner, the Mountain Room serves dishes of hearty Western fare like charbroiled steaks, baked mountain trout, and seasonal stews that are expertly executed, with visual appeal as well as hitting the mark gastronomically. The surprising wine list, including some choice California vintages, is more than respectable, and then there are the worth-every-calorie dessert options—cherry cobbler, apple pie, and flourless almond pound cake. Reservations are only accepted for large groups; otherwise, seating is first-come, first-served. This policy usually means there's a wait—a good 15 to 30 minutes is average—but you can pleasantly while away the time with a classy cocktail in the rough-hewn bar, where rock climbers down microbrews as they brag about the day's accomplishments. Request a window table, from which you may catch sight of the famous Yosemite Falls. The view is a powerful enhancement to what is already the finest cooking you'll find in Yosemite Valley, if not the entire park. *Yosemite Lodge at the Falls, Northside Dr., Yosemite Village; 209/372-1274.* **$$–$$$**

Wawona Dining Room. The Victorian-era Wawona Hotel is a civilized retreat from the hurly-burly of Yosemite Valley. Its genteel dining room is cheered by picture windows and unique hand-painted lights displaying images of giant sequoia trees. It's deservedly popular for its hearty, pioneer-style breakfasts of bacon, eggs, country sausage, buttermilk waffles, cowboy flapjacks, and the like. Also drawing in crowds are the expansive Sunday brunch buffets and Western barbecue cookouts on select Saturday summer evenings. Expect standard American fare at lunch, but more creative, often seasonally inspired cuisine for dinner, such as espresso-grilled flatiron steaks and West Indies spice-rubbed chicken with banana chutney and butternut squash. Martinis are the specialty of the hotel bar. Reservations are advised for dinner. *Forest Dr., off Wawona Rd.; 209/375-1425.* **$$–$$$**

Curry Village. At this historic tents-and-cabins camp in Yosemite Valley, families and outdoor athletes can fuel up for a full day's worth of adventures. If you're in a hurry in the morning, grab an icing-rich cinnamon roll or oversized lemon-poppyseed muffin from the Coffee Corner. Later in the day, fork into a fresh-baked pizza and a salad on the tree-shaded deck, which insulates you from the constant commotion of visitors touring the valley just outside the

★ Veg Alert! ★

Cafe at the Bug in Midpines is particularly vegetarian- and vegan-friendly, with several veg choices on the menu for each meal, from frittatas to lasagna, plus some tofu-substitution options.

fence; order a hot sandwich or burger combo at the bar; or pick up a gooey, not-exactly-good-for-you but oh-so-satisfying and overstuffed burrito and other Mexican fare from the take-out taqueria. The dining pavilion lays out all-you-can-eat breakfast and dinner buffets, which tend to be disappointingly bland, but filling. Most eating options at Curry Village are only open during the summer season. *Southside Dr., Curry Village; 209/372–8333.* **$–$$**

Dining Outside Yosemite
See the price chart on p. 275.

Erna's Elderberry House Restaurant. This sumptuous restaurant at the Château du Sureau bed-and-breakfast off Highway 41 south of the park dramatically effects French provincial ambience with its candelabras and fine-art oil paintings. Even more unforgettable is the polished service from attentive wait staff. The chef's prix-fixe dinner menu ($95) changes nightly but usually includes bistro classics like Belgian endive and tomato terrine, Jerusalem artichoke soup, herb-crusted rack of lamb, and dark-chocolate soufflé for dessert. Vegetarians are happily accommodated upon request. Stars of the wine cellar include hard-to-find California and Austrian vintages. *48688 Victoria Lane, Oakhurst; 559/683–6800.* **$$$$**

The Branding Iron Steakhouse & Saloon. Just off Highway 41, not far from the park's south entrance, this ranch cookhouse is a social place for old-fashioned steak dinners, plus ginormous burgers and hog-wild desserts, such as deep-fried cheesecake and prize-winning brownies. On Thursday nights, swing by for barbecue chicken and ribs, or wait until Friday to try the prime rib and home-cooked chili. There is a small menu with kids' fare, too. The restaurant is only open for dinner, from Wednesday to Saturday during peak summer months and shorter hours in winter. *Sierra Sky Ranch, 50552 Road 632, Oakhurst; 559/658–2644.* **$$–$$$**

Evergreen Lodge Restaurant. West of the park's Big Oak Flat Entrance Station, off Highway 120 near Hetch Hetchy, this old-fashioned mountain resort has a cozy restaurant that offers much more than the usual roadside fare. Breakfast includes delicately fried French toast with berry compote and New York strip steak with eggs. If you're in a hurry, order up coffee, pastries, or a deli lunch to go from the general store. Once the sun sets, the 1920s-era main lodge and tavern beckon with filling entreés such as bison and elk tenderloin, along with microbrews and tasty bar snacks like molasses barbecue chicken wings and Angus burgers. It's the resort's restful ambience, so far from the highway traffic and the nonstop crowding of Yosemite Valley, plus a stellar Californian wine list, that put it over the top. *33160 Evergreen Rd., Groveland; 209/376–2606.* **$$–$$$**

Whoa Nellie Deli. A more unlikely roadside spot there never was: this regular ol' gas station on the east side of the Sierra Nevada mountains has a chef-run deli serving sophisticated meals. It's only open during summer, usually from May through September, but it's worth the drive for innovative soups, barbecue chicken, and grilled portabello mushroom sandwiches, as well as specialties like buffalo meat loaf, lobster taquitos, and house-made cheesecakes. Some of the outdoor patio tables have distant views of Mono Lake. *Tioga Gas and Gift Mart, 22 Vista Point Rd., Lee Vining; 760/647–1088.* **$–$$**

Cafe at the Bug. Although it's a 25-mile drive west of the park along Highway 140, this alternative-minded hostel and cabins complex has a crunchy, hippie-flavored cafe that's one of the best bargains in the Yosemite region. Set on thickly wooded grounds, the communal wooden dining room dishes up hearty hikers' dinners such as honey-mustard roasted salmon or grilled pork chops with mashed potatoes. The choices for vegans and vegetarians are plentiful, too. Drop by in the morning for muesli, omelettes, and pancakes, and to pick up sack lunches before hitting the trail later. *Yosemite Bug Rustic Mountain Retreat, 6979 Hwy. 140, Midpines; 209/966–6666.* **$–$$**

⊕ SEQUOIA AND KINGS CANYON NATIONAL PARKS

Except for Wuksachi Lodge in Sequoia, in-park accommodations are no-frills. You'll nonetheless pay a premium to stay in the parks, but it is well worth it to spare yourself the long, often winding drive from even the closest towns. Besides, the chance to sleep near the giant forests of sequoia trees or in the belly of the Kings Canyon beside a roaring river is exactly what you've come to the parks for.

This section covers lodgings inside Sequoia and Kings Canyon national parks, in the Giant Sequoia National Monument of the Sequoia National Forest, and in gateway towns outside the parks. Reservations are essential from Memorial Day through Labor Day. Because these parks are so close together, you could overnight in one park and day-trip to the other. This won't work if you base yourself in a more remote area, however, such as Mineral King or Cedar Grove.

LODGING IN SEQUOIA AND KINGS CANYON

See the price chart on p. 275.

These places are not renowned for their comfort, but they're the only places in the park and while not very memorable, they are convenient for putting you close to all of the action.

Wuksachi Lodge. The most deluxe hotel in Sequoia National Park, the Wuksachi Lodge offers a mixed bag to guests. North of Lodgepole village and the Giant Forest, the tall-ceilinged lobby of this wood-and-stone hotel is as impressive as its common areas, where you can sink into a plush chair by the fireplace and sip an Irish coffee from the bar. The lodge's 102 cookie-cutter hotel rooms with private baths, telephones, and TVs are actually located in three-story satellite buildings more reminiscent of a two-star roadside motel. They're quite a long walk from the front desk, snack and gift shop, and restaurant, too. Discounts for AAA members make it a better deal. Wi-Fi access is available only in the hotel lobby of the main building. For dining with views, the lodge dining room (*see* Where to Eat in Sequoia and Kings Canyon National Parks, *below*) serves breakfast, lunch, and dinner.

The rustic yet elegant lobby and common areas of the Wuksachi Lodge make a good first impression on overnight visitors.

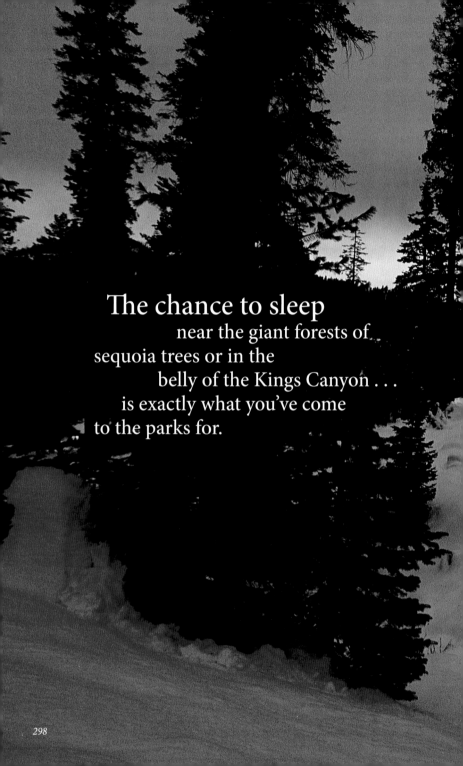

The chance to sleep
near the giant forests of
sequoia trees or in the
belly of the Kings Canyon . . .
is exactly what you've come
to the parks for.

64740 Wuksachi Way, off Generals Hwy.; 801/559–4930, 866/807–3598; www.visitsequoia.com. **$$$**

Cedar Grove Lodge. Near where Highway 180 ends in the Kings Canyon beside the Kings River, this basic two-story lodge has 18 bare-bones motel-style rooms with queen beds and telephones, plus three more lodge rooms with patios overlooking the river. While you won't want to spend much time in these thin-walled, somewhat cramped accommodations, they are your only choice in this beautifully remote area of Kings Canyon National Park. The lodge is usually open from late May through early October. *Hwy. 180, Cedar Grove; 559/565–0100, 866/522–6966; www.sequoia-kingscanyon.com.* **$$**

John Muir Lodge & Grant Grove Cabins. Named after the famous Sierra Nevada conservationist, this rustic place offers the only accommodations in busy Grant Grove village. The lodge has just a few dozen standard rooms with shabby-chic country furnishings, including patchwork quilts on the beds but no TVs or telephones. You can also stay in one of the 41 thin-walled cabins (choose either hard-sided or soft-sided) at the back of the property and be surrounded by trees. These basic wooden and canvas-tent cabins in Grant Grove share public bathhouses; the wooden cabins have heating and electricity, but the tent ones do not. The most popular cabins are the nine duplex wooden cabins with private baths and the "Bath Cabin 9" (also called the Honeymoon Cabin), all of which have electricity, heating, carpeting, and Mission-style furnishings. Rooms in the lodge are available year-round, but the cabins are open only in summer. *Hwy. 180, Grant Grove; 559/335–5500, 866/522–6966; www.sequoia-kings canyon.com.* **$–$$**

LODGING OUTSIDE THE PARKS

See the price chart on p. 275.

Montecito Sequoia Lodge. Off a tree-lined side road in the Sequoia National Forest between Sequoia and Kings Canyon national parks, this family-oriented summer camp offers lakeside lodgings year-round. Established in 1946, the resort today operates on the old-fashioned "all inclusive" plan, where accommodation rates include three meals a day (but not always family-camp activities, which can be separate and optional). Choose from 38 upscale motel-style rooms (some with views) scattered in lodges around the property, or one of the 16 more rustic cabins with wood-burning stoves, electrical heating, and shared bathhouses with showers—and mountain views. During the summer, the resort puts on different themed family camps each week, which makes the atmosphere somewhat rambunctious. Family camp activities include open-mike and variety-show nights, special outdoors activities and arts-and-crafts workshops for kids, and theme parties. Most people who stay here in summer come for the family camps, so you may feel like an outsider if you stay there independently during that time. In winter, the resort is the best place near either park for snow sports. Enjoy family-style buffet dinners, with homemade ice cream in the resort's dining room (*see* Where to Eat Outside Sequoia and Kings Canyon National Parks, *below*). *63410 Generals Hwy; 559/565–3388, 800/843–8677; www.mslodge.com.* **$$–$$$**

Sequoia Village Inn. Just outside the south entrance to Sequoia National Park, this cozy family-run lodge is ensconced in a grove of oak trees just off the highway. The lodge's 10 rooms, all in wooden cottages and chalets, provide more privacy than other roadside motels. Although they can be buggy—bring your insect repellent—the rooms have more amenities that you might expect, including air-conditioning, satellite TV, and kitchenettes or full kitchens; there's also an outdoor swimming pool. No restaurant or dining hall is on-site. *559/561–3652; 45971 Sierra Dr. (Hwy. 198), Three Rivers; www.sequoiavillageinn.com.* **$$–$$$**

Silver City Mountain Resort. Near the end of the treacherously winding road into the Mineral King Valley in southern Sequoia National Park, you will find this privately owned collection of a dozen rustic cabins and Swiss chalets. Most have knotty pine walls and tin roofs befitting this historical mining settlement. While far from luxurious, they are usually restful places to lay your head. Some of the comfier cabins and Swiss chalets are equipped with full kitchens, and the biggest have stone fireplaces and claw-foot bathtubs. Eight of them have electricity and private baths, and those that don't instead come equipped with kerosene lamps and have access to a shared shower house. This resort is a good getaway if you want to be near spectacular mountain hiking trails. The market and diner offer limited options, so bring any supplies you may need with you. The resort is usually open from late May through mid-October. *Mineral King Rd.; 559/561–3223 in summer, 559/734–4109 in winter; www.silvercityresort.com.* **$–$$$**

Sequoia Motel. The town of Three Rivers, near the south entrance to Sequoia National Park, has a smattering of more expensive motels, but this humble property is a stand out for its hospitality and help-ful service. The fewer than a dozen standard motel-style rooms with pretty flower beds are rustic but cheerful. Or you can choose one of the few on-site cabins, some of which have full kitchens, private baths, and outdoor decks for stargazing. If you're a guest who likes to read, the Library guest room is furnished with floor-to-ceiling bookshelves and has an extra-long bed. In summer, guests have access to an outdoor swimming pool. *559/561–4453; 43000 Sierra Dr. (Hwy. 198), Three Rivers; www.sequoiamotel.com.* **$–$$**

Sequoia River Dance B&B. On quiet, oak tree–shaded grounds by the Kaweah River, this family-run inn with five guest rooms is ideal for relaxing hideaways. Most rooms have shared bath and a few, such as the Crystal Hill Room with an antique brass queen-size bed, have river views. You can lounge on the lawn and listen to the river run, or pop in a video or DVD in the common area, a nice perk since there are no TVs in the rooms. The owners welcome pets and don't have any age restrictions on children. The inn is a short drive to Sequoia National Park's south entrance. Breakfast includes an ever-changing roster of homemade creations by your hosts, former restaurant chefs, who may surprise you with fresh-baked, fruity scones or a vegetable frittata to start your morning. *40534 Cherokee Oaks Dr., Three Rivers; 559/561–4411; www.sequoiariverdance.com.* **$–$$**

CAMPGROUNDS IN AND AROUND SEQUOIA AND KINGS CANYON NATIONAL PARKS

See the price chart on p. 275 and the camping chart on p. 305–307.

Sequoia and Kings Canyon National Parks offer more than a dozen campgrounds totaling more than 800 campsites (some of which are seasonal), with more camping available in the Sequoia National Forest surrounding the parks. All campgrounds regularly fill up on summer weekends and holidays. A few National Park Service and USDA Forest Service campgrounds accept summer camping reservations. Make reservations online at www.recreation.gov or by calling 877/444–6777.

If you arrive without a reservation during peak times, your best chances of finding a first-come, first-served site still available are in more remote areas of the parks (for example, Cedar Grove in Kings Canyon National Park or Mineral King in Sequoia National Park). To avoid frustration, stop in at the main visitor centers to ask about availability before making the long drive out to these spots. Pay showers are available at Grant Grove and Cedar Grove in Kings Canyon National Park, and at Lodgepole and Stony Creek villages and Silver City Mountain Resort near Mineral King in Sequoia National Park.

If you'd rather not pitch your own tent nor carry a camp stove and food into the wilderness, the **Bearpaw High Sierra Camp** (*www.visit sequoia.com*) is an 11.5-mile hike along the High Sierra Trail starting from Crescent Meadow in Sequoia National Park. Open from mid-June until mid-September, it offers private canvas tents, flush toilets, hot showers, and a catered breakfast and dinner for about $175 per night. Box lunches are available for an additional fee. For reservations or to check last-minute availability, call 866/807–3598 after January 1.

In the Giant Sequoia National Monument, the **Sequoia High Sierra Camp** (*www.sequoiahighsierracamp.com*) is only a 1-mile hike from the Marvin Pass trailhead off Big Meadows Road. It offers more deluxe canvas-tent cabins with hand-carved furnishings, high-thread-count linens, and feather-down pillows, as well as flush toilets and hot showers. Overnight rates of around $250 include a chef-prepared dinner and breakfast and a boxed picnic lunch. The camp is typically open from mid-June through early October; make reservations by calling 866/654–2877.

Also in the Giant Sequoia National Monument off Big Meadows Road, the **Big Meadow Guard Station** built by the Civilian Conservation Corps in the 1930s is available for rent between mid-June and mid-October. Guests must supply their own bedding, cooking equipment, and toiletries. For more information, contact the **Hume Lake Ranger District** (*35860 E. Kings Canyon Rd. [Hwy. 180], Dunlap; 559/338–2251; www.fs.fed.us/r5/sequoia*). Make reservations online at www.recreation.gov or by calling 877/444–6777.

The campgrounds in Sequoia and Kings Canyon offer pretty settings for a relaxing getaway, though none have any bells and whistles (or even RV hookups). Those around Lodgepole and Grant Grove get quite busy in summer with vacationing families, as Cedar Grove deep inside Kings Canyon and the hotter, drier Sequoia foothills campgrounds near Ash Mountain. Mineral King is even more remote and has less-developed campsites that attract a more hard-core set of outdoor adventurers (watch out for those marmots!). Campgrounds in the national forest lands between Kings Canyon and Sequoia national parks can be just as popular, although they generally fill up after the national park campgrounds do. The exception to this is at Hume Lake, where easy access to water sports and summer vacation–friendly amenities such as a convenience store and take-out burger and ice-cream shop make car camping more fun for families, especially if you have young kids.

WHERE TO EAT IN SEQUOIA AND KINGS CANYON NATIONAL PARKS

See the price chart on p. 275.

The main tourist areas of Sequoia and Kings Canyon national parks—Lodgepole, Grant Grove, and Cedar Grove villages—all have snack bars, delis, grills, or basic restaurants for convenient meals on the run and grocery markets for stocking up before picnics and campfire cookouts. In summer, usually nightly from mid-June through August, you can have "Dinner with a Ranger" during a family-style Western barbecue cookout at Wolverton Meadow in Sequoia National Park. Buy same-day tickets at Wuksachi Lodge (*64740 Wuksachi Way, off Generals Hwy.; 801/559–4930*) or the Lodgepole market (*Lodgepole Village, off Generals Hwy.*).

Wuksachi Lodge Dining Room. Walk through the tall-ceilinged, artistically appointed hotel lobby to find this rustic-looking restaurant, a short drive north of the Giant Forest and Lodgepole village. Open year-round, it has a stone fireplace and panoramic windows looking out onto groves of lodgepole pine and fir trees. The seasonal, often organic menu of hearty dinners may include pan-seared mountain trout or juniper-crusted duck breast with autumn squash. Lunch is a more casual affair (mostly just sandwiches and salads), and breakfast is an all-you-can-eat buffet. There's full cocktail service from the hotel bar. *64740 Wuksachi Way, off Generals Hwy.; 801/559–4930.* **$$–$$$**

DINING OUTSIDE SEQUOIA AND KINGS CANYON NATIONAL PARKS

See the price chart on p. 275.

Fugazzi's California Bistro. In downtown Visalia, less than an hour's drive west of Sequoia National Park, Fugazzi's is an urbane downtown eatery with colorfully painted walls and sofas that are divinely comfortable. Perch at the bar with a martini, or nab a table and nosh on fresh, oversize salads or satisfying bowls of Cal-Italian pastas. There are some inventive thin-crust pizzas too, like Thai chicken with peanut sauce and artichoke-topped pies. The list of California wines and domestic microbrews is an especially welcome sight after a long day's hike. *127 W. Main St., Visalia; 559/625–0496.* **$$–$$$**

Montecito Sequoia Lodge. In the Giant Sequoia National Monument, between Sequoia and Kings Canyon national parks, this mountain resort with A-frame buildings and old-fashioned wooden cabins puts on a chef-made spread of above-par buffet meals that are sometimes available to nonguests (always call ahead to check).

The log cabin-style dining room feels just like summer camp when you were a kid, and it's often full of ravenous families sharing meals that might feature grilled fresh tilapia, corn salad, and homemade ice cream and berry pies. If there's a wait, kick back on the outdoor deck, which has beautiful forest and sunset views. *63410 Generals Hwy; 559/565–3388.* **$$–$$$**

Hummingbirds. At Clingan's Junction, this antique-looking diner with clinker brick walls and a chain saw–carved statue of a bear is a good bet along Highway 180 en route to Kings Canyon National Park. Chicken-fried steak, liver and onions, and fish-and-chips are among the comfort food standards served at dinner, while lunch fare sticks to burgers and hot and cold sandwiches. At breakfast, order the "Ranch Hand Special" (two eggs, two pancakes, thick-sliced ham, and hash browns) to fuel up your body for your day's adventure in the parks. *35591 E. Kings Canyon Rd. (Hwy. 180), Squaw Valley; 559/338–0160.* **$–$$**

Sierra Subs & Salads. The town of Three Rivers is just a short drive to the south entrance of Sequoia National Park. This take-out deli makes creative, fresh deli sandwiches and salads, healthy vegetarian wraps, and grilled panini like the Black Bear Grill, with roast beef and Ortega chilies, or the Potwisha Portabella, with seasoned mayo and mushrooms on fresh-baked shepherd's bread. Enjoy your meal at one of the few picnic tables at the side of the road, or get a boxed picnic lunch and fruit smoothie to go. *41717 Sierra Dr. (Hwy. 198), Three Rivers; 559/561–4810.* **$**

CAMPING IN AND AROUND THE NATIONAL PARKS

All of the following campgrounds have drinking water available, unless otherwise noted. Those marked with an asterisk (*) are located outside the national park boundaries, and are not operated by the NPS. There are no hookups for RVs in these campgrounds. The RV column on the chart indicates if road access is acceptable and sites are large enough for RVs; some have pull-through sites, while others are back-in only.

CAMPGROUND NAME	AREA/PARK	OPEN	RESERVATIONS	# OF SITES	FEE	RVs	FACILITIES
Atwell Mill	Mineral King/ Sequoia	Late May– late Oct.	No	21	$12	No	ADA site, vault toilets
Azalea	Grant Grove/ Yosemite	Year-round	No	110	$18	Yes	Flush toilets
* Big Meadows	Off Generals Hwy.	May–Oct.	No	25	Free	Yes	Vault toilets (no potable water)
* Buck Rock	Off Generals Hwy.	May–Oct.	No	5	Free	No	Vault toilets (no potable water)
Buckeye Flat	Foothills/Se- quoia	Late Apr. – early Sept.	No	28	$18	No	ADA site, flush toilets
Canyon View	Cedar Grove/ Yosemite	Varies May– Oct.	Yes (for large groups only)	28	$18–$35	No	Small/large group sites, flush toilets
Cold Springs	Mineral King/ Sequoia	Late May– late Oct.	No	40	$12	No	Vault toilets
* Convict Flat	Hwy. 180	May–Oct.	No	5	Free	No	Vault toilets (no potable water)
Crystal Spring	Grant Grove/ Yosemite	Late May– mid-Sept.	No	50	$18–$35	Yes	Small-group sites, flush toilets
Dorst	Giant Forest/ Sequoia	Late May– early Sept.	Yes	204	$20	Yes	RV dump station, flush toilets
* Horse Camp	Off Generals Hwy.	May–Oct.	No	5	Free	Yes	Equestrian sites, vault toilets (no potable water)

Name	Location	Season	Reservations	Sites	Fee	Pets	Facilities
* Horse Creek	Off Hwy. 198, west of Foothills Entrance Station	Year-round (some sites)	Yes (some sites)	80	$16–32	Yes	RV dump station, flush toilets, hot showers
* Hume Lake	Hume Lake	Mid-May–late Sept.	Yes	74	$19	Yes	Flush toilets, Wi-Fi Internet access
* Landslide & Tenmile	Hume Lake	May–Oct.	No	31	$15	No	Vault toilets (no potable water at Landslide)
Lodgepole	Giant Forest/Sequoia	Year-around	Yes (summer only)	214	$18–$20 (in winter $10)	Yes	RV dump station, flush toilets
Moraine	Cedar Grove/Yosemite	Varies May–Oct.	No	120	$18	Yes	Flush toilets
Potwisha	Foothills/Sequoia	Year-round	No	42	$18	Yes	ADA site, RV dump station, flush toilets
* Princess	Hume Lake	Mid-May–late Sept.	No	90	$17	Yes	Family sites, RV dump station, vault toilets
Sentinel	Cedar Grove/Yosemite	Late Apr.–late Oct.	No	82	$18	Yes	ADA site, flush toilets
Sheep Creek	Cedar Grove/Yosemite	Varies May–Oct.	No	111	$18	Yes	Flush toilets
* Stony Creek	Off Generals Hwy.	May–Oct.	Yes	49	$19	Yes	Flush toilets
Sunset	Grant Grove/Yosemite	Late May–mid-Sept.	No	157	$18	Yes	Flush toilets
South Fork	Foothills/Sequoia	Year-round	No	10	$12 (free Nov.–Apr.)	No	Vault toilets (non-potable water available in summer only)
* Upper Stony Creek	Off Generals Hwy.	May–Oct.	No	18	$15	Yes	Vault toilets

Geology, Flora, and Fauna

The sun rises aboe Mt. Whitney and its needles.

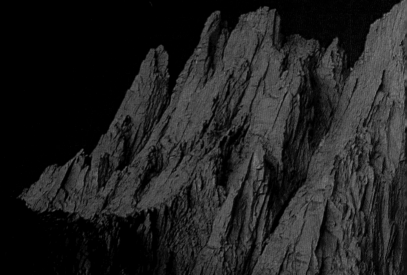

The incredible biodiversity of the Sierra Nevada mountains and its parks is as intriguing as its geological history: Not for nothing was Yosemite declared a World Heritage Site in 1984. There's so much of it to see and fortunately there's still time.

Environmental pollution, harmful introduced species, and loss of habitat can't keep the parks down. The extraordinary and once-endangered peregrine falcon is among the creatures making a comeback, and the giant sequoia forests are healthier than they've been since the arrival of the first European pioneers and immigrants in the 19th century. Yosemite, Sequoia, and Kings Canyon today protect more than 250 native species of vertebrates (possessing backbones, for the most part) and 1,200 kinds of vascular plants (those with conductive tissue that allows them to breathe and move water and food throughout their bodies).

The parks' wildflowers include
Indian paintbrush.

World-famous climber Peter Croft
treks up the north ridge of Mt. Conness
in the Sierra Nevada mountains, on the
eastern edge of Yosemite National Park.

Mesmerized by the Merced River in Yosemite Valley.

⟜ GEOLOGY

The Sierra Nevada mountain range is the highest in California and its Mt. Whitney is the highest peak (14,505 feet) in the contiguous United States. The Sierra Nevada range, the crest of which easily rises above 13,000 feet as it passes through Yosemite National Park, divides the central valley of California lying to the west from the lowlands of the Great Basin Desert spreading to the east. In Sequoia National Park, the Great Western Divide parallels the Sierra crest, while in Kings Canyon National Park, the monumental Monarch and Goddard divides are massive ridges pointing west from the Sierra crest.

This entire region once lay at the bottom of an ancient sea. At sea bottom, layers of sediment were compacted into sedimentary rock. Then, as the oceanic plate started to slide beneath the North American continent, in a process called subduction, it provoked an intense period of volcanic activity along the West Coast. Magma from this molten oceanic plate either pushed above the surface in volcanic explosions or cooled underground and became granite. These granite reserves, called plutons, are aggregated into even larger masses of rock called batholiths, which tilted and raised along fault lines to form the Sierra Nevada range. This same gigantic process of shifting rock continues today, but it won't make them taller, because the mountains are being weathered down by erosion at the same rate that they're growing. Erosion is also exposing underground granite and exfoliating the granite you can already see, creating such unforgettable formations as Yosemite's Half Dome.

The light playing off Half Dome at different times of the day.

As the Sierra Nevada mountains are uplifted and tilted over time, rivers including the Tuolumne, Merced, Kings, and Kern have cut deep canyons into the west side of the range. Ice Age glaciers formed along the crest of the Sierra Nevada, from where they slipped and slid over the exposed granite rock domes and cliffs, leaving evidence of glacial polish (usually smoothed or grooved surfaces where pebbles scraped as they were carried along by the glaciers), such as you can see from Yosemite's Glacier Point. Most importantly, these glaciers softened the sharp V-shaped valleys of the mountain range into wider U-shaped valleys, most famously in Yosemite Valley, but also at Cedar Grove in Kings Canyon National Park.

When the glaciers retreated, they left behind moraines (fields of glacial debris, ranging from small silt to large rocks) and lake basins, many of which are increasingly filled in with sediment, as is the case with the Yosemite Valley's famous Mirror Lake.

FLORA

GIANT SEQUOIA

Easily identified by its massive girth and towering height, the giant sequoia grows only on the western slopes of the Sierra Nevada at elevations of 4,500 to 7,000 feet. Its seed-bearing cones are surprisingly small, measuring just a few inches long. Its bark, softer than that of other pines, also reveals dark wine-red stains; far from nefarious, these discolorations stem from the tannin inside, which helps these long-lived giants survive wildfires, an important process without which new sequoias would never sprout nor grow. The biggest known giant sequoia is the General Sherman Tree, which is growing in Sequoia National Park's Giant Forest.

Wildfires: A Friend of the Forest

Not all wildfires are disasters. In many cases they're essential to a forest's health. This was not a popular view in the 1930s, when the National Park Service and the U.S. Forest Service began what would be three decades of aggressively suppressing fires. The federal government partly reversed its position in the '60s, reasoning that financial burden of stanching many of these fires outweighed saving natural and cultural resources from destruction. Also changing the government's tune was scientific research showing that wildfires were essential to the natural life cycle of woodland forests, findings that ultimately led to a new national environmental policy.

Nowhere was this new policy of permiting wildfires to burn with minimal containment more critical than in Sequoia and Kings Canyon national parks, where the policy was first tested. These areas were key due to a finicky pine cone. The giant sequoia tree cones can only release their seeds in very hot and dry conditions and can only germinate successfully on bare mineral soil that has been cleared of competing plant growth. Both conditions usually occur after a wildfire.

Today, technical fire crews in the national parks identify forested areas that have not burned in a long time and regularly initiate prescribed burns to clear out underbrush, which reduces the potential for disastrously large-scale fires that could wipe out an entire ecosystem for decades. As you travel in the parks, especially in summer, keep an eye out for prescribed fires. Firefighters are often on hand to answer questions.

CALIFORNIA POPPIES

In the Sierra foothills early in spring, California poppies yield their silky, fan-shaped petals, which vary in hue from deep orange to pale yellow. You might spot them on roadsides throughout the parks, from lower-elevation valleys to mixed conifer forests, where hillsides and grassy meadows may appear carpeted in gold. California's state flower is tolerant of drought and grows well in poor soil. An extract from this showy flower was once used medicinally by Native Americans as an extremely mild sedative, as the California poppy is only a distant relative of the opium poppy, from which more potent narcotics are derived. The California poppy's medicinal uses by indigenous tribes included relieving toothaches and sleeplessness and ridding children's scalps of lice.

BRISTLECONE PINE

If you thought the giant sequoia was long-lived, well, you'd be correct, but the title for oldest tree on earth goes to the bristlecone pine. This gnarled tree can live to be more than 3,000 years old and grows on the east side of the Sierra Nevada mountains, among other places in the western United States. Hiding out in remote groves just below the timber line, the bristle-cone pines are twisted and often have dead wood exposed. Blame both characteristics on the rough winds that batter these thin-air dwellers, which grow incredibly slowly through short summer and deep-freeze winters in dry, almost desertlike soil. The pine owes its name to its cones with claw-like bristles and scrub-brush branches densely filled with needles.

LODGEPOLE PINE

In the mixed-conifer forests of the Sierras, telling the many types of pines apart can pose a challenge if you don't know the trick, which is sizing up the different cones and examining the branches to count how many needles are in discrete clusters on the branches. If the needles are paired, you're likely looking at a lodgepole pine, which as its name suggests, grows remarkably straight and tall. The name derives from the Native Americans' use of the thin trunks to construct tepee frames. Lodgepole cones are relatively small, only a few inches long in most cases. As with giant sequoias, lodgepole cones need wildfire-like heat before they'll release their precious seeds to sprout in the newly scarred, bare mineral soil of a partly denuded forest floor.

PONDEROSA PINE

If the long needles come in threes and the exteriors of the cones are prickly to touch, chances are you've come upon a ponderosa pine. Another telltale sign is that the flaky and pale bark of older ponderosa pine trees, which are also known as yellow pines, takes on the appearance of pieces of a jigsaw puzzle all fitted together. If you get up close to any specimens, you may find that the bark has an faint scent of vanilla. Perhaps the most common trees on the western side of the Sierra Nevada mountain range, ponderosas have served as an abundant source of lumber in forests throughout California that are not protected as they are in the national parks.

SNOW PLANT

The stalky, short snow plant, whic[h]
is red all over from stalk to fleshy
flowering stem, is one of the mos[t]
unique plants in the Sierra Nevad[a]
region. It is impossible not t[o]
notice it poking above forest floor[s]
carpeted by pine needles, espe[-]
cially when it pops up at the edg[e]
of melting patches of snow startin[g]
in May. The contrast between it[s]
bright reddish color and the dee[p]
greens of the forest or stark whit[e]
snow can be startling. This beauti[-]
ful specimen is like a vulture o[f]
the plant world, preying on othe[r]
decomposing plant matter in th[e]
surrounding soil.

SUGAR PINE

When it comes to pines, the sugar
is king. The largest known of the
species, sugar pines are capable
of stretching upwards of 200 feet
above the forest floor. Their cones
are proportionally enormous,
growing up to 18 inches long and
so heavily laden by scales that their
posture tends to take on an accor-
dion-like droop. Sugar pines yield
clusters of needles that grow in
groups of five, another way to help
distinguish them from other pines.
Native Americans and early pioneers in the Sierra Nevada would
carve the sugar pine's bark to
encourage the release of a slightly
sweet tree resin that could then be
chewed like gum.

FOXTAIL PINE

The foxtail pine is an irregular, jagged tree that exists on rocky granite outcroppings and slopes at elevations above 9,000 feet. A native of California, the foxtail pine is found in very few places outside Sequoia and Kings Canyon national parks, where it is one of the most common subalpine trees. Foxtails grow surprisingly low to the ground, with bushy branches filled with needles in groups of five that curl around like its namesake animal's tail. Its reddish-brown bark is remarkably thick, acting as insulation during the long winters. Foxtail pines adapt to harsh conditions by growing slowly; with luck, one may live to be 1,000 years old.

LUPINE

Low-lying lupine plants are common throughout the Sierra Nevada, especially alongside hiking trails and in the valleys. Although there are many lupine varieties, most display vertical rows of blueish-purple flowers that resemble small pods when closed. Of the several dozen species, only some lupines in the region have proved to be poisonous, and only if ingested. Other common lavender-colored wildflowers in the region include larkspur, which grows several feet (yes feet, not inches) tall at elevations above 5,000 feet, and the sweet-scented sky pilot, a rare specimen that only grows at elevations above 10,000 feet.

FAUNA

BIGHORN SHEEP

In the high country of the Sierra crest, muscular bighorn sheep can be seen scrambling on rocky granite outcroppings and along mountainsides. In winter they descend to lower elevations on the east side of the range, where green grazing lands are more plentiful during the colder months. However, loss of habitat, hunting (which is now prohibited), and increased predation by mountain lions has driven down the numbers of bighorn sheep in the Sierra Nevada. Now protected as an endangered species, bighorns can be spotted mostly in the high country, for example, around Tioga Pass in Yosemite. Like their fellow park residents, the mule deer, bighorns rut in autumn, when antlered males fight each other dramatically over mates. Rams have heavy, curled horns, while ewes' horns are short and slightly bent. From afar, it's easy to spot both sexes' white rumps, which stand out brightly against their furry brown coats.

BLACK BEAR

The region's most celebrated mega-fauna is the black bear. Most have inky black fur, though a golden-tan or cinnamon-color is not uncommon. Unlike grizzlies, which were wiped out in California in 1922, black bears don't have a shoulder hump. They're much smaller than grizzlies, measuring about the same height as a human adult, but weighing more (averaging up to 600 pounds), depending on their age and sex. They also have larger ears than their formerly endangered grizzly cousins. Although they naturally forage most often for acorns and berries, black bears are omnivores. They hibernate lightly for up to seven months during the winter, and at lower elevations that see more moderate winters they may not sleep much at all. Their populations are spread equally throughout the Sierra Nevada range. You've got a good chance of seeing one by visiting from late spring through early autumn, when the bears are most active. They're also prevalent in the Sierra Nevada backcountry.

OUR BEAR BRETHREN

"Bears are made of the same dust as we, and breathe the same winds and drink the same waters. A bear's days are warmed by the same sun, his dwellings are overdomed by the same blue sky, and his life turns and ebbs with heart-pulsings like ours, and was poured from the same First Fountain. And whether he at last goes to our stingy heaven or no, he has terrestrial immortality. His life not long, not short, knows no beginning, no ending. To him life unstinted, unplanned, is above the accidents of time, and his years, markless and boundless, equal Eternity. God bless Yosemite bears!"

—John Muir, *John of the Mountains: The Unpublished Journals of John Muir*, 1979.

STELLER'S JAYS

Bright blue Steller's jays are a ubiquitous annoyance in all three parks due to their relentless attempts to steal food from picnickers and campers. Of course, it's not really their fault, as these intelligent birds have quickly become accustomed to humans who have invaded their natural habitat. If you can get past their most irritating habit, try to admire their tenacity for survival; they range freely across the western half of the North American continent, all the way from Alaska to Mexico. They will eat almost anything and naturally feed on all types of fruits and berries, as well as nuts, which they can hold with their feet as they pound the hard shell open with their beaks. Not to be confused with the blue jay, the Steller's jay has a darker upper body with a jet-black head and prominently peaked crown.

MULE DEER

Often seen grazing in meadows and forests are mule deer, with their black-tipped tails. Their name comes from the shape of their ears, which resemble mules' ears. Their unusual gait—all four feet can hit the ground at once—gives them an advantage over predators, as they move faster over scrubby terrain and can change directions instantly. Like bighorn sheep, mule deer rut in autumn, when males clash antlers over mates. Human incursions into the wilderness, notably with modern highways, have made the mule deer's seasonal migrations between the Sierra Nevada high country and the foothills more difficult, sometimes resulting in starvation and deadly auto collisions. Drive carefully in the parks, especially at dawn and dusk.

PEREGRINE FALCON

A predatory bird once faced with extinction, peregrines now may be spotted with binoculars as they nest from March through July in the granite walls and domes of Yosemite National Park. In summer, mature birds migrate into the Sierra Nevada high country. Similar in size to a crow, these "duck hawks" are slate-blue or brownish-black with prominent white throats and black markings on their cheeks that resemble mustaches or sideburns. Thanks to the world-record-breaking speed of their dives, peregrine falcons are able to hunt and feed on other birds also in flight. Their impressive wingspan may extend almost 4 feet.

CALIFORNIA MOUNTAIN KINGSNAKE

With black, red, and white stripes along its entire lengthy body, this snake is often confused with the venomous coral snake. But no worries here: the coral snake doesn't live in these parts, and the mountain kingsnake isn't poisonous. Instead, it kills its victims—mostly lizards, mice, and other small rodents—by constriction. While humans don't interest them in the slightest, these mighty powerful predators infamously prey on other snakes (thus giving them the royal title of "kingsnake"), everything from harmless gopher snakes to the most venomous rattlers.

GREAT GRAY OWL

The seldom-seen great gray owl lacks the tufted ears that are common to many other species of owls in this region. Their ears are asymmetrical, which together with their enormous, disc-shaped faces, permit them to focus on the sounds of their prey. There are estimated to be less than 100 great gray owls left in the Sierra Nevada mountains, which form the southern boundary of the owls' habitat. North America's largest owl still resides in the higher-elevation forests of Yosemite, however, so while you probably won't spy one, you may hear its deep-throated voice echoing through the trees in spring.

MARMOT

Yellow-bellied marmots live high up in the Sierra Nevada mountains, where they make their homes among the granite rock piles of talus slopes and along riverbanks. These rocky strongholds help protect these furry ground squirrels (and one of the largest rodents in North America) from such natural predators as eagles and hawks. Marmots are among the most curious and disarmingly fearless animals you'll meet in the parks, most often along high-country hiking trails and also in the Mineral King Valley of Sequoia. Marmots have an unusual addiction: they've developed a taste for antifreeze coolant, and they'll go to great lengths to get it.

MOUNTAIN LION

Although the mountain lion is an occasional predator, chances are you won't see one of these solitary, stealthy cats at any of the three parks. That doesn't mean they're not out there, closely watching and wondering if you'll notice them. Also called cougars, these enormous carnivores live throughout the Sierra Nevada, from the foothills up through the forests and into the mountains. They're tawny colored, can be 8 feet long, and weigh up to 200 pounds. They're capable of taking down a mule deer or elk, though not a black bear, the only creature in the region that outsizes them. Attacks on humans are not unheard of but are rare.

FLORA

CALIFORNIA BUCKEYE

A deciduous tree, the California buckeye—aka California Horse Chestnut—is common in the western Sierra Nevada foothills, where it blooms with very long and fragrant clusters of white and pale pink flowers, usually in late spring or early summer. But you have to hurry to see them: to conserve water, they drop their flowers as soon as summer heats up.

MANZANITA

The manzanita, noted by its crooked branches, is the most common shrub at lower elevations in the Sierra Nevada foothills, where to the delight of rabbits, squirrels, and other small house-hunting mammals, it grows 3 to 6 feet high in dense thickets on hillsides. Hikers are less pleased by the plant, given its obstructionist tendency to sprawl through the tangled undergrowth of the native chaparral.

INCENSE CEDAR

With its scent of earthy incense and cinnamon-colored bark, the cedar can reach almost 200 feet tall. At Kings Canyon's Cedar Grove, the sheer number of incense-cedars growing in a narrow canyon is thought to intensify their fragrance, especially when strong winds are blowing. The cedar's durable wood is often lurking beneath the yellow coat of the everyday No. 2 pencil.

POISON OAK

If you see tripartite leaves on that low-lying shrub along the trail, recall the summer camp mantra, "leaves of three, let them be." You're looking at poison oak, which can also manifest itself as a leafless, twiggy plant. If you've been exposed to its toxic oil, you'll generally start to feel an almost irresistible urge to scratch the exposed area, where an allergic red rash will usually break out within an hour or two. The sooner you wash the affected skin, the better. (*See* the Practical Information chapter for more steps to take.)

FAUNA

BATS

The caves within Yosemite, Sequoia, and Kings Canyon teem with bats. More than half of the bat species here are rare enough to be listed on endangered species lists. Although not threatening to humans, bats do carry and can transmit dangerous diseases such as rabies, so caution is advised while caving. Enormous bat colonies can be observed whirling and flying out of caves en masse at dusk for feeding time, returning around sunrise. You can also observe bats when they roost in snags—dead, hollowed-out trees still standing in the forest after lightning strikes and wildfires.

MOUNTAIN YELLOW-LEGGED FROG

These critically endangered relatives of the western toad are among the amphibians you may spot croaking alongside higher-altitude mountain lakes and streams. If you could get close enough to one before it hopped away, you'd discover an odor of garlic. The frogs lay their eggs in lakes and streams so cold that the larvae must survive underwater throughout the long winter. When they emerge onto land, their bellies and the underside of their back legs are colored a pale yellow. The now forbidden practice of stocking alpine lakes with trout, which feed on the frogs' eggs and larvae, is responsible for the frogs' alarming decline.

WESTERN FENCE LIZARD

Moving fast as a gathering thunderstorm atop rocks and along the forest floor, the western fence lizard is instantly recognizable by the iridescent blue patches on the belly and throat of adult males, who proudly display these blue-colored parts to intimidate rivals. The "push-ups" you'll probaly see them do—moving their front limbs up and down quickly—is a defensive move that also attracts mates. Generally about 6 inches long, these lizards feed on insects and spiders, and in turn become food for snakes and predatory birds.

Practical
Information

◉ BEST TIMES TO VISIT

The national parks covered in this book are open year-round. **Summer**—basically from Memorial Day through Labor Day—is when tourism peaks. The busiest months are July and August, when the high country of the Sierra Nevada is relatively snow-free. If you're looking to escape the worst crowds, avoid the parks on a holiday weekend.

The quietest times when you can still take advantage of warmer weather are the week before Memorial Day and the week after Labor Day. The first half of June is also a good time to visit, because all of the park roads are typically open but the biggest crowds haven't arrived yet. It's also well before the late-summer thunderstorms.

Spring is an especially busy time in Yosemite National Park (though not as busy as summer). Everyone comes to see waterfalls at their fullest, when they're fed by snowmelt, usually in May. Wildflowers bloom over a period of several months, starting in March or April in the Sierra Nevada foothills region, then moving upward in elevation through the parks, with high-country meadows not peaking until July.

Autumn is a much quieter period in the parks because fall foliage is not very brilliant in evergreen forests. In September and October, many visitor services start shutting down for the season. On the plus side, the solitude in the parks is refreshing, and you may have hiking trails all to yourself, especially if you visit Tuolumne Meadows in Yosemite National Park, Mineral King in Sequoia National Park, or Cedar Grove in Kings Canyon National Park just before their respective roads close for the winter.

Winter is an unusual time to visit the parks, but it can be very rewarding in its own way. Although many park roads are either closed for the season or subject to winter-storm closures, some areas of each park stay open even when snow falls, usually between November and April. Yosemite has the most winter-time attractions, ranging from special celebrations in Yosemite Valley to a family-friendly ski school at Badger Pass. In Sequoia and Kings Canyon national parks, you can go snowshoeing or cross-country skiing among the groves of giant sequoias in winter. For more winter-specific info, *see* the feature boxes at the end of each national park chapter.

AVERAGE TEMPERATURE HIGHS AND LOWS BY MONTH

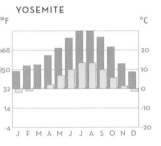

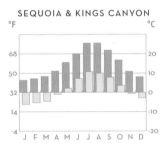

FESTIVALS AND SEASONAL EVENTS

SPRING

Springfest, Yosemite. This high-spirited winter carnival happens at Badger Pass Ski Area during the last week of ski season (usually late March). Expect costume contests, ski races, and all sorts of family-oriented play in the snow. *209/372-8430; www.yosemitepark.com.*

SUMMER

Earth Day, all three parks. The activities vary from year to year, but the festivities for Earth Day, April 22, generally include guided hikes, family-friendly eco-activities, and volunteer cleanup and restoration of the great outdoors. *209/372-0200; www.nps.gov/yose. 559/565-3341; www.nps.gov/seki.*

National Park Day, all national parks. This nationwide festival on August 25 honors all of the country's national parks. It's celebrated with special ranger-led walks, talks, and campfire programs, as well as with movies and other activities geared to families. *209/372-0200; www.nps.gov/yose. 559/565-3341; www.nps.gov/seki.*

Perseid meteor shower, all three parks. Caused by particles of comet dust crashing into Earth's atmosphere, this natural fireworks show peaks in the night sky between midnight and sunrise (the timing varies each year) on August 11 and 12. *209/372-0200; www.nps.gov/yose. 559/565-3341; www.nps.gov/seki.*

Strawberry Music Festivals, Yosemite. Concerts by local artists in multiple musical styles plus outdoor fun for the family are at the heart of these events over Memorial Day and Labor Day weekends at the city of San Francisco's Camp Mather, near Hetch Hetchy. *209/984-8630; www.strawberrymusic.com.*

Tuolumne Meadows Poetry Festival, Yosemite. This free festival of writing and music featuring poetry workshops, open readings and musical jams, and spoken-word performances takes place in August at the Parsons Memorial Lodge. *209/372-0200; www.nps.gov/yose.*

FALL

Celebrate Sequoias Festival, Sequoia. Take guided walks through the giant sequoia groves in early September during this family-friendly celebration of music and art. *559/565-3341; www.nps.gov/seki.*

WINTER

Bracebridge Dinners, Yosemite. While the food is wonderful, come for the dazzling setting and performances. In mid-December, The Ahwahnee hotel dining room is transformed to look like a 17th-century English manor's great hall for a series of holiday feasts. The gourmet fare might include Maine lobster terrine and Angus beef tenderloin, as well as hot mulled wine and plum pudding in honor of the holiday. The meals are accompanied by Renaissance-style performances with music, singing, and dancing. Advance reservations are essential. *801/559-4949; www.bracebridgedinners.com*

Chefs' Holidays, Yosemite. The Ahwahnee brings gourmet food to the forefront during this event held mid-January through early February. Meet the star chefs of famous kitchens from San Francisco to New York City, along with California winemakers, then learn their secrets at cooking classes and demonstrations, followed by gala dinners. Advance reservations are essential. *801/559-4884; www.yosemitepark.com.*

Heritage Holidays, Yosemite. In early March it's the time for old-fashioned galas that pay homage in style to the Roaring Twenties, with such enticements as vintage fashion shows, historic hotel tours, live jazz orchestras, and dancing at a grand ball. Advance reservations are essential. *801/559-4884; www.yosemitepark.com.*

Nordic Holiday Races, Yosemite. At Badger Pass, this seasonal competition takes off over a weekend in early February. Everyone is welcome to register in ad-

vance for the 16-kilometer classic striding race, where prizes are awarded for the best skiers' costumes, the winners of the downhill telemark race (in which most people time themselves just for fun), and the champions of the freestyle skate race that goes all the way out to Glacier Point and back—a whopping 35-kilometer trip. *209/372-8430; www.yosemitepark.com.*

Trek to the Tree, Kings Canyon. On the second Sunday of December, up to 100 Christmas carolers gather at the base of the General Grant tree, where park rangers lay a wreath of greenery in honor of the nation's military veterans. *559/565-3341; www.nps.gov/seki.*

Vintners' Holidays, Yosemite. Throughout November and into early December, The Ahwahnee hosts this oenophilic extravaganza, with wine tastings galore, meet-and-greets with California winemakers, and gala dinners. Advance reservations are essential. *801/559-4884; www.yosemitepark.com.*

 COMMUNICATIONS

INTERNET

High-speed wireless Internet access is not common inside the parks. A few free Wi-Fi hot spots are found at park lodgings, including The Ahwahnee and Yosemite Lodge at the Falls in Yosemite National Park, in the hotel lobby of the Wuksachi Lodge in Sequoia National Park, at the John Muir Lodge at Grant Grove in Kings Canyon National Park, and near the front desk at the Montecito-Sequoia Resort in the Giant Sequoia Monument of the Sierra National Forest. Both The Ahwahnee and the Yosemite Lodge at the Falls have self-serve, fee-based Internet kiosks available to the public, but beware: they don't work reliably.

PHONES

Cell-phone coverage is very limited in the parks. Some networks and some types of mobile phones will work in certain areas, while others won't, but none are very reliable. In Yosemite National Park, places in the Yosemite Valley and along Tioga Road have spotty coverage. In Sequoia and Kings Canyon parks, you may get minimal reception in the Foothills and Grant Grove areas. Instead of relying on your cell phone, before your trip consider buying a prepaid phone card that you can use with pay phones, which are scattered throughout the parks, usually at visitor centers, campgrounds, lodges, markets, and gas stations.

ENTRY FEES AND PASSES

A seven-day entry pass for any of the three parks (including the Hume Lake District of the Sierra National Forest) costs $20 per car. An annual pass for Yosemite National Park costs $40; for Sequoia and Kings Canyon, it's $30. The annual "America the Beautiful" National Parks and Federal Recreation Lands Pass costs $80. Purchase the pass at any park entrance station, or in advance online at http://store.usgs.gov/pass. For U.S. citizens and permanent residents, seniors aged 62 and older pay $10 for a lifetime pass valid for entry to all national parks and federal recreation lands, while those with a permanent disability receive a free lifetime pass.

Special wilderness permits are required for backpacking in the wilderness of the parks. You should reserve these permits as far in advance as possible, especially for weekend trips and during the peak summer season. Wilderness regulations vary for each park; *see* the individual park chapters for helpful details, including costs and how to apply for permits.

⊕ GETTING TO THE PARKS

By Air

Rental cars are available with advance reservations at each of these airports.

Fresno Yosemite International Airport (FAT) is the closest airport to all three national parks. Connecting flights from gateway hubs to this regional airport are infrequent. The airport is 7 miles northeast of downtown Fresno, off Peach Avenue, north of Highway 180, and it is 65 miles from the south entrance of Yosemite National Park and 50 miles to the west entrance of Sequoia and Kings Canyon. *559/621–4500; www.flyfresno.org.*

San Francisco International Airport (SFO) is northern California's busiest airport. It is served by most domestic and many international airlines. The airport is 13 miles south of San Francisco, off Highways 101 and 380, and it is 200 miles from the Arch Rock entrance of Yosemite National Park and 200 miles to the west entrance of Sequoia and Kings Canyon. *650/821–8211 or 800/435–9736; www.flysfo.com.*

Oakland International Airport (OAK), in the East Bay area, is served by some domestic and international airlines. The airport is 10 miles south of downtown Oakland via I-880, off Hegenberger Road and 98th Avenue, and it is 180 miles from the Arch Rock entrance of Yosemite National Park and 225 miles to the west entrance of Sequoia and Kings Canyon. *510/563–3300; www.flyoakland.com.*

Mineta San José International Airport (SJC), in the South Bay area, is served by many domestic and some international airlines. It's as close to all three parks as the other Bay Area airports: 195 miles from the Arch Rock entrance of Yosemite National Park and 205 miles to the west entrance of Sequoia and Kings Canyon. The airport is 4 miles northwest of downtown San Jose, off Highway 101. *408/501–0979; www.sjc.org.*

Sacramento International Airport (SMF), served by some domestic and international airlines, is handy for Yosemite National Park, just 150 miles from the park's Big Oak Flat Entrance Station entrance; it is 235 miles from the west entrance of Sequoia and Kings Canyon national parks. The airport is 12 miles northwest of downtown

Sacramento, off I–15 via Airport Boulevard. *916/929–5411; www
sacairports.org.*

Los Angeles International Airport (LAX) is Southern California
busiest airport. It is served by most domestic and many internation
airlines. It's convenient for southern Sequoia National Park, ju
225 miles from the park's Foothills Entrance Station. It is 250 mile
from the Big Stump Entrance Station to Kings Canyon and 250 mile
from the south entrance of Yosemite National Park. The airport is 1
miles southwest of downtown L.A., off Sepulveda Boulevard, west o
I–405 (San Diego Freeway) and north of I–105 (Century Freeway
310/646–5252; www.lawa.org/lax.

Reno/Tahoe International Airport (RNO) in western Nevada i
served by many domestic and some international airlines. It's a goo
choice for entering Yosemite National Park from the east side whe
the Tioga Road is open (usually June until October). The airport is
miles southeast of downtown Reno, east of South Virginia Street a
Plumb Lane, off U.S. Highway 395, and it is 150 miles from the eas
entrance of Yosemite National Park. There is no automobile entranc
on the eastern side of Sequoia and Kings Canyon national park
775/328–6400; www.renoairport.com.

By Car

The following routes are functional highways to get you most quickl
to the parks from major urban areas nearby. For California roa
conditions, call 800/427–7623.

Yosemite Valley is about a two-hour drive from Fresno, 3½ hour
from Sacramento, four hours from San Francisco, and more than fiv
hours from Los Angeles. It's three or more hours to the park from
Reno, Nevada, which is usually only an option between June an
October, depending on whether or not the road is snow-free.

The Foothills Entrance Station of Sequoia National Park is
1½-hour drive from Fresno, four hours from Sacramento, and 4½
hours from either San Francisco or Los Angeles. Kings Canyo
National Park's Grant Grove area is a 1½-hour drive from Fresno
four hours from Sacramento, 4½ hours from San Francisco, and fiv
hours from Los Angeles.

From Fresno: to reach Yosemite, take Highway 41 north, continu
north on Wawona Road, and take Highway 140 east into the valley
To reach Sequoia travel via Highway 99 south, then drive east o
Highway 198 past Visalia for about an hour to the Foothills Entranc
Station near Three Rivers. To reach Sequoia or Kings Canyon, tak

Highway 180 east to the Big Stump Entrance Station, past which you can turn north toward Kings Canyon or south toward the Giant Forest area of Sequoia.

From Sacramento: to reach Yosemite, take Highway 99 south to Stockton, then Highway 4 east to Copperopolis, detour onto County Road E-15 southeast to Yosemite Junction, and join Highway 120 east, then Highway 140 east. To reach Sequoia or Kings Canyon, take Highway 99 south to Fresno, then Highway 180 east to the Big Stump Entrance Station, past which you can turn north toward Kings Canyon or south toward the Giant Forest area of Sequoia.

From San Francisco: to reach Yosemite, cross the Bay Bridge on I-80 into Oakland, then take I-580 east toward Stockton, detour onto I-205 past Tracy, jog north onto I-5, drive east on Highway 120, and finally take Highway 140 east into the valley. To reach Sequoia or Kings Canyon, cross the Bay Bridge on I-80 into Oakland, then take I-580 east toward Stockton, detour onto I-205 past Tracy, jog north onto I-5 past Tracy, drive east on Highway 120, take Highway 99 south to Fresno, and finally Highway 180 east to the Big Stump Entrance Station, past which you can turn north toward Kings Canyon or south toward the Giant Forest area of Sequoia.

From Los Angeles: to reach Yosemite, take I-5 north to Highway 99 north to Fresno, then continue as above. In winter, the drive along Highway 140 east of Merced on Highway 99 is a much easier approach route to Yosemite Valley. To reach the Foothills Entrance Station of Sequoia National Park, take I-5 north and connect to Highway 99 north, then drive east on Highway 198 past Visalia for about an hour to the Foothills Entrance Station near Three Rivers. To reach Kings Canyon, take I-5 north and connect to Highway 99 north, then drive east on Highway 198 to Visalia, take Highway 63 north past Orange Cove, then Highway 180 east through Squaw Valley and Dunlap to the Big Stump Entrance Station.

From Reno: when the Tioga Road is open (usually from June until October), it's possible to enter Yosemite National Park from the east side of the Sierra Nevada mountains on Highway 120, which branches off U.S. Highway 395 outside the town of Lee Vining. There is no eastern entrance for vehicles for Sequoia and Kings Canyon national parks.

From Yosemite to Kings Canyon & Sequoia: from Yosemite Valley it's a 2½-hour trip south on Highway 41, then east along Highway 180 to the Generals Highway, which connects Sequoia and Kings Canyon parks. If you turn left at the junction of Highway 180 and the Generals

Highway, it's a 15-minute drive north to Grant Grove, from where it's another hour's drive to Cedar Grove, both in Kings Canyon National Park. If you turn right at the junction, it's a 45-minute drive southeast to Lodgepole and one hour's drive to the Giant Forest Museum, both in Sequoia National Park.

 GETTING AROUND

BY BICYCLE

In Yosemite National Park, bicycles are allowed only on paved roads and trails. In Sequoia and Kings Canyon parks, bicycles are allowed on paved and unpaved roads where cars are also permitted, and on paved recreational trails (e.g., connecting campgrounds). Bicycles are not allowed on hiking trails in the parks and may not go off-trail in wilderness areas. All riders under age 18 must wear a helmet. In Yosemite Valley, you can rent bicycles (weather permitting) for an hour or a day from the Yosemite Lodge at the Falls or at Curry Village.

BY BUS AND SHUTTLE

In Yosemite National Park, there are several bus routes with **free shuttle buses** in the park; all but one are seasonal (*see* the chart, *opposite*). Starting from Yosemite Valley, there are also **private shuttle buses** (*209/372–4386; www.yosemitepark.com*) that offer tours of Glacier Point and Tuolumne Meadows. For the narrated four-hour tour to Glacier Point, buses usually depart the Yosemite Lodge at the Falls three times daily between late spring and early fall. For the eight-hour narrated tour up to Tuolumne Meadows, buses pick up passengers at Curry Village, Yosemite Village, and the Yosemite Lodge at the Falls once daily between July and early September. These private rides can serve hikers as well: if you are planning a one-way hiking or backpacking trip down into the Yosemite Valley, you should park your car in the valley, then use these buses to access trailheads off Glacier Point Road and Tioga Road. Reservations, which are especially recommended in summer, are accepted up to seven days in advance (prepayment may not be required). Unfortunately there are no free shuttles serving hikers in a similar fashion, so you have to take the tour, even if all you really need is a trailhead shuttle.

Yosemite's Free Shuttles

SHUTTLE SERVICE	ROUTE STOPS	HOURS OF OPERATION	TIME OF YEAR
Yosemite Valley	Major points of interest in eastern Yosemite Valley, including lodgings, stores, trailheads, and viewpoints	Daily 7 am—10 pm	Year-round
El Capitan	Yosemite Valley Visitor Center, El Capitan, and the Four-Mile trailhead	Daily 9 am—6 pm	Summer
Wawona–Mariposa Grove	Wawona general store and the gift shop near the South Entrance Station area to the Mariposa Grove	Daily 9 am—6 pm	Spring through fall
Tuolumne Meadows	Tuolumne Meadows lodge, campground and store, visitor and wilderness centers, Olmsted Point, Tenaya Lake, and various trailheads	Daily 7 am—7 pm	Mid–June to early September
Tuolumne Meadows (to Tioga Pass)	Tuolumne Meadows Lodge, Mono Pass, and Tioga Pass	Daily four round-trips between 9 am and 5 pm	Mid–June to early September
Badger Pass	Between Yosemite Valley and Badger Pass	Twice daily	Ski season (usually from mid-December through March)

Yosemite Area Regional Transportation System (YARTS) public buses (*877/989–2787; www.yarts.com*) travel along Tioga Road (Highway 120), connecting the Yosemite Valley Visitor Center with Crane Flat, White Wolf, Tuolumne Meadows, and Lee Vining and Mammoth Lakes on the east side of the Sierra Nevada. This route operates once daily in each direction during July and August, weekends only in June and September, weather permitting.

In Sequoia National Park, **free shuttle buses** operate between late May and early September. The green route connects the Giant Forest Museum with the General Sherman Tree and the Lodgepole and Wuksachi village areas. The gray route loops from the Giant Forest Museum out to Moro Rock and Crescent Meadow. For updated route schedules, consult the free park newspaper *The Guide*, or call 559/565–3341.

Between the town of Visalia and the Giant Forest Museum, the **Sequoia Shuttle** (*877/287–4453; www.sequoiashuttle.com*), for a fee, makes five daily runs in each direction, stopping in Three Rivers and at the park's Foothills Visitor Center. This shuttle operates between Memorial Day and Labor Day weekends. Advance reservations and prepayment are required.

There are no shuttle buses (free or otherwise) currently operating in Kings Canyon National Park.

BY CAR

Most visitors drive themselves around the parks, although the shuttles listed in the previous section will help avoid parking hassles. Traffic jams are a common problem in summer, when there are long lines at park entrance stations and frequent delays along all of the main park roads. At peak times, some day-use **parking lots** at viewpoints and trailheads fill completely before noon, especially in the Giant Forest area of Sequoia National Park, and in Yosemite Valley, at Mariposa Grove, and along Tioga Road near Tuolumne Meadows in Yosemite National Park.

In general, **navigating around the parks is easy**, with the exception of Yosemite Valley, where a network of one-way roads can be confusing for first-time visitors (consulting the free park newspaper and map brochure will help you avoid backtracking).

The **speed limit** varies on roads around the parks, ranging from 15 mph in congested areas up to 45 mph on highways such as Tioga Road (Highway 120). Other regulations limit the length of vehicles that may travel on narrow, twisting mountain roads, which are not recommended for RVs or trucks towing trailers.

If you're driving slowly to enjoy the scenery, **pay attention to other drivers on the road behind you**, and frequently pull over to let faster traffic pass on two-lane park roads. If you catch sight of wildlife, pull completely off the road instead of causing traffic jams and accidents by stopping suddenly in the middle of the highway. **Be cautious driving at night**, when wildlife is more apt to suddenly run across the road or stand in the middle of it. This is especially true on twisting, narrow park roads, such as the Kings Canyon Scenic Byway.

There are some **gas stations** in the parks, but they're not all open year-round, and only a few have 24-hour credit-card pumps. So it's best to fill up your car's gas tank before arriving in the parks. Gas stations are in Yosemite National Park at Crane Flat, Wawona, and Tuolumne Meadows; there's a repair shop in Yosemite Valley. In national forest-service lands around Sequoia and Kings Canyon national parks, there are gas stations at Stony Creek, Hume Lake, and the Kings Canyon Lodge.

Because the winters are so severe in the Sierra Nevada mountains, **frequent road construction is the norm inside the parks during the summer months**. In late spring and early fall, watch out for slushy, even icy, conditions on roads that have just been opened or are about to close for the season.

Winter road closures are common in all three parks (for details, *see* the special winter-travel features at the end of each national park chapter). In winter, always carry tire chains. For the latest road conditions in Yosemite National Park, call 209/372–0200; for Sequoia and Kings Canyon national parks, call 559/565–3341.

You also want to be sure that your car is in good condition before visiting the parks; towing services are time-consuming and costly, and the nearest pay phone may be miles away from where your car breaks down. Membership in an auto club like AAA (*www.aaa.com*) can help with roadside emergencies, including locking your keys in the car, running out of gas, or needing a tow.

⊙ HEALTH AND SAFETY

Yosemite, Sequoia, and Kings Canyon national parks can feel like the ultimate outdoor playgrounds—but remember that these wild places involve critical risks. Every year, visitors get injured and sometimes there are serious or even fatal accidents. Even if you're planning a low-key trip in well-traveled areas of the parks, be prepared and familiarize yourself with the essential health and safety issues and tips. A little preparation and a cautious approach will go a long way toward keeping you safe. The advice given below is not intended to be a substitute for professional medical advice, which you should seek in the event of any illness or accident while visiting the parks. National Park Service rangers who are qualified as EMTs can offer free assistance to visitors.

As is true in most places in the United States, **for ambulance, fire, and police emergencies in the park, dial 911.**

From Moro Rock's summit in Sequoia National Park you overlook the Great Western Divide.

ALTITUDE SICKNESS

Commonly known as "altitude sickness," Acute Mountain Sickness (AMS) can strike even if you have never experienced problems before at high altitudes (generally defined as above 8,000 feet). Although altitude sickness affects some park visitors in high places like Yosemite's Tuolumne Meadows or Mineral King in Sequoia National Park, AMS is more likely to affect backpackers and climbers. Symptoms, which typically appear within 10 hours after first arriving at high altitudes, include headaches, dizziness, loss of appetite, nausea (possibly vomiting), insomnia, and extreme fatigue. If symptoms do not resolve, or they worsen within the first 24 to 48 hours, get to a lower elevation immediately.

If you continue to stay at the same elevation or ascend further before symptoms resolve, you are at risk for developing high-altitude cerebral edema (HACE), marked by loss of muscular control and altered mental status, or high-altitude pulmonary edema (HAPE), evidenced by increased shortness of breath, persistent coughing, and chest pain.

The best way to avoid altitude sickness is to allow yourself plenty of time to acclimatize before exerting yourself (e.g., sleeping at high elevations before hiking there the next day). To further lessen your chances of altitude sickness, drink plenty of water and either cut back on or avoid alcohol altogether.

Heat Exhaustion and Heatstroke

Protect yourself from the sun by wearing sunscreen and a hat, especially at higher elevations. Also don't overexert yourself outdoors, especially on hot days, and be sure to stay well hydrated—always carry extra water with you on hikes. Dehydration can lead to heat cramps, heat exhaustion, and heatstroke.

Heat cramps occur when your muscles spasm after sweaty exertions; the best treatment is to rest, drink water, and gently stretch and massage the afflicted areas.

Symptoms of heat exhaustion include headaches, nausea, dizziness, thirst, fatigue, and increased heart and respiratory rates. Move into the shade immediately, drink water, fan yourself, and pour water on your head while you rest.

Another serious condition that can result from dehydration and overexposure to the sun and intense heat is heatstroke, which may give you flushed skin, a loss of coordination, an altered mental status, and seizures. It is potentially fatal and requires immediate cooling off and medical attention.

Hypothermia and Frostbite

Hypothermia, which is when the body loses heat to the environment faster than it can produce it, may happen when you are exposed to cold, wet, and/or windy conditions. Early symptoms of hypothermia include the "umbles" (i.e., stumbling, fumbling, mumbling), which worsen as you lose motor control. Signs that the condition is progressing are uncontrollable shivering, increased heart and respiration rates, and cold, pale skin. If the hypothermia continues to advance, you eventually reach a severe state in which the shivering stops.

The best treatment for hypothermia is to change into dry clothes, adding insulating layers, and to take shelter from the elements. Drinking plain water and eating carbohydrates (e.g., energy bars) may help hasten your recovery, too. You may have heard that using direct body heat to warm hypothermic people and giving them hot beverages can help, but the results of recent medical studies suggest this isn't necessarily true. Wrapping them up warmly and giving them clean water and carbs to consume seems to work best.

Frostbite is another hazard in cold conditions. Always dress appropriately for cold weather and watch for any exposed skin that appears too white, waxy, numb, or cold. To treat superficial frostbite, do not massage the affected area. Instead, use skin-to-skin warming techniques (e.g., placing cold fingers under arms) and seek shelter in a warm place. Medical attention is necessary for all cases of frostbite.

Lightning

Always check the weather forecast before setting out on any hike. Do not attempt to hike over mountain passes, tackle summits or peaks, or climb any granite domes when thunderstorms are approaching. If lightning flashes, descend immediately and get off of any exposed ridges or high places. Also, avoid standing or being immersed in water. You want to make sure you are not the tallest thing in the immediate area, and you want to stay clear of all current-conducting materials. Throw all metal objects away from you, including hiking poles and backpacks that have metal stays. Many lightning-related fatalities can occur from electricity running through the ground; sitting on a camping pad rolled up into a ball will help insulate you from this.

Poison Oak and Ticks

The most common afflictions for hikers, especially in the Sierra Nevada foothills region, are poison oak and ticks. Poison oak is a plant with distinctive tripartite leaves (remember "leaves of three, let them be"), although it can appear as a twiggy shrub. It's toxic year-round. If you think you've been exposed, wash the affected areas immediately. Oral antihistamines and topical treatments may help relieve the itchy, oozing rash that often follows. For severe allergic reactions, seek medical help.

The best prevention for tick bites, which can lead to Lyme disease and other serious illnesses, is to use insect repellant containing DEET and to perform tick checks regularly while in the woods. Wearing light-colored clothing with your pants tucked into your socks will help. To remove a tick, pull slowly and steadily on the body of the tick with tweezers, being careful not to crush the tick or to pull too quickly and forcefully, and thus leave the tick's head inside the wound, as that may cause greater infection. With the patient application of slow and steady pressure, the insect will eventually back itself out and let go.

Enjoy the sounds of running water alongside you while hiking in the parks—but don't drink it without purifying it first.

STREAMS, RIVERS, AND WATERFALLS

Although experts disagree on whether contracting giardia is a risk in the Sierra Nevada, it's better to be safe than sorry. So don't drink water from any natural (i.e., untreated) source inside the parks without first either bringing it to a rapid, rolling boil or treating it with purification tablets.

Streams and rivers are particularly dangerous places to swim in late spring and early summer, when winter snowmelt from the Sierra Nevada mountains causes extremely cold, fast-moving water that can knock you off your feet and sweep you away in an instant. Moving boulders and other underwater debris can pin down even strong swimmers, resulting in serious injuries or drowning.

Exercise caution when fording streams and rivers along hiking trails. Avoid water crossings above your knees. If you must cross, use a hiking pole while crossing at an angle to the current, preferably linking arms with your companions and loosening your backpack straps in case you need to disentangle yourself quickly.

If you see a black bear while in the parks, keep your distance and let it be. But if the bear threatens you, make noise and look big.

When waterfalls peak in late spring and early summer, nearby hiking trails can become dangerously slippery. Playing around waterfalls—for example, by rock climbing alongside them or by swimming in deceptively calm-looking pools above them—is risky, and potentially fatal if you are swept over the top of the falls or caught in a whirlpool.

Wild Animals

Nothing is more important for visitors than to learn to share the park safely with wild animals. To avoid any potentially threatening encounters with wildlife in the park, it's good to follow a few simple guidelines. For instance, a good rule of thumb is to **never hike alone**. In places where rattlesnakes might be hiding—for example in dense vegetation or around blind corners on hiking trails—stomping your feet (snakes are deaf, but they can feel vibrations through the ground) or gently poking through fallen foliage with a hiking pole from a safe distance, to roust any reptiles before you might accidentally step on them, are both good ideas.

Never feed a bear or any other wildlife, including birds and deer. It's important to keep any food or scented items (e.g., soap, candy, empty bottles, bags of garbage, sunscreen, coolers, even baby wipes and car seats) safely locked out of sight in the trunk of your vehicle. Better yet, use the bear-proof lockers provided in parking lots inside the national parks. Doing so prevents bear break-ins, which not only cause extensive property damage to your car, but also hurt the wildlife. The same advice applies while camping in the parks. Keep a clean campsite, and you won't have any unwelcome visitors, whether deer, squirrels, Steller's jays, or black bears. It's worth noting that black bears that become habituated to humans eventually become more aggressive and have to be destroyed, which is why feeding wild animals is a federal offense. Remember: "A fed bear is a dead bear."

If you feel threatened by a black bear, stand your ground, gather any small children to your side, and make yourselves look as big as possible; then make as much noise as you can—shout and bang metal objects together, for example. But you only need to do this if the bear is doing something that makes you feel afraid. If the bear is just foraging for berries or tearing apart a log to get at the delicious ants underneath the bark, there's no need to scare it (or yourself). Just give the bear the right of way on the trail, for example, by moving off to the opposite side and waiting until it lumbers by. If a black bear does make a sudden move toward you, that's the time to react dramatically.

TAKE NOTHING BUT PICTURES,
LEAVE NOTHING BUT FOOTPRINTS

When you visit national parks, the wild natural beauty around you easily inspires good deeds of eco-consciousness. A good way to start is to use the recycling bins in the parks to dispose of glass and aluminum containers.

In addition to recycling, you also need to pay attention to what you're throwing away and where you're throwing it. Littering is of course a no-no. But what some don't realize is that litter includes cigarette butts, which aren't very biodegradable and have been known to cause immensely destructive wildfires in the parks. Dispose of cigarette butts in trash cans located in developed areas of the parks. Additional smoking restrictions may apply in late summer, when wildfires are more likely due to dry tinder-box conditions in the forests and canyons. If a dumpster is full, look for an emptier one to leave your garbage in, and be sure to latch the dumpster securely before leaving—dumpsters that are overflowing or not latched securely will attract wild black bears. Also, don't throw away any propane canisters in dumpsters; they are hazardous material, which you should instead take home with you and dispose of at the appropriate hazmat dump site in the town where you live.

You also do not want to feed or harass local wildlife, nor let your pets run wild. This is not only to protect the parks' natural ecosystems and to preserve wildlife-watching opportunities for all, but also to ensure the safety of your pets (*see* Pets in the Park, *below*).

It's important to be careful where you walk and drive in the parks. Avoid short-cutting trails, which can lead to erosion and landslides, and don't wander off-trail into fragile meadows, which can become easily trampled to death. Also do not drive off-road or park off the pavement; your car may damage tree-root systems and even start wildfires in dry, grassy areas. Bicycle on paved roads only. If you can, take advantage of park shuttles or walk wherever possible. This reduces traffic congestion as well as pollution.

Although it is tempting to pick wild-flowers or gather pine cones to take home with you, it's illegal to remove any natural objects or cultural artifacts (such as Native American arrowheads and pioneer-era tools) from the parks.

If you're heading into the backcountry overnight, the park rangers who issue your wilderness permit will brief you on relevant regulations and Leave No Trace (LNT) principles of outdoor ethics. Here are a couple LNT guidelines that apply to day hikers as well:

• Always pack out what you pack in (that includes food scraps and toilet paper!).

• Do not dispose of human waste near any water sources, such as streams and rivers.

For more information on the Leave No Trace principles, see the Web site *www.lnt. org.*

Also note that there are no grizzlies anywhere in these parks, only black bears. (The last grizzly bear was extirpated from California in 1922.)

Mountain lions are most active at dawn and dusk, but you may encounter one anytime while hiking. Although it is rare to notice them before they notice you, if you do sight a mountain lion, make yourself look big and back away slowly from the animal (moving fast makes you look like prey instead). Other potentially harmful animals that hikers may encounter include rattlesnakes and spiders, most dangerously tarantulas, brown recluses, and black widows. As noted above, **always watch where you step, sit, and place your hands outdoors**. And remember to check inside your shoes for any nasty critters before putting them back on your feet after swimming or tent camping.

If you run across pack mules and horses on trails, stand quietly on the uphill side of the trail and make eye contact with the riders, then follow any further directions they may have.

See also the Warning: Marmots Ahead box in the Sequoia National Park chapter.

PETS IN THE PARKS

Pets must be on a leash at all times in the three national parks. They are typically allowed on paved roads and paved trails (e.g., in campgrounds) only in developed areas of the parks, but they're never allowed on hiking trails or anywhere in the backcountry wilderness. If you want to go hiking with your dog, leashed pets *are* allowed on hiking trails in the Sequoia National Forest around Kings Canyon and Sequoia national parks.

 TIME

California is on Pacific Standard Time (PST), which is eight hours behind Greenwich Mean Time (GMT), except during Daylight Saving Time (DST), when the clocks move ahead one hour, from the second Sunday in March until the first Sunday in November.

It's helpful to be aware of sunrise and sunset times while visiting the parks, so that you get an early enough start in the morning and, more importantly, so you don't get caught after dark on an unfamiliar hiking trail. To find out the times for sunrise and sunset, check the free park newspapers or ask at visitor centers.

⊕ VISITOR INFORMATION

At park entrance stations, rangers will hand you a glossy, foldout map providing a basic overview of the park. More detailed maps, as well as interpretive hiking trail brochures, are sold at park visitor centers. Details of National Park Service visitor centers are given in each of the national park chapters.

In summer, rangers inside these visitor centers may be overwhelmed with visitors, so be patient. Or skip the wait entirely: the most common visitor questions are often answered in the free park newspapers, *Yosemite Today* in Yosemite and *The Guide* in Sequoia and Kings Canyon. Published seasonally, they contain the most accurate, up-to-date information that you may need during your visit, including hours of operation for all visitor facilities and services, schedules of ranger-guided programs and activities, maps of shuttle bus routes, and campground overviews.

In Yosemite Valley, visitor information is also available from the Sierra Club at LeConte Memorial Lodge.

ONLINE RESOURCES

DNC Parks & Resorts at Yosemite: *www.yosemitepark.com.* Visit this site for lodging and activity info and reservations through the official park concessionaire. It's also a good place to find package deals.

National Parks Conservation Association: *www.npca.com.* The NPCA carries a Park Stories podcast series on its Web site, along with select articles from its *National Parks* magazine and general information on all of the national parks.

Sequoia and Kings Canyon national parks: *www.nps.gov/seki.* These twin parks' official Web site covers all the visitor essentials, including helpful seasonal travel info, black bear safety tips, and road construction advisories.

Sequoia Natural History Association: *www.sequoiahistory.org.* Another nonprofit natural history association, SNHA offers an online bookstore, field seminar "edventures" in the park, and helpful links to partner agencies throughout the southern Sierra Nevada.

Sierra Club: *www.sierraclub.org.* The national conservation organization's Web site explains its efforts to restore Yosemite's Hetch

Hetchy and protect giant sequoias. It also has a good overview of the life and work of its founder and Yosemite savior, John Muir.

Yosemite National Park: *www.nps.gov/yose.* The park's official Web site delves into everything you might want to know, including travel tips, current road conditions, and up-to-date park info from the Yosemite Today newspaper, as well as video podcasts.

Yosemite Association: *www.yosemite.org.* The online presence for Yosemite National Park's nonprofit natural history association provides savvy practical info, live webcams that show current images of the park online, and "Nature Notes" on Sierra Nevada wildlife.

Useful Phone Numbers

Yosemite National Park: *209/372-0200.*

Sequoia and Kings Canyon national parks: *559/565-3341.*

California Department of Fish and Game (license sales): *559/243-4005.*

Recorded Weather Forecasts (National Weather Service): *559/498-0375.*

RECOMMENDED READING

Blehm, Eric, *The Last Season,* 2007. Long-winded but still riveting investigation of the life and surprising death of Randy Morgenson, a dedicated wilderness ranger in Sequoia and Kings Canyon national parks. It examines the personal sacrifices made by seasonal National Park Service (NPS) rangers.

Denny, Glenn, *Yosemite in the Sixties,* 2007. A visual documentary of photos taken in the 1960s heyday of rock climbing in the Yosemite Valley from the perspective of pioneers of the sport living in raucous Camp 4.

Frye, Michael, *The Photographer's Guide to Yosemite,* 2000. An insider's guide including maps for shutterbugs looking to capture perfect images of Yosemite National Park in every season and at any time of day.

Ghiglieri, Michael P., and Farabee, Charles R., *Off the Wall: Death in Yosemite,* 2007. By turns macabre and comedic, this well-researched accounting of how visitors have met their untimely ends in Yosemite National Park is irresistible.

Huber, N. King, *Geological Ramblings in Yosemite,* 2008. This roadside guide dives into the ancient geological forces that have shaped what visitors will see in the national park today.

Laws, John Muir, *The Laws Field Guide to the Sierra Nevada,* 2007. Fun, colorfully illustrated naturalist's guide to the flora and fauna of the Sierra Nevada region, including national parks and national forests.

Lee, Gaylen D., *Walking Where We Lived: Memoirs of a Mono Indian Family,* 1999. Personal tale of how Native American ways of life in the eastern Sierra Nevada region have changed over generations.

Lee, Stetson, ed., *The Wild Muir: 22 of John Muir's Greatest Adventures,* 2008. Excerpts from early conservationist John Muir's most extreme outdoor adventures, with woodcut illustrations by Fiona King.

Madgic, Bob, *Shattered Air: A True Account of Catastrophe and Courage on Yosemite's Half Dome,* 2005. A cautionary tale about hikers who made an ill-fated decision to climb Half Dome in the face of an oncoming thunderstorm.

Muir, John, *The Yosemite,* 1912. Famous advocate for Yosemite National Park and the Sierra Nevada region pens his observations of the valleys and the high country, dating from his first explorations in 1869. The Yosemite Association's 2001 edition includes color photographs by Galen Rowell is a beauty.

Radanovich, Leroy, *Images of America: Yosemite National Park and Vicinity,* 2006. For historians, this unique collection of images of the Sierra Nevada region in the late 19th and early 20th centuries features its little-known pioneer, mining, and military history.

Scott, Amy, *Yosemite: Art of an American Icon,* 2006. Insightful essays accompany this museum-quality collection of artworks, ranging from Native American basketry to modern photography.

Secor, R. J., *The High Sierra: Peaks, Passes, and Trails,* 1999. An authoritative guide to backcountry mountaineering and trekking in the Sierra Nevada high country.

Sibley, David Allen, *The Sibley Field Guide to Birds of Western North America,* 2003. The definitive guide for birders is comprehensive yet compact enough (in its paperback edition) to carry in a backpack.

Stillman, Andrea G., and Szarkowski, John, eds., *Yosemite and the High Sierra,* 1994. Beautiful reproductions of landmark photographs by Ansel Adams, accompanied by excerpts from the photographer's journals written when Adams traveled in Yosemite National Park in the early 20th century.

Storer, Tracy I., Usinger, Robert L., and Lukas, David, *Sierra Nevada Natural History,* 2004. A scientific field guide for amateur naturalists who want to learn more in-depth information about the region, with color plate inserts and helpful black-and-white illustrations and sketches.

Wiese, Karen, *Sierra Nevada Wildflowers,* 2000. Perfect for beginning wildflower watchers, this handy identification guide covers more than 230 kinds of flora growing in the Sierra Nevada region.

Index

Tuolumne Meadows in
June after a snow storm.

Acknowledgments

⊕ FROM THE AUTHOR

Writing this book would not have been possible without the help of all of the national park employees that I've met during the last 15 years as I have frequently visited Yosemite, Sequoia, and Kings Canyon national parks. Special thanks are owed to my former colleagues at Kings Canyon National Park. Gratitude is due to Jennifer Paull, one of the most insightful editors that I've had the pleasure of working with. Biggest thanks of all go to Mike Connolly Jr., without whom I would not have made such a comeback from a serious accident. It was also Mike who introduced me to wild black bears in Redwood Canyon, and who has since accompanied me on all of my trips into the Sierra Nevada high country.

⊕ FROM THE PUBLISHER

All photographs in this book are by Chris Falkenstein unless noted below.

14, Library of Congress Prints & Photographs Division. **Best Experiences:** *21 (top) and 28-29, Robert Holmes.* **History of the Parks:** *42-43, 44, 46, 47, 50, and 51, Library of Congress Prints & Photographs Division. 52, Yosemite Research Library, National Park Service. 53 (top), Library of Congress Prints & Photographs Division. 53 (bottom), Porterville Public Library. 54 and 55, Library of Congress Prints & Photographs Division. 56, Christophe Testi/Shutterstock. 57, Yosemite Research Library, National Park Service. 61, Igor Karon/ Shutterstock.* **Yosemite National Park:** *92, SuperStock/age fotostock. 127, Bryan Brazil/Shutterstock.* **Spotlight on Supersized Sights:** *158 (top right), Robert Holmes. 159 (top left), Yenwen Lu/iStockphoto. 159 (top right), Nicole Paton/Shutterstock. 159 (bottom), Eric Foltz/iStock-photo. 160 (left), Alexandra Picavet/National Park Service. 161 (left), Christoph Rückert/Kirsten Auferkorte. 161 (right), Library of Congress Prints & Photographs Division. 167, Robert Holmes.* **Sequoia National Park:** *168-69, Robert Holmes. 170, John Seiler/iStockphoto. 171, Gail Curteman Cole. 172, Pierrette Guertin/iStockphoto. 178-79, 182-83, 184, and 185 (top), Robert Holmes. 185 (bottom), Yevgen Timashov/ Shutterstock. 187 (top and bottom), 188-89, and 192-93, Robert Holmes. 196, Library of Congress Prints & Photographs Division. 198-99 (all), Robert Holmes. 200 and 201, Robert Holmes. 205, National Park Service. 208, Yenwen Lu/iStockphoto. 210 (left), Jens Stolt/*